Here Lies Bitterness

Here Lies Bitterness

Healing from Resentment

Cynthia Fleury

Translated by Cory Stockwell

polity

Originally published in French as *Ci-gît l'amer. Guérir du ressentiment*
© Editions Gallimard, Paris, 2020

This English edition © Polity Press, 2023

This book is supported by the Institut français (Royaume-Uni) as part of the Burgess programme.

Polity Press
65 Bridge Street
Cambridge CB2 1UR, UK

Polity Press
111 River Street
Hoboken, NJ 07030, USA

All rights reserved. Except for the quotation of short passages for the purpose of criticism and review, no part of this publication may be reproduced, stored in a retrieval system or transmitted, in any form or by any means, electronic, mechanical, photocopying, recording or otherwise, without the prior permission of the publisher.

ISBN-13: 978-1-5095-5103-3
ISBN-13: 978-1-5095-5104-0 (paperback)

A catalogue record for this book is available from the British Library.

Library of Congress Control Number: 2022935679

Typeset in 10.5 on 12 pt Sabon
by Fakenham Prepress Solutions, Fakenham, Norfolk NR21 8NL
Printed and bound in the UK by CPI Group (UK) Ltd, Croydon

The publisher has used its best endeavors to ensure that the URLs for external websites referred to in this book are correct and active at the time of going to press. However, the publisher has no responsibility for the websites and can make no guarantee that a site will remain live or that the content is or will remain appropriate.

Every effort has been made to trace all copyright holders, but if any have been overlooked the publisher will be pleased to include any necessary credits in any subsequent reprint or edition.

For further information on Polity, visit our website:
politybooks.com

CONTENTS

Part I

Bitterness: What the Man of Resentment Experiences   1

1. Universal Bitterness   3
2. Individual and Society in the Face of Resentment: Rumbling and Rumination   5
3. The Definition and the Manifestations of Resentment   7
4. The Inertia of Resentment and the Resentment Fetish   10
5. Resentment and Egalitarianism: The End of Discernment   14
6. Melancholy in a State of Abundance   18
7. What Scheler Could Teach to the Ethics of Care   22
8. A Femininity of Resentment?   24
9. The False Self   26
10. The Membrane   28
11. The Necessary Confrontation   31
12. The Taste of Bitterness   33
13. Melancholic Literature   35
14. The Crowd of Missed Beings   37
15. The Faculty of Forgetting   42

CONTENTS

16. Expecting Something from the World 45
17. The Tragedy of the Thiasus 47
18. Great Health: Choosing the Open, Choosing the Numinous 49
19. Continuing to Be Astonished by the World 53
20. Happiness and Resentment 57
21. Defending the Strong against the Weak 59
22. Pathologies of Resentment 61
23. Humanism or Misanthropy? 66
24. Fighting Resentment through Analysis 68
25. Giving Value Back to Time 71
26. In the Counter-Transference and the Analytic Cure 73
27. To the Sources of Resentment, with Montaigne 79

Part II
Fascism: The Psychological Sources of Collective Resentment 83

1. Exile, Fascism, and Resentment: Adorno, 1 85
2. Capitalism, Reification, and Resentment: Adorno, 2 92
3. Knowledge and Resentment 96
4. Constellatory Writing and Stupor: Adorno, 3 100
5. The Insincerity of Some, the Cleverness of Others 104
6. Fascism as Emotional Plague: Wilhelm Reich, 1 107
7. The Fascism within Me: Wilhelm Reich, 2 111
8. Historians' Readings, Contemporary Psyches 123
9. Life as Creation: The Open Is Salvation 130
10. The Hydra 133

vi

CONTENTS

Part III

The Sea: A World Opened to Man   139

  1. Disclosure, According to Fanon   141
  2. The Universal at the Risk of the Impersonal   148
  3. Caring for the Colonized   155
  4. The Decolonization of Being   160
  5. Restoring Creativity   164
  6. The Therapy of Decolonization   169
  7. A Detour by Way of Cioran   174
  8. Fanon the Therapist   178
  9. The Recognition of Singularity   183
10. Individual Health and Democracy   189
11. The Violation of Language   193
12. Recourse to Hatred   197
13. The *Mundus Inversus*: Conspiracy and Resentment   200
14. Toward an Enlargement of the Ego, 1   205
15. What Separation Means   208
16. Toward an Enlargement of the Ego, 2: Democracy
    as an Open System of Values   211
17. The Man from Underground: Resisting the Abyss   215

Notes   227

vii

This book is based on a decision, a commitment, an axiom: its intangible principle or regulating idea is that man, the subject, the patient, has the power to act.[1] It is not a question of wishful thinking, or of taking a falsely optimistic view of people. It is a question of a moral and intellectual choice—a wager that we are capable of acting. It is above all a way of insisting on the respect due to those who are in treatment, for the patient is an agent—the agent par excellence. Thinking about patients responsibly means accepting their capacity to leave denial behind in order to confront reality. Life, even in its banal routines, affirms this capacity even as it sometimes contradicts it. As for my own life, I ceased long ago to entrust it to facts alone. Battling resentment teaches us that a certain tolerance for uncertainty and injustice is necessary.[2] What we find on the other side of this confrontation is the possibility of expanding ourselves.

— I —

BITTERNESS

What the Man of Resentment Experiences

— 1 —

UNIVERSAL BITTERNESS

Where does bitterness come from? From suffering and from a lost childhood, one might say from the outset. Starting from childhood, something is played out between bitterness [*l'amer*] and this Real that shatters our serene world. Here lies mother, here lies the sea [*Ci-gît la mère, ci-gît la mer*].[3] We all take different paths, yet we are all familiar with this link between potential sublimation (the sea), parental separation (the mother), and pain (bitterness)—this melancholy that does not come about all on its own. I don't believe in essentialism (without a doubt, many have died from or by way of its illusions); instead, I support a dialectical approach. Bitterness, the mother, the sea, it's all tied together: the mother is also the father, the parent, that which precedes separation, that from which we don't want to separate, that which takes on meaning only in the light of separation, that which we have to become on our own, parents for others, whether or not they are our own children, parents in the sense that we take on something of the need for transmission.

Bitterness must be buried; above it, something else will grow and come to fruition. No earth is ever damned for eternity: a bitter fertility founds the understanding that is to come. The distinction between confronting bitterness and burying it is not very important: in treatment with patients, we do both, one after the other, one in spite of the other; here as well, there is always a remainder, as though something incurable persisted, but it is still possible to locate "stances": places where the health of the soul finds its footing.[4] The task of the patient is to multiply these stances.

It is with the following words that Ishmael, at the beginning of Melville's book dedicated to the tireless quest for the white whale,

3

PART I

describes a sort of unease that constrains him, and at the same time—
above all—an existential resource to which he aspires:

> Whenever I find myself growing grim about the mouth; whenever it is
> a damp, drizzly November in my soul; whenever I find myself invol-
> untarily pausing before coffin warehouses, and bringing up the rear of
> every funeral I meet; and especially whenever my hypos get such an
> upper hand of me, that it requires a strong moral principle to prevent
> me from deliberately stepping into the street, and methodically
> knocking people's hats off—then, I account it high time to get to sea
> as soon as I can.[5]

Getting to the sea . . . Melville also writes of the need to "see the
watery part of the world,"[6] and we understand that what is at stake
in the motif of the sea is not navigation, but an existential open
expanse, a sublimation of the finitude and lassitude that fall upon
subjects without them knowing how to respond, because there is no
response. All they can do is navigate, cross, go toward the horizon,
find a place where they are able to live once more in the here and
now. They have to distance themselves to avoid "knocking people's
hats off," to avoid the roar of their mounting resentment. "If they but
knew it, almost all men in their degree, some time or other, cherish
very nearly the same feelings towards the ocean with me."[7] Ishmael
thus knows very well that none of this is personal, that the need for
the ocean alleviates the feeling of abandonment that is there in all of
us from the beginning, a feeling that punctuates our lives, like a sad
refrain reminding us that the countdown to death is always there, and
that there is no meaning in the origin or in the future—only, perhaps,
in this desire for immensity and weightlessness that water, the sea, and
the ocean represent.[8] "What do you see?—Posted like silent sentinels
all around the town, stand thousands upon thousands of mortal men
fixed in ocean reveries."[9] So long as these reveries predominate, they
constitute a kind of barrier against a more intimate and dangerous
darkness—in other words, bitterness, and its crystallization that
inevitably opens out onto resentment.

— 2 —

INDIVIDUAL AND SOCIETY IN THE FACE OF RESENTMENT

Rumbling and Rumination

At this point, you might say: "So what? Everyone is familiar with resentment. Nothing this common, no matter how bad it is, can be a serious problem for the individual or for society." In response, I join Cornelius Castoriadis, philosopher and psychoanalyst by trade, in espousing the idea that people are radically different from one another when it comes to their ability to keep their own resentment at a distance. It may seem that an awareness of resentment would allow us to avoid falling prey to the petrification that ensues from it. But in fact, this is not true of all people, or of all societies. "What can I aim for when psychoanalyzing an individual? Certainly not the suppression of this obscure depth, my unconscious or his unconscious—an undertaking that would be murderous if it were not impossible. What I can aim for is to establish another relationship between the unconscious and consciousness."[10] The individuation of a being, his subjectivization, and what Wilhelm Reich will later call his "capacity for freedom" all arise from the creative and serene relationship between consciousness and the unconscious.[11] Castoriadis reminds us of the decisive truth of analysis, not only for a subject, but for the society in which this subject lives:

> The entire question is whether the individual has been able, by a happy accident or by the type of society in which he has lived, to establish such a relationship, or whether he had been able to modify this relationship in such a way as not to take his fantasies for reality, to be as lucid as possible about his own desire, to accept himself as mortal, to seek the truth even if it should cost him, et cetera. Contrary to today's prevailing imposture, I have affirmed for a long time that there is a *qualitative difference*, and not only a difference of degree,

PART I

between an individual thus defined and a psychotic individual or one so heavily neurotic that he can be described as alienated, not in the general sociological sense, but in the quite precise sense that he finds himself expropriated "by" himself "from" himself. Either psychoanalysis is a swindle, or else it intends precisely this end, a modification of this relationship such as we have described it.[12]

What is at stake here is the advent of a man who is qualitatively different from his peers, and who would hold a key to humanism and to the society in question.

Inversely, people who are alienated cannot participate in the building of any common world except for one that embodies a process of reification. The aim of psychoanalysis is just as political as it is therapeutic.

For current power, other people are things, and all that I want goes against this. The person for whom others are things is himself a thing, and I do not want to be a thing either for myself or for others. I do not want others to be things, I would have no use for this. If I may exist for others, be recognized by them, I do not want this to be in terms of the possessions of something external to me—power; nor to exist for them only in an imaginary realm.[13]

Castoriadis here paints the wretched but well-known picture of the dynamics of objectification—indeed, "thingification"—as an organizing principle of society as a whole and also of intimate relations, because these relations are indissociable from the drive-related conflicts that reign within individuals. The stakes are both individual and social: one must not consider others or oneself as things because doing so will consolidate the collective mechanism of resentment, leading men and societies to sunder their prospects through these resentmentist means—making it almost impossible to overcome psychic and social alienation.[14]

6

— 3 —

THE DEFINITION AND THE MANIFESTATIONS OF RESENTMENT

Max Scheler defined resentment with great clarity in the book he devoted to it in 1912, just before the First World War (a terrible time of lethal drives): "the repeated experiencing and rumination of a particular emotional response reaction against someone else, which leads this emotion to sink more deeply and little by little to penetrate the very heart of the personality, while concomitantly abandoning the zone of action and expression."[15]

The key term for understanding the dynamics of resentment is "rumination": something that is chewed and re-chewed, and that furthermore possesses the characteristic bitterness of food that has been worn down by chewing. Rumination is itself that of another rumination, in the sense that what is at stake in it from the outset is reliving an emotional "re-action" that in the beginning could have been addressed to someone in particular. But as resentment goes on, its addressee becomes increasingly indeterminate. Loathing becomes less personal and more global: it can come to strike individuals whom the emotional reaction did not originally concern, but who at some point were caught up in the extension of the phenomenon. From this point a double movement is at work that is reminiscent of the one described by Karl Polanyi:[16] the more resentment gains in depth, and the more the person is impacted in his core and in his heart, the less he is able to maintain his capacity for action; as such, his ability to express himself creatively weakens. It eats away at him, digs into him. And with every rekindling of this resentment, compensation becomes more and more impossible: the need for reparations, at this point, is unquenchable. Resentment leads us down this path—no doubt illusory, but no less cruel for being so—of impossible reparations, and indeed of their rejection. Obtaining these impossible reparations—which do in fact exist—would require invention, creation, sublimation. But dealing with resentment means penetrating a zone that stings painfully, and which therefore resists any attempts to project light onto it—or rather, by way of a reversal (like a sort of inverse stigmatization), affirms a certain enjoyment of its darkness.[17] "This rumination, this constant rekindling of the emotion, is thus very different from a mere intellectual recollection of the emotion and of the events that gave rise to it: it is a reexperiencing of the emotion itself, a renewal of the original feeling—a re-sentiment."[18]

How, then, to resist the continuous pressure of this painful reliving? We see here that there is a possible link to the phenomenon of trauma, which produces a "breach" in the psyche.[19] The breach thus plays upon what was initially a wound, a blow, or an inability to heal over, and turns it into a yawning gap, one that is active, at times intense, at times chronic. In the face of the jolts brought on by this gap, which are fed by rumination, the work of the intellect and of rational thinking remain helpless.

Undoubtedly we should not give up so quickly on the performativity of this work of reason, but let us be realistic about the limitations of rational argument: let us accept that it is difficult to resist the jolts of a sadness that seeks to confine within itself envy, jealousy, contempt for others and eventually for oneself, the sentiment of injustice, the desire for revenge. It ends up gnawing at you, as Scheler writes:

> Perhaps the most suitable German word would be *Groll*, which indicates an obscure, suppressed, gnawing rancor that is independent of the ego's activity, and which little by little engenders a long rumination of hatred and animosity that does not contain a specific hostile intention, but nourishes any number of such intentions.[20]

Groll is rancor, the fact of *holding a grudge* against someone, and we can see how this holding of grudges takes the place of the *will*, how bad energy is substituted for vital and joyous energy: how this falsification of the will, or rather this prevention of *good will* (this privation of the *will for . . .*), how this bad object deprives the will of a good direction—how it deprives the subject. It requires him to stop focusing on it. But as resentment goes on, indecision becomes all the greater, and the ability to turn away from it all the more difficult. It contaminates everything. The gaze gets caught up in its immediate surroundings rather than crossing into new territory, resulting in a boomerang effect that rekindles resentment. Everything becomes a bad sign, one that is not there to be dodged but rather so

BITTERNESS: WHAT THE MAN OF RESENTMENT EXPERIENCES

that one can remain captive to reexperiencing. The subject becomes "fat": he loses his mental and physical agility, so necessary to the possibility of movement. Too full, closed in, the subject is on the border of nausea and its continuous heaving; he can cry out all he wants, but these cries will only appease the nausea for a very short time. Nietzsche spoke of intoxication,[21] while Scheler evokes "self-poisoning" to describe the "malice"[22] of resentment. The latter gives rise to a "more or less permanent deformation of the meaning of values as well as the ability to make judgments."[23] The impact of resentment thus attacks the sense of judgment, which is tainted, eaten away from within—already beginning to rot. From this point, producing informed judgments—which could lead to a redemption from resentment—becomes difficult. What is needed is to identify resentment's echo or even its aura, though this term is too noble to be used to designate what is rather a spreading, a servile contamination that, with the passage of time, will find justifications that are worthy of the name. The faculty of judgment henceforth puts itself in the service of maintaining resentment rather than deconstructing it. Such is the sullying aspect of the phenomenon, which employs the instrument that could be used for liberation (the faculty of judgment) to maintain servitude and alienation—for there is indeed servitude in the face of the lethal drive. "Slave" morality is already at play here, in the fact of submitting oneself to rumination.

— 4 —

THE INERTIA OF RESENTMENT AND THE RESENTMENT FETISH

One can and one must refuse rotting food and nourish oneself otherwise, but in this state of mind, the subject prefers carrion. The preference for rotting elements is essential to the workings of resentment, for the latter cannot be thought of as retaliation, as a legitimate defense, as a simple reaction. Indeed, it often arises from a non-reaction, from a renunciation of action. It consists in having kept things within oneself. I'm not saying that one should never keep anything inside oneself, but the resentful subject has "suspended" time, as though to hate better and for a longer period. Attempts to combat this must penetrate vengeance, which is a very peculiar type of hope—a decaying hope, but one whose energetic force can be very intense. "Revenge is distinguished by two essential characteristics. First of all, the immediate reactive impulse, with the accompanying emotions of anger and rage, is temporarily or at least momentarily checked and restrained, and the response is consequently postponed to a later and to a more suitable occasion."[24]

Quick retaliations are not enough to make resentment disappear, for in truth, resentment is not simply a question of re-action (or its absence): it also falls within the purview of rumination—the decision to ruminate or the impossibility of not ruminating. It is no simple matter to choose between a definition of resentment as *impotence* (to do something), and another definition that ends up conceding that there is a choice in favor of this impotence. This is undoubtedly a matter of degree and of the disability brought on by resentment, which is more or less accepted. One can be caught in the trap of resentment while at the same time trying to extricate oneself from it, refusing to settle for its viscous grasp. One is here on a knife's

BITTERNESS: WHAT THE MAN OF RESENTMENT EXPERIENCES

edge: vengeance and rumination, but also refusing to succumb to it completely, not wanting to succumb completely.

Moreover, vengeance is not resentment: vengeance is terrible, and it contaminates like resentment, but it remains directed, determined, in the sense that it is possible for it to be assuaged. Scheler believes that the desire for vengeance falls away once revenge has been exacted, but I am not so certain: vengeance knows how to move about and locate a new object. Leaving in one's wake this lethal dynamic, this energy of decay, is anything but simple. But with resentment, none of this is true. Its very aim seems to be the prevention of all moral overcoming; its goal is to ensconce itself in failure—to ensconce you in failure, you who try to create a solution.

We see this at work very clearly in certain tenacious forms of psychosis: in the way the patient puts all his energy into trying to prevent a solution, to cause doctors and medicine as a whole to fail, to produce only blockages. No overcoming is accepted: undoubtedly, accepting overcoming would produce a new collapse that the patient does not want to take on, and hence, dysfunction as a mode of functioning is preferred. Resentment's only talent—and in this it excels—is to embitter: to embitter personalities, to embitter situations, to embitter outlooks.[25] Resentment prevents opening, it closes, it *forecloses*: no escape is possible. The subject is perhaps outside of himself, but in himself, eating away at the self, and as such eating away at the only mediation possible with the world.

Even if resentment with regard to having (envy) and resentment with regard to being (jealousy) must be differentiated, it is possible to consider them together. This is precisely the accomplishment of resentment: eating away at the interiority of the person and not only at his desire for acquisition; shaking his ability to maintain his identity. "Envy does not strengthen the acquisitive urge, it weakens it,"[26] writes Scheler, and the more envy grows, the more it renders the subject impotent, and the more it changes his discontent with regard to his possessions into an ontological discontent, which is much more devastating: "'I can forgive everything, but not that you *are*—that you are *what* you are—that I am not what you are—indeed that I am not *you*.' This form of envy goes to the other's very existence, an existence that, as such, smothers us, and is felt to be an unbearable reproach."[27] Here, the trap closes in around the subject. For while it is possible to believe that recuperating the ability to possess (goods) will end up appeasing him, no one believes that appeasement is possible for a subject consumed by a hatred for the other, a hatred nourished by overflowing fantasies.

PART I

When the subject oscillates within this breakdown—which tends toward a breakdown of his own self—healing or any form of removal from this grasp becomes extremely complicated. Here we must posit a regulating idea: healing is possible, but clinical work is undoubtedly insufficient for the required care, and for the continued transmission of this care. The therapist is human, and we have to grapple with this inherent insufficiency of the cure. It is impossible to get beyond resentment without the will of the subject taking action. It is precisely this will that is missing, buried each day by the subject himself, so as to avoid facing up to his responsibility, his spiritual task, his moral obligation to overcome.

Only the destruction of the other can possibly bring some form of enjoyment, some "pleasure principle" allowing one to face up to a reality that is unbearable because it is judged to be unjust, unequal, humiliating, not worthy of the value one attributes to oneself. Resentment is a delirium of victimization: delirium not in the sense that the individual is not a victim—he is, at least potentially—but because he is in no way the only victim of an unjust order. The injustice is global, undifferentiated; of course, it concerns the individual in question, but the complexity of the world means that it has no precise destination or recipient. Victim compared to what? To whom? Within which framework of values and expectations? It is one thing to temporarily define oneself as a victim and to recognize oneself as such for a moment; it is quite another to consolidate one's identity exclusively on the basis of this "fact" which is undoubtedly more subjective than objective. What is at stake is a "decision" made by the subject to choose rumination: to choose the enjoyment of what harms, whether this enjoyment is conscious or, as is generally the case, unconscious. The "delirium" arises because of alienation—non-perception of responsibility in the repetition of the complaint—and because the subject does not see that he is actively working within the mechanics of rumination. He refuses to look away, to renounce the idea of reparations, knowing that all reparations are illusory because they will never be at the level of the injustice that he feels. The subject must close the chapter, and this is what he does not want to do. We are undoubtedly dealing here with the definition of "grievance" put forth by François Roustang, which must always be dissociated from suffering. Grievance always means "bringing forth a grievance," which is undoubtedly commendable in the juridical sphere; in the psychological and emotional sphere, however, we must depart from this model so as to avoid being eaten away by our grievances, and shutting ourselves off in an

BITTERNESS: WHAT THE MAN OF RESENTMENT EXPERIENCES

all-consuming rage. Let us also recall the Freudian lesson about the denial of reality, which nicely evokes what is at play in resentment. The subject who is enamoured with resentment does not go so far as to deny reality (since he suffers from it), but his resentment functions like a sort of fetish.[28] What is a fetish used for? Precisely to replace a reality that is unbearable for the subject. In other words, if it is so difficult for the subject to relinquish a grievance, it is because the grievance functions as a fetish: it procures for him the same pleasure; it screens off what must be avoided; it allows him to bear reality, to mediate it, to make it seem less real. The grievance becomes the only inhabitable reality through the pleasure principle that it provides, and the resentment fetish comes to act as an obsession. Resentment not only serves to maintain the memory of that which was experienced as a wound, but also allows for the enjoyment of this memory, as though it were keeping alive the idea of a punishment.

— 5 —

RESENTMENT AND EGALITARIANISM

The End of Discernment

Scheler describes it perfectly: resentment employs the faculty of judgment to denigrate everything that could encourage it to reform itself and hence to disappear. Resentment has an extremely strong capacity for self-preservation:

> The common man is only satisfied if he feels that he possesses a value that is at least equal to others; he acquires this feeling either by negating (by falsifying) the qualities of those to whom he compares himself, in other words by a specific "blindness" to these qualities; or—and here lies the basis of *ressentiment*—he falsifies the *values themselves* which could bestow excellence on any possible objects of comparison.[29]

It would thus be healthy for him to be able to recognize his equality with others without the need to negate the qualities of these others. One possibility for elaborating an antidote to resentment lies in the notion of perceived equality. The structure of resentment is egalitarian: resentment arises the moment the subject senses that, while he may be unequal, he is only wronged because he is equal. Simply feeling oneself to be unequal is not enough to bring about this sense. The frustration develops on the terrain of the *right to*. I feel frustrated because I believe something to be my due or my right. The belief in a right is necessary to experience resentment. At least, this is the theory of Scheler and his Tocquevillian heirs, who believed that democracy was essentially a regime that brought about resentment precisely because the notion of egalitarianism was one of its inherent concerns.

It is not a question here of negating the necessity of equality for avoiding resentment—this echoes the "ultra-solution" of the Palo

BITTERNESS: WHAT THE MAN OF RESENTMENT EXPERIENCES

Alto School,[30] which consists in killing the patient to eradicate the disease: "The operation was successful but the patient died."[31] Let us return to the previous citation from Scheler: if the "common" man is only satisfied by the feeling of possessing equal value, this does not mean that he truly possesses such a value, but that he must have the illusion of doing so. In other words, the "common world" persists by giving everyone the right to illusions about their own value. Furthermore, that which undoubtedly renders a man common, or at least assigns him a residence within mediocrity, is his incapacity to recognize the value of others, and his simultaneous belief that this will help him to extract himself from his own inadequacy. But inventing superiority has never brought about superiority. On the contrary, knowing how to admire others and recognize their value is a true antidote to resentment, even if it demands, at first, greater mental fortitude. Even so, denigrating others is not enough for resentment. A further step is necessary: that of the indictment. And since this indictment lacks any real object, it veers toward denunciation, disinformation. The corpse must be fabricated because there has not been any murder. From here on in, the other will be guilty. A form of "universal depreciation" ensues.

This "complete repression" sets in motion "a complete negation of values," says Scheler, a "hateful and explosive animosity."[32] Because this is also what being "fat" means: holding within oneself an explosion, something ignitable, a deflagration that can consume everything without discernment. Resentment aims to destroy discernment, such that one can no longer make distinctions and aims single-mindedly for a *tabula rasa*. It is the logic of an oil stain that spreads everywhere, leading to an inability to grasp the origin or the cause of the affliction, which from this point becomes more difficult to assuage. The sheer breadth of the damage becomes so great that the sphere of solutions shrinks, bringing about an inverse *ethos*, a "general disposition" to produce hostility instead of welcoming the world. One regresses, folds back upon oneself, because evolution seems too threatening—a synonym for loss.

It is logical for discernment to be affected when the subject is overwhelmed by his resentment. Discernment is the act of separating, setting aside, and differentiating so as to better grasp the specificity of things and avoid generalizations; it is a disposition of the mind that allows one to make clear and healthy judgments. It is a disposition of health, from the physical standpoint but also from that of the psyche; it is the disposition of one who takes pleasure in, rather than feeling renounced by, the complexities of rational thinking.

15

PART I

Discerning and feeling can sometimes be equated, in the precise sense that discerning is the capacity to feel fully and without confusion, to sense and to recognize, to identify without mixing things up. It is clear that the times in which we live put this aptitude for discernment at risk, even if they do not prevent it outright: the saturation of information (often notably false information), and the reductionism evinced by new forms of public space (notably social networks), nourish incessant assaults on discernment, which inherently possesses the wrong rhythm to resist them. Discernment presupposes time, patience, prudence, and an art of scrutinizing, observing, and anticipating: one discerns silently and with bated breath, seeing without being seen, disappearing so as to allow that which is observed to behave naturally. Discernment presupposes stepping back in the very situations in which the resentmentist subject sees himself as protagonist. Discernment was for a long time a completely spiritual value, specifically Jesuit,[33] permitting people to clarify their motivations[34] and to purify their emotions. In the work of Ignatius of Loyola and Francis de Sales, God is that which allows one to discern; "God" is more precisely divine grace, the time that allows the subject to transform internally. Here, of course, philosophy undertakes a secularization of the notion of discernment, and the only state of law that is worthy of the name—the social contract—must serve to protect the time necessary to undertake the transformation of self and world. The loss of discernment is the first symptom of narcissistic pathologies and psychotic disturbances.

Finally, let us not believe in the existence of objects worthy of being ruminated upon. No object—even that of learning about death—can save rumination from its sad lot, which is to weaken people. The famous idea that "to philosophize is to learn how to die"[35] can lead us to believe that we must never forget our finitude, that it must constantly ring out in our minds, making us able to love everything, to overturn everything. Nothing of the kind is true. Montaigne, who is one of the greatest defenders (in the wake of Socrates) of the need to learn how to die,[36] himself alerts us to a possible misinterpretation of this: with age, he discovers that learning about death is in no way a rumination—on the contrary, giving in to it consigns us to misunderstanding. "To see the exertions that Seneca imposed upon himself in order to steel himself against death, to see him sweat and grunt. . . . His burning emotion, so oft repeated, shows that he himself was ardent and impetuous."[37] In other words, believing that death is the aim of our lives does not manage to extract us from a precisely lethal agitation. Rumination on death does not produce a liberating analysis

16

of death. "We confuse life with worries about death, and death with worries about life."[38] Consequently, Montaigne opts for a definition of death that is just as essential, but that doesn't allow it to be the purpose of life. It is not a "goal" but a simple "end."[39] Metaphysics is elsewhere: it moves about in the region of the invention of life.

— 6 —

MELANCHOLY IN A STATE OF ABUNDANCE

Scheler sees democratic regimes as inherently more inclined to resentment. Tocqueville had already perceived this in his own time, characterizing egalitarianism as an evil that strikes man, and highlighting the fact that he becomes more sympathetic to equality as conditions become more equal. This is a logical phenomenon, but one that is difficult to control. The least example of inequality wounds the eye, he said, and the insatiability of the individual where equality is concerned can be devastating. Already, he was dealing with the evil that is melancholy in a state of abundance.[40] I never tire of returning to this passage[41] because it identifies a key element of immature democratic behavior—a perverse behavior that causes what is most exceptional in this system to rot, namely its demand for equality and the work it undertakes to bring this equality about.

Is this perversion unavoidable? I don't believe so. It is a matter of education, one that plays out on the level of Foucault's "government of the self," the only framework that permits a "government of others" worthy of the name, and that respects the egalitarian challenge always faced by democracy. For Scheler, resentment is obviously not the result of perfect democracy, but of a democracy that is lacking—which always ends up being the reality of democracy, though this must not be taken as an invalidation of the latter. Resentment, Scheler notes, "would be slight in a democracy which is not only political, but also social and tends toward equality of property."[42]

Resentment is produced by a gap between recognized and uniform political rights and a reality of concrete inequalities. This coexistence of formal rights and the absence of concrete rights produces collective resentment. This is undoubtedly true. But in contrast to Scheler, I believe that resentment is more structurally inherent in humans,

BITTERNESS: WHAT THE MAN OF RESENTMENT EXPERIENCES

because in an egalitarian economic situation, it transforms into a need for symbolic recognition, demanding ever more egalitarianism or projecting hatred onto others (a hatred that arises from insufficiently analyzed personal factors). This does not mean that our societies do not produce a potential for resentment[43] when their inequalities are revived. Feeling "offended," humiliated, and impotent gives rise, at first, to a withdrawal into the self, indeed a form of acquiescence that is the result of being knocked down. Happily, the subject soon gets back up. But if the initial blow lasts, if it is repeated, and if one gets the feeling that it comes about due to the actions of a growing number of individuals (an elite, for example), the offense becomes an all-explanatory framework that makes the subject its prisoner and comes to seem inevitable.

This leads to two possible results: on the one hand, the subject may waste away; on the other, he can seek to overturn the stigma, in other words to enter the terrain of victimhood, the fact of defining himself from this point on as the "offended" one, and to use this new identity in a tyrannical way—resentment being the first step on the road to terror. The violence with which Scheler takes egalitarianism to task is reminiscent of the critique of Nietzsche, who sees egalitarianism as directed by the morality of slaves who wish to weaken others so as to feel equal to them. Behind the inoffensive demand for equality there often lies, according to both of these thinkers, an egalitarian perversion: the fear of not being up to snuff, a sad and terrible emotion: "Only he who is afraid of losing demands universal equality."[44] This is of course a very conservative and disparaging view of equality (which is perceived merely as an instrument employed to reach egalitarianism), one that overlooks equality's importance for human dignity. Nonetheless, the analysis of resentment here is justified, because it nicely reveals the way resentment falsifies values in the manner of a sophist, whose eloquence often attempts to mask a spiritual weakness. Resentment can be articulated with eloquence, but generally the two split apart quite quickly, because there is a link of kinship between values and the fact of being cultured. Negating all values obliges one to denigrate culture or intellectualism.

Scheler pursues his analysis by calling the common man a "weakling." We must understand this to mean a spiritual weakness, which will soon require the assent of the masses to be perceived as legitimate. "But soon the need for binding forms of judgment will reappear."[45] In fact, since the judgment in question is merely a decaying opinion, the masses are necessary to give the subject of resentment the consistency that he does not possess on his own,

19

PART I

which subsequently allows him to go in search of a little of this potential for resentment in others. For as everyone knows, no one is a stranger to spiritual weakness. "The man of *ressentiment* is a weakling, he cannot stand *alone* with his judgment. . . . Universality, or the consent of all, thus replaces the true objectivity of values."[46]

The test of solitude can serve as a rampart against the damage of resentment, to the extent, on the one hand, that it remains an act that makes individuation possible, and on the other hand because an individual who chooses to confront solitude, even one that gives rise to immense bitterness, remains less damaging to others, because he is confined within himself. In searching out the consent of all, the subject of resentment displays the traps of the conformism within which he is caught. Judgment often presents itself as the outgrowth of a critical mind—similar to the development of paranoid conspiracy theories—but in truth this is thinking at a base level. This form of judgment is a falsification of values for two reasons: first, because it presents itself as a new ordering of values, deposing the hierarchy of those currently in effect; second, because it borders upon moral relativism or nihilism.

The Nietzschean thesis that Christianity is a delicate flower of resentment[47] is well known. It is contradicted by Scheler, who understands resentment as the source of a new form of morals, and more specifically as a form of modern morals, one typical of contemporary bourgeois societies whose ideal is precisely the bourgeoisie. Scheler's thesis is thus antimodern. Further, he champions a very elitist Christianity, one that is quasi-aristocratic and antithetical to modern humanitarianism; its essence is not democratic, as is sometimes claimed in reflections on the notion of Christian love. For Scheler, Christianity is an absolute stranger to all ideas of the equality of human values, as evidenced by the distinction between hell, heaven, and purgatory. Scheler is completely correct in this, but the fact remains that Christianity espouses the idea that people are equal in their dignity, and views forgiveness as a possibility.

The current reinforcement of individualism in our societies can at the same time produce a fertile breeding ground for resentment to the extent that the individual breaks away from society, only glimpsing his responsibility if he is able to distinguish it from that of others. The first reflex of this individual is to make others responsible for perceived dysfunctions; the second is to conclude that he is not responsible for the shortcomings of others. The individual can no longer bear collective responsibility; at the same time, whenever the possibility of assuming individual responsibility is given to him,

BITTERNESS: WHAT THE MAN OF RESENTMENT EXPERIENCES

he judges it to be a collective responsibility in disguise. In summary, resentment is the psychic trick that consists in believing that everything is the fault of others. The subject of resentment invites everyone else to recognize their shortcomings, but as soon as the occasion arises for him to assume his own responsibility, he considers himself to be above reproach. This is the difference between a Christian morality, which brings everyone together in their collective responsibility, and individualistic democratic morality, which claims to make individuals responsible. "The Christian idea of the moral solidarity of mankind appears not only in ideas such as 'we all sinned in Adam' and 'we were all resurrected in Jesus,' but also in the notion that we should all feel collectively responsible for our faults, . . . that everyone shares in the merits of the saints, and that the 'poor souls' can be redeemed by the moral works of others."[48] Inversely, the morality of slaves, as Nietzsche describes it, always seeks "to *limit* responsibility as much as possible, to explain individual faults through extrinsic activity, and holds that one must not owe anything to anyone."[49]

— 7 —

WHAT SCHELER COULD TEACH TO THE ETHICS OF CARE

It is thus not easy to take up the challenge of advocating for collective solidarity, a common feeling of responsibility (even if this responsibility does not seem to fall upon us), and at the same time advocate for an individualism of responsibility, one that is real and that does not seek to transform itself by merely calling upon the responsibility of others. This is the challenge of the assumption of maturity: having enough humility to bear your own responsibility, and enough lucidity not to sink into resentment as soon as others shirk their duties. Scheler may condemn the resentment of the common man, but he does just as much to condemn bourgeois humanitarianism: the false pity that says "it pains me" in a poor imitation of Christian mercy— what Althusser would call the Internationale of good intentions, and indeed what he defines as the perverted altruism that is nothing more than hot air. Scheler would undoubtedly be a fierce opponent of "the ethics of care," or rather of the caricatured version of it, according to which the vulnerable end up being placed under house arrest, and serial state handouts become a way of life. Scheler quotes a passage from Goethe in which the latter worries that the world will become "'a vast hospital, where each will be his fellow man's humane sick-nurse,'"[50] and associates social legislation with the "'poetry of sickness and morbidity.'"[51]

Everyone will recognize here the conservative denunciation of socialism, but also the slippery slope that an ethics of care must be able to avoid: the promotion of moral weakening behind a façade of communicational compassion. The emphasis on moral rigidity in right-wing thought can be useful here: it permits one to see one's own weakening, yet keep this weakening from becoming systematic. Take, for example, this critique of the socializing or Christianizing view

BITTERNESS: WHAT THE MAN OF RESENTMENT EXPERIENCES

that serves as an antechamber of democracy, and more specifically of an egalitarian regime: Scheler argues that Jesus was in no way a republican advocating the love of the neighbor in the way that people today advocate for human rights; in making this argument, Scheler reveals himself to be just as much of an ideologue as his adversaries. And he reverts once more to Nietzscheanism by recalling that Christ's love is not a "soft" love, that he in no way exalts "those whose instincts are too weak for enmity,"[52] or, as Nietzsche calls them, "'domesticated carnivores.'"[53]

Here as well, it is interesting to recall that resentment cannot be satisfied by the incapacity to be hostile, but only by the deliberate choice not to get bogged down in this incapacity—to surpass it. Just as in clinical work, aggressive impulses are identified as the inability to act (all the while that they give the illusion of being actions), it must be understood that the refusal of violence remains an act, a form of acting, that in no way derives exclusively from cowardice. Refusing hostility or refusing violence is not reserved only for "weaklings": it also belongs to the domain of spiritual firmness, or in any case must seek to belong to it. Furthermore, as is easily verifiable by looking both at history and contemporary reality, those who are "too weak for enmity" are only so in a conjectural manner: they too will spew forth hostility when there is the slightest possibility of expressing it without paying the price. It is therefore necessary to remain vigilant. Resentment is a poison that is all the more lethal for being fed by time, which enlarges it and allows it to reach down into our cores. As Scheler recalls, love in its Christian conception is an act that belongs not to sensations but to the mind—in other words, to decisions and to a sense of duty and responsibility.[54]

— 8 —

A FEMININITY OF RESENTMENT?

The fact that women, according to Scheler, are more exposed to the dangers of resentment should not be taken in an essentialist way: the claim refers to the patriarchal structure in which women are integrated, or rather trapped. Rancor remains the arm of "weaklings"; maligning others remains the easiest way to bring about performativity in speech, all the more so when the ability to act has been taken away. Scheler's conservatism, which is difficult to swallow, must be deconstructed, just like his antisemitism. His ode to the woman who is "the most properly feminine"[55] might charm those who jeer the emancipatory and feminist elements of modernity; my aim in pointing to it here is to show how an often just description of resentment does not necessarily protect us from our own resentment, and that the work of deconstruction should always first and foremost be undertaken on oneself. That said, it is good to remember the extent to which pathologies are integrated into eras, and that the two are difficult to separate, even if certain pathologies are personal in nature.

Let us take hysteria, which for a long time was considered to be feminine, even though it refers above all to a particular conditioning that for a long time was imposed on woman: the reduction of her world, a confinement within the private and the petty, a virtual house arrest, prohibition of the grandeur of the outside world and of self-growth. In today's clinical settings, the forms of hysteria, where they persist in democratic societies, are just as masculine as they are feminine, because they come about within lives that are—alas—more egalitarian for the fact of being submissive. It would have been better if submissiveness had lost ground in our so-called modern societies, which it has done in certain regards—but only by widening its circle

BITTERNESS: WHAT THE MAN OF RESENTMENT EXPERIENCES

of impact, and hence logically including men. Whence the blatant reversal whereby the bearers of resentment are not women (who are busy testing the waters of their emancipation—a real enough phenomenon, even if a lackluster one) but men, "common" men, to employ Scheler's adjective. They have been demoted, contemptuously qualified as "excess" and "useless," those who have "had their day," or who simply have the feeling of having had their day, and whose sole experience has become that of loss.

— 9 —

THE FALSE SELF

Nostalgia for what one once had can be a very effective poison for the soul. Donald Winnicott describes this rancor as one of the essential elements for the definition of the "false self"—the false personality that the subject invents to defend himself against what he considers threatening for his identity, his health, and the life of his psyche. This is a basic and at times necessary technique of dissimulation, but it cannot last: at some point, the false self takes root and becomes more and more difficult to distinguish from the self. Marc Angenot also places it at the heart of his description of the "resentmentist ego": "The ego of resentment is a sort of 'false self,' the simulacrum of a personality, full of obstinacy, arrogance, grudges, and hostility—behind which hides a fragile, sheep-like, and enslaved real ego."[56]

The concept of the "false self" is key for grasping the nature of the psyche of the man of resentment: just as he reacts rather than acting, he also *is not*—he wears a mask, even if he is not aware of doing so. Indeed, he unceasingly refuses to examine his own consciousness, to consider that he might have some responsibility for his situation. He forever opts for bad faith and shuts himself within it:

> He turns away completely from the inward way along which he should have advanced in order truly to become a self. In a deeper sense, the whole question of the self becomes a kind of false door with nothing behind it in the background of his soul. . . . He behaves very discreetly with the little bit of reflection he has within himself, fearing that what he has in the background might emerge again.[57]

Another key point for understanding the false self is the latter's submissiveness. This is the criterion that it shares with resentment:

BITTERNESS: WHAT THE MAN OF RESENTMENT EXPERIENCES

the subject practices the "false self" to hide from himself what he believes to be the strength of the other, or what he believes to be the desire of the other, which must thus be satisfied; he ends up oscillating within resentment when this desire is revealed to be inalienable and hence impervious to his tricks. In Winnicott's work, there are several degrees of the "false self," certain of which are no threat to the interior of the subject, as long as the latter protects this interior from attacks from without and from the toxicity of his environment. Behind this "false self" the "real self" always endures, aware of the split he imposes upon himself, but not necessarily suffering any of the violence of this split, for he knows that it will not last and that it will be necessary for him to break with it to return to the path of real action.

— 10 —

THE MEMBRANE

A return to the Nietzschean will to power allows us to understand the scope of the challenge of the modern age: that of the confrontation with the void, the "absurdity of becoming,"[58] and overcoming the erosion provoked by the latter. Modernity is without a doubt the moment when man becomes a subject, or rather becomes more aware of the notion of the subject, a notion that is illusory and contradictory, but that opens onto the possibility of *agency*, the attempt to become an agent, without deluding oneself with one's own mastery. Modernity, thus, is an encounter with the absence of meaning and with the entirely personal possibility of creating one—a meaning that will often founder, that can at times become intertwined with a more common and collective one, but that will not necessarily resolve all the challenges of "making sense."

It is unnecessary to grope about for the "extortionate conclusion"[59] of nihilism, because nihilism is also a belief system. The idea that "nothing has meaning," if it is taken systematically, takes on the appearance of a belief, and manifests man's presumptuousness: "He negates the presence of that from which he cannot derive meaning."[60] Trying to examine this belief in a profound manner can also lead to resentment, and thus it is best to be wary of it, to remain vigilant where its possible force is concerned, to keep away from the sentiment of purposelessness that it can induce, to make sure that any flirtations one might have with it are rare. "The nihilistic question 'for what?' is rooted in the old habit of supposing that the goal must be put up, given, demanded *from outside*—by some *superhuman authority*. Having unlearned faith in that, one still follows the old habit and seeks *another* authority that can *speak unconditionally* and *command* goals and tasks."[61]

BITTERNESS: WHAT THE MAN OF RESENTMENT EXPERIENCES

Nihilism thus has something in common with resentment, something that puts the outside into play, a decentering that in reality is not a decentering at all. Decentering consists in simply displacing the center of power, in submitting oneself to the outside. Not that the subject never submits himself to the outside—he undeniably does. But just as irreducibly does he not do so. Resentment, just like nihilism, forgets this primary truth: that there exists an inside and an outside, a fine membrane that separates the individual from the world, the self from what is outside it. This membrane preserves man from madness in that it allows him to extract himself from situations in which he is confronted with the obligations of submission, violence, or emptiness. This membrane is undoubtedly thin, it can undoubtedly be damaged, and the erosion of self bears witness to its possible corrosion, but most of the time it remains present. The disappearance of this membrane in the psyche occurs only in extreme cases: torture, being forced to perpetrate acts of cruelty on those we love, or experiences of the impossible that require the subject to split into two, perhaps definitively.

"We are freer than ever to gaze in every direction, and we do not perceive limits anywhere."[62] Today, the common sentiment is a little different: it generates a new anxiety, that of a void, certainly, but also that of something worse: the illusion of a fullness that is beginning to wither, and that leaves the subject at a loss for words. Yet a simple glance at the clinical treatment of patients, and notably young patients, shows that the sense of a void continues to add new victims, that our immense modern space is not easy to grasp, that the young are shattered by this realm in which fullness and nothingness seem at first to be indistinguishable, demanding the effort of a lifetime to tell them apart from one another. Nietzschean techniques of exhilaration to confront the void are, furthermore, extremely ingenious, allowing us to understand that resentment and entertainment are not so different, the latter being the path chosen by the "weakest" to avoid the void and the failure to get beyond it. Entertainment remains a mediocre way to resist the attacks of resentment, one that is effective in the short but not the long term: our need for it must constantly be fed. In the end, it is quite logical for the risk of indigestion to be the opposite of digestion—of the ability to make do and to synthesize diverse elements. The opposite of this terrible feeling of emptiness, Nietzsche continues, is "the intoxication by way of which the whole world seems to be concentrated within us, which causes us to suffer from an excessive fullness."[63] How can fullness be excessive? This is the proof that it has begun to spoil, that it is nothing but a parody of

PART I

fullness, and again we are caught in "accountants' tricks" to "fulfill our petty pleasures" in the hope of calming our feeling of emptiness, all the while that the resentment of others is already rumbling in the distance—those others who went down the same path of petty pleasures, but from whom these pleasures were confiscated.

Resentment is also born from this aborted entertainment, from this will for entertainment that has been frustrated, from this illusion of believing that the subject could avoid confronting his own solitude, that he could make others the basis of the whole of his misfortune—but this is absurd in the sense that these "others" also experience themselves as so many subjects, subjects who are not responsible for him, who are no less constrained by the feeling of emptiness, trying to focus on their own lot. There is, within resentment—at least in its durability, in its deepening, in its establishment at the heart of the subject—a denial of responsibility, a transfer to others of the responsibility for the world and thus for himself; in summary, a magisterial illusion whereby he forgets about the membrane that separates the inside from the outside.

— 11 —

THE NECESSARY CONFRONTATION

Resentment is a failure of the soul, the heart, and the mind, but let us recognize that a relationship to the world that has not passed through the trials of resentment is insufficiently tested. One must glimpse the specter of resentment to understand the risk of a subjectivation that would be completely delivered from it. I believe that this risk, within the analytic cure, is the most substantial of all. Montaigne, in his wisdom, recognizes that a virtue that has not been the object of temptation for vice would not be particularly important. In this sense, one might consider resentment to be a challenge for every soul that seeks to affirm itself as virtuous:

> The word virtue has a ring about it which implies something greater and more active than allowing ourselves to be gently and quietly led in reason's train by some fortunate complexion.
> A man who, from a naturally easy-going gentleness, would despise injuries done to him would do something very beautiful and praiseworthy; but a man who, stung to the quick and ravished by an injury, could arm himself with the arms of reason against a frenzied yearning for vengeance, finally mastering it after a great struggle, would undoubtedly be doing very much more.[64]

Resisting the appetite for vengeance, entering into conflict with resentment itself and not with the object of resentment (which would mean a falsification of the combat), being conscious of the offense and as such going beyond it rather than submitting to it: this is indeed something "active," which demands at once an ability to symbolize and an ability to engage with the surrounding world. Montaigne in no way posits himself as the most virtuous of men—quite the contrary. He possesses a delightful humility—one that is real without being self-indulgent—with regard to his own insufficiency. As to the questions of whether he has been able to master the resentment within him, and whether he has had the good fortune of not often being confronted by it, he responds through his second hypothesis: "If I had been born with a more unruly complexion I am afraid my case would have been deserving of pity. Assays of myself have not revealed the presence in my soul of any firmness in resisting the passions whenever they have been even to the slightest degree ecstatic."[65] He chalks up his happy lot in life to his natural wisdom. He nonetheless recognizes within himself an essential aversion to harmful ecstasy; indeed, he derives no pleasure from the expression of his vices and as such keeps himself at a distance from them, with the help of an alert and completely efficient character: "I prune my own vices and train them to be as isolated and as uncomplicated as possible."[66] This trait of not holding his vices dear, borrowed from Juvenal, is testament to an effort he undertakes on his own person, that of forcing himself to constrain that which threatens to overflow him, and of taking the responsibility for doing so upon himself.

— 12 —

THE TASTE OF BITTERNESS

Not giving in to resentment, sublimating that which is incurable, resisting the devastation that it can cause: it is possible to transform resentment into simple disenchantment or melancholy and to withdraw from the world. Montaigne also teaches this art of bitterness, that of knowing how to make do with bitterness by not subjecting oneself to the illusion of purity or absoluteness. This is not easy, because bitterness alters one's taste. "We can savor nothing pure,"[67] writes Montaigne, before deferring to Lucretius, poet of nature, who was well aware of the anxiety that afflicts man: "from the very fount of our delights there surges something bitter which gives us distress even among the flowers."[68]

Such is undoubtedly the specificity of human life and its pleasures: it takes shape against a background of finitude and insufficiency. There is no pleasure and no moment of relief that is not ephemeral; nothing is ever healed in a definitive manner so long as the final truth—inevitable—rumbles in the distance. And this is not even to mention the wounds that are always scattered across life, and that alter once more the taste of life. All of this necessitates an ability to appreciate the taste of bitterness: this would undoubtedly be the stoic lesson par excellence. Not intentionally bringing about bitterness, but knowing how to taste it without flinching once it arrives: "Pour me out your bitterest cups!" writes Catullus.[69] And Montaigne describes joy as a form a "severity," far removed from the sickly-sweet images of commercialized happiness, which is always tied to a price—a *pretium doloris*, we might say. Bitterness is the price that must be paid for this absence of illusion, and it thereby confers a form of purity on the taste that remains. Undoubtedly this is the choice: on the one hand, total illusion, one without bitterness but that causes

PART I

us to miss all possible perception of true taste; on the other hand, a real bitterness that, once it is sublimated, allows a certain form of sweetness to appear, one that is terribly subtle, vulnerable to expectations, but is nonetheless of a great and magnificent rarity.

— 13 —

MELANCHOLIC LITERATURE

Bitterness was once a great literary and poetic object. Verlaine is incontestably one of its most gifted experimenters, even if the taste that he leaves us with is more pungent than delicate. This is the horizon of the *Poèmes saturniens*, that great ode to the sons of Saturn, who have "a good share of misfortune and a good share of bile," and from whom imagination is not merely an ally because it can render reason inept, not knowing what to make of this "ideal that collapses." But the ode betrays its own failure, because even though it narrates it is not reducible to the imagination. On the contrary, it soars up and offers forth to the souls of those who read it as a different form of blueness. Thanks to Verlaine, its bitterness turns into the foam of the sea, a total landscape, the possibility of coloring the whole world with a hue that seems sad, but whose charms are apparent to all those with more attentive eyes.

Victor Hugo, so competent when it comes to sublimation, was able to depict the man caught up in bitterness without giving in to him, instead pushing him to become an other. He speaks of men-oceans. Describing them, he thinks of Dante, of Shakespeare, of Michelangelo, those illustrious and talented geniuses who traversed the ebbs and flows of life, this "inexorable coming and going, this noise of all the winds, that blackness and that translucency, that vegetation peculiar to the deep."[70] These are the men-oceans who create immense bodies of work, who are touched by grace at the very moment they confront the abyss. Not that this abyss produces (as if by magic) its opposite. In no way. Hugo calls these men "eagles flecked with foam,"[71] who are capable of "that smoothness after an upheaval,"[72] those who do not give in to shipwrecks—for there are indeed shipwrecks. "It is all one whether you look at these souls or at the ocean,"[73] he continues:

this is without a doubt one of the greatest homages we can give to those who experience bitterness and discover its strange flavor; they know how to enlarge our world; they know how to reconnect us to it, all the while that we are caught in the nets of our own disarray, without any style.

Nietzsche speaks very differently, because with him bitterness turns into aridity. But his collusion with poets is nonetheless real: "That the destruction of an illusion does not produce truth but only one more piece of ignorance, an extension of our 'empty space,' an increase of our 'desert.'"[74] Neither Saturn nor the ocean, but the desert. "Our" empty space, "our" desert: singularity and the proper reside here in an imperceptible way, one that is not always pleasant. There is still a subject or a self there in this emptiness who seems to have nothing to do with us—who does not seem to be addressed to us. But the very fact that this subject or self is from the outset posited as a man means that we are indeed addressed by it. Believing in addresses such as this one is an error, like forgetting that the subject is nothing more than one point of view within an infinity, knowing that he also possesses many other possible points of view upon this desert. We remain, for ourselves, the only possible mediation of the world, or at least the only irreducible one. We cannot not pass by way of ourselves. We invent terms such as "one" and "self" to create distance, and rightly so. We take aim at the disappearing self to attempt to approach the real and also to approach others, but the only support provided to us is that of the self. For some, this is the sad reality, while for others, it can be something else as well: the attempt to go beyond "slave morality," to return to a Nietzschean register, inscribing it within a Hegelian inheritance.

— 14 —

THE CROWD OF MISSED BEINGS

Many things should be noted concerning this morality of insufficiency that takes pleasure in itself. "The crowd of missed beings is overwhelming; their blissful insouciance and their sense of security (their absence of any interest in the collective evolution of man) is even more so. How it can all collapse."[75] The crowd of missed beings echoes the herd, the rabble, the slaves: properly speaking, those who refuse ordeals, who bridle in the face of difficulty, refuse frustration, refuse the test of life because it can bring about the death of the subject. Nietzsche's theses might seem binary, because undoubtedly there is, on the one hand, the master, and on the other, the slave. But there is also, within oneself, the dialectic of both, as Hegel stipulates:

> It is only through staking one's life that freedom is won; only thus is it proved that for self-consciousness, its essential being is not [just] being, not the *immediate* form in which it appears, not in its submergence in the expanse of life. . . .[76]

The risk of death is not a mere image, it is quite real: the subject becomes master because he combats, because he confronts a risk that can get the better of him. This is a risk that others refuse to confront due to a fear of vacillating, which thus produces real vacillating—this is the approach of the slave. For Nietzsche, resentment is precisely the form of thinking that belongs to the masses, the vile and undifferentiated man who believes himself to be a victim when he is the one responsible for this indifferentiation, when he has deliberately chosen the absence of risk—enjoyment, in other words: the Nietzschean term is "intoxication." Resentment is a softness of the soul. This seems

PART I

counter-intuitive for us, as much because it is nauseating as because its acidity is stimulating and can give the illusion of an intense taste. The "crowd of the misshapen," as Nietzsche calls it: the herd versus the exceptional man. Let us try to understand the fear of making oneself exceptional, or rather the ardent desire to be exceptional without paying the price: wanting to pay the price of the herd and at the same time wanting distinction doesn't work. We return here to the notion of *pretium doloris*, which is indispensable to subjectivation, to the emancipation or the escape of the minority. The subject cannot avoid taking this vital risk of thinking, this risk of irreversible separation, if he wants to embark upon the adventure of the subject:

> The beginning of the slaves' revolt in morality occurs when *ressentiment* itself turns creative and gives birth to values: the *ressentiment* of those beings who, denied the proper response of action, compensate for it only with imaginary revenge. Whereas all noble morality grows out of a triumphant saying "yes" to itself, slave morality says "no" on principle to everything that is "outside," "other," "non-self": and *this* "no" is its creative deed. This reversal of the evaluating glance—this *essential* orientation to the outside instead of back onto itself—is a feature of *ressentiment*: in order to come about, slave morality first has to have an opposing, external world, it needs, physiologically speaking, external stimuli in order to act at all—its action is basically a reaction.[77]

Choosing resentment consists precisely in choosing non-action—installing a compensatory regime in the imaginary and not in the real. It consists, furthermore, in constituting oneself "in opposition to" without grasping the structural exhaustion of the situation, because always constituting oneself in relation to another means weakening one's own subjectivity, making it dependent, and living in a sort of panopticon within which one is the primary prisoner. It is experiencing oneself as *second to*, as a "valet," as the one subject to consequences and stranger to causes. It makes one ill. The one who incessantly compares himself ends up turning himself into a measure, or rather placing his being within a sequence so as to compare it to that of another—an other who, since he is singular, is inherently incomparable. The will to compare betrays the emptiness that moves us, the fear of being nothing, so we search and we compare to ensure that we are better or, inversely—to point to a form of alienation that is different but no less damaging—that we are inferior: this is what becomes unbearable, so much so that it is necessary to sully our values and denigrate the other in order to invalidate this comparison that has given us such a poor image of ourselves.

Assuming the *pretium doloris* does not only mean taking the risk of thought or of action, but also detaching ourselves from the need for reparations. To take this risk—that of not seeking amends for the injustice that has been committed—is to stop waiting for reparations as a *deus ex machina*, and to emotionally (not just theoretically) liberate ourselves from expectations. It is to take the risk of healing the wound ourselves, accepting that, while we are not always the best doctors for ourselves, a decision needs to be made. The border we must cross to make this decision is that of having the courage to no longer await reparations: not necessarily to forgive, but to turn away from the obsessive wait for reparations, the need to shut ourselves away within the need for reparations. Abandoning our grievance and even the justice of this grievance, taking this risk: not capitulating, but deciding that the wound will be somewhere other than within our mediocre exchanges with the other. Renouncing justice—not the idea of justice, but the idea of being, or asking others to be, the armed wing of this justice. There will perhaps be justice at some point—the quest for it can exist—but only on the condition that it not bring about resentment, that it not use the hatred of the other as a motor. Our entire history, the entire historical path of our civilization, is constructed upon this. It is thus by no means easy to abandon this classic motor of history and implement something different: a justice that conceives of itself through action, engagement, invention, sublimation, and not reparations. Of course, reparation protocols, which are the product of institutions, are essential, even with all their shortcomings. These protocols often constitute the central core of public policy. But we're speaking here of the individual: how he escapes his own resentment, how he extracts himself from the prison of social injustice, and also the prison formed by his own mental representations. Or how he finally comes to understand that one cannot repair that which was wounded, broken, humiliated: one repairs "elsewhere" and "otherwise"; that which is to be repaired does not yet exist.

Nietzsche takes another step in this denunciation when he claims that modernity has caused the ill, the weak, the mediocre, or the herd to triumph, and that it has brought about the era of resentment on a global scale. This denunciation of the modern age, compared to a hypothetical and valiant ancient age, is easy to deconstruct: a virtually absolutist denunciation such as this one ends up doing a disservice to Nietzsche's argument. Rather than denunciation, let us employ

PART I

interpretation—as Nietzsche's work suggests—to attempt to grasp the breadth of his thought and of what follows from it. Choosing resentment means choosing the herd in ourselves, taking aim at the acidity of others to make our own acidity resonate. Nietzsche calls this the herd instinct. "The man of *ressentiment* is neither upright nor naïve, nor honest and straight with himself. His soul *squints*; his mind loves dark corners, secret paths and back-doors, everything secretive appeals to him as being *his* world, *his* security, *his* comfort; he knows all about keeping quiet, not forgetting, waiting, temporarily humbling and abasing himself."[78] Undoubtedly the man of resentment does not see his own deception; undoubtedly he has no consciousness of possessing the *ambitions of the small*, of having chosen weakness, occupied as he is with feeling the fever of acidity and believing in its magical powers, because henceforth he often opts for a belief in magic—in reparations that fall from the sky—even though he may be entirely atheistic. But resentment and superstition work in concert, and those who are enamoured with resentment believe in looking for compensation for injustices—thus prohibiting themselves from the only remedy, that of action. They believe that reaction can bring about compensation. They believe in the enemy, the very enemy that they have entirely constructed—for we should recognize that it is not easy for a healthy soul to have enemies.

It is true that each of us can be confronted with someone whom we consider to be an immense danger—a barbarian, or simply an enemy in the sense that he wants to destroy us. It is thus impossible, at least if we want to keep ourselves safe and protect those we love, to confront this other in the hopes of striking him down. But here it is not a question of that. Resentment fabricates enemies not in order to defend itself—as if these enemies wanted to decimate the man of resentment—but rather to wish for their death. Men of resentment, of course, will claim the opposite, explaining that their lives are jeopardized by these notorious "others." But the truth is more difficult: the enemies in question are not even enemies, because they share their ideals with the men of resentment: the latter seek to put themselves in the place of the so-called enemies, which proves that the very category of the enemy has been usurped. "Imagine 'the enemy' as conceived of by the man of *ressentiment*—and here we have his deed, his creation: he has conceived of the 'evil enemy,' '*the evil one*' as a basic idea to which he now thinks up a copy and counterpart, the 'good one'—himself!"[79]

I consider that the struggle against resentment is the main objective of the analytic cure, but I also believe that there are no reparations

BITTERNESS: WHAT THE MAN OF RESENTMENT EXPERIENCES

at the end of the journey. It is not rare for patients to arrive for treatment with this desire: fix what is broken, live like they lived before the drama or the trauma. Later, they understand that there will be no backtracking, that the work is one of creating and not repairing, and that without this creation there will be only regression. In fact, what they aim for in this fantasy of a return to the past is a state of carefreeness, the illusion of happiness, indeed happiness itself—and this remains possible. But the happiness in question will never be the old happiness. It will be something that never existed, and it is quite impressive when the patient is able to tackle this challenge: creating what never existed. It is normal for the patient to waver, to feel incapable of taking up this challenge. But finding a form of health means setting out on the road of creation and of possible emergence.

— 15 —

THE FACULTY OF FORGETTING

Nietzsche, Freud, and Deleuze come together in their descriptions of the unconscious and conscious double movement of the principle of resentment and its functioning. Starting from the Freudian framework of the topical hypothesis, we understand how a stimulus has been received and kept as a memory trace by the unconscious, and is then revived, as it were, by a new stimulus (this one contemporary): the "momentary" trace thus becomes more "permanent."[80] Resentment would therefore not exist without conscious revival: the stimulus would remain at the unconscious and even traumatic level, but would not necessarily become resentment. Deleuze reminds us that for Nietzsche, great souls are marked by an ability to forget. We might evoke here the ability to repress, but this is not exactly the same thing as forgetting: it lacks the latter's innocence. It is undeniable that true forgetting can be a real force, for it permits us to arrive at something different—it allows for something else to emerge; it is thus a sort of unconscious dynamic of regeneration, one that is of course outside of the definition of a cognitive deficit. Forgetting has too often been viewed only from the standpoint of consciousness, as an insufficiency, when from the standpoint of the unconscious it can have an immense vital power, one that is subsequently validated by consciousness. Because in fact, if consciousness forgets what the unconscious retains, the subject can feel ill at ease and experience what is called the return of the repressed. But it seems difficult to deliberately aim for forgetting: is voluntary forgetting still forgetting? It is also clear that those who experience resentment do not forget it. But one must avoid here the error of viewing the man of resentment as the protector of memory, as the one who never forgets what has happened. This is not the case. The stimulus received by the man of resentment is

BITTERNESS: WHAT THE MAN OF RESENTMENT EXPERIENCES

irreparably mediated by him. In other words, what is received is not necessarily what happened, or in any case is only a small part of what happened. The problem is not that he never forgets but that what is retained in his memory has already been falsified, and will be all the more falsified by its conscious revival—which, furthermore, does not require the same object, due to the sheer amount of what has been felt. As we have already seen, resentment can very easily do without an object and hence a particular memory. It is not to be found in forgetting but in falsification, not because the stimulus received is necessarily different from the original reality, but because the man of resentment, lacking humility, believes that stimulus and reality are one, missing the distinction between them. It is possible to recover from not making distinctions on an unconscious level—this is the very task of analytical work. By contrast, not making distinctions on the conscious level is decidedly inadequate. This is the defining weakness of resentment: it deceives itself, believing, to top it all off, that it has not forgotten, when in fact it has forgotten the confusion that it brings about.

The faculty of forgetting is a way of protecting ourselves from resentment, with the essential proviso that we must not equate forgetting with the mere desire to forget.

> When *ressentiment* does occur in the noble man himself, it is consumed and exhausted in an immediate reaction, and therefore it does not *poison*, on the other hand, it does not occur at all in countless cases where it is unavoidable for all who are weak and powerless. To be unable to take his enemies, his misfortunes and even his *misdeeds* seriously for long—that is the sign of strong, rounded natures with a superabundance of a power which is flexible, formative, healing and can make one forget. . . .[81]

It is certain that true awareness of the tragic constitutes the true stakes of the literary and philosophical work of Nietzsche: I am speaking of a deep understanding of the notion of the tragic, and in a way its acceptation, not to justify or provoke it but simply to understand that there is an essential difference between the subject and the real, and between what we call truth and the real itself. Taking oneself seriously depends on not understanding the tragic in a facile way.

Jankélévitch employs terms that are clearly close to those of Nietzsche in pointing toward a very similar reality, even though these thinkers may appear to be opposed. When Jankélévitch writes that it is not necessary to believe oneself to be tragic, that it suffices to simply be serious, he points to the same thing as Nietzsche: a keen understanding of the real and of its pain, an inevitable sense of *pretium doloris*, but also an absence of sentimental, victimizing, and discursive reclamation of this sentiment. It is not necessary to take oneself seriously or to make pronouncements about seriousness at all: it is enough to arrive at an acceptation that does not veer toward a complacent and reactionary renunciation of resentment. Furthermore, another sense of "it is enough" emerges here: an "it is enough" that is not vindictive, that is evidence of a moral obligation to move on, which gestures toward the emergence of a new awareness.

Nietzsche recalls Aristotle's error in assimilating the tragic and depressive affects such as terror and pity: "If he were right, tragedy would be an art dangerous to life: one would have to warn against it as notorious and a public danger."[82] Art, putting itself in the service of pessimism, would negate itself, he continues. Tragedy must instead be understood as a "tonic," an opportunity for a cathartic dynamic and not a ruminative repetition. In other words, the tragic must move in the direction of action, not of the simple reaction that is the very opposite of action. Tragedy, for Nietzsche, does not teach resignation: "a *preference for questionable and terrifying things* is a symptom of strength; . . . It is the *heroic* spirits who say Yes to themselves in tragic cruelty: they are hard enough to experience suffering as a *pleasure*."[83] It is no doubt easier—let us say more self-evident—for the artist to sublimate the tragic. The challenge appears more complicated for the non-artist, the one who does not have a technical and methodological reflex for sublimation: the non-artist must thus experiment with his own artistic path, which will not necessarily result in a literary or artistic work, but which will arise from the same libidinal process, the same investment into the world, and the same ability to seize the tragic, all the while keeping his own venomous thoughts at bay.

— 16 —

EXPECTING SOMETHING FROM THE WORLD

Nietzsche said it: the man who escapes resentment does not escape it right away—it is always the fruit of labor. And his work incessantly repeats this: his vigilance steers us toward sublimation rather than simply allowing ourselves to be satisfied with sublimation. This is one of the Freudian definitions of culture: "Sublimation of instinct is an especially conspicuous feature of cultural development; it is what makes it possible for higher psychical activities, scientific, artistic or ideological, to play such an important part in civilized life."[84] Sublimation is the aptitude that is necessary for the individual subject, isolated or caught in the snares of society: it is the ability to construct something of one's own neuroses, and to weave them together with those of others (which are all the more difficult to digest); it is an almost alchemic talent for making of the drives something other than a work of regression, of turning them toward something beyond themselves, of wisely employing the creative energy that runs through them.

For we must understand that energy is lacking: it is renewable, but every subject has his own rhythm of renewing, and burning his energy via objects that do not lend themselves to this consumes and endangers ecosystemic resilience. "Since a man does not have unlimited quantities of psychical energy at his disposal, he has to accomplish his tasks by making an expedient distribution of his libido."[85] Analysis allows us to understand the libidinal functioning of a being: how its energy comes to be concentrated on this or that object, and how, by concentrating too much on an object, energy consumes itself, begins to run in place, without the possibility of being recharged; how we must learn the "expedient distribution of the libido," because it is the same energy that runs through body and

PART I

mind, through the investment we make into society and the one we are capable of distributing outside of society. The rules here vary: some of us know how to employ this energy in writing, in public life, in sexuality; others must "choose" or put up with the fact that this energy is not infinite, that it must be oriented, that it is necessary to choose even though we would prefer to do otherwise.

Freud did not try to hide his everyday sexism, which was based on a phenomenon proper to his era: namely, the place of a stronger form of hysteria in women than in men. The Freudian error is to overlook this historical specificity and hence to essentialize women.[86] If women are caught within resentment, it is not because they are no longer the object of masculine attention—or at least less so—but rather because they are deprived of their own libidinal investment. If we are not able to invest in the world by means of our own libido, we die a slow death as we toss about within resentment, using the latter as a defense mechanism. It is here, as it happens, that the mingling of personal effort and societal effort is decisive. Because there are certainly structural conditions that produce resentment. This does not mean that we have to submit to them, but we should recognize that the situation is more difficult for he—and more often she—who has to confront them. It is thus the duty of politics, of a rule of law worthy of the name, to produce conditions that do not reinforce resentment, permitting the greatest number to libidinally invest into the world—not only to permit what Winnicott refers to as the hope for an expectation that is filled by the world, but also the provision of means to achieve it.[87] No individual can simply rely upon this duty of the state and its rule of law to produce this: the state is nothing without the perpetual effort of individuals who work to create ways to combat resentment. For all that, the individual is not the only one responsible for democratic dysfunction—above all, for the complacency that consists in not considering the maintenance of the structures that feed resentment as a serious problem. Hoping in the world does not mean denying frustration, but rather inscribing the latter within an order of symbolization and meaning. If the individual is persuaded that he cannot expect anything from the world, he closes himself off to it, and this alters his "receptivity to pleasure and unpleasure," thus destining him to an "obtuseness of mind" and "a gradual stupefying process."[88]

— 17 —

THE TRAGEDY OF THE THIASUS

But the tipping point, counterintuitive as this may be, comes when we oppose the certain meaning of the tragic to resentment, and also oppose the correct understanding of tragedy to the spirit of seriousness, instead seeing in it the possibility of a challenge to joy. Tragedy always goes beyond that which is *my* tragedy. Tragedy is tragic because it is universal, because from the outset the *I* cannot stand up to it or tackle it; the *I* simply does not measure up—they are not on the same terrain. To say *I* is to posit the world as *my* world, which is undoubtedly necessary for the subject, but which cannot constitute the last word. Because if it does so, its path comes to be divided into resentment, on the one hand, and a superiority complex, just as absurd, on the other: illusion against illusion. One can always say *I*, but real individuation must bring us beyond this position so that we can undertake Mallarmé's adventure of a disappearing *I*.

I don't invoke Mallarmé by chance. He is first and foremost the author of an essential work of mentorship,[89] and he is also the one who helps Deleuze to understand the sense of the tragic in Nietzsche, so as to go beyond the limits of the traditional understanding of the tragic. For it is true that the *deus ex machina* is often considered as that which allows no way out, as that which descends upon man and leaves him no possible refuge. Here, the tragic comes to appear as a *roll of the dice*—every bit as overwhelming, abrupt, and impossible as a roll of the dice, but as such, bursting with a potential for sublimation and deciphering (that at times still resists both of these).

"The glad tidings," Deleuze writes, "are tragic thought, for tragedy is not found in the recriminations of *ressentiment*, the conflicts of bad conscience or the contradictions of a will which feels guilty and responsible. The tragic does not even fight against *ressentiment*, bad

PART I

conscience or nihilism. According to Nietzsche it has never been understood that the tragic = the joyful. This is another way of putting the great equation: to will = to create. We have not understood that the tragic is pure and multiple positivity, dynamic gaiety. . . . The dicethrow is tragic."[90] This is a thought that one must attempt to live, without being seduced only by its poetry.

When dealing with patients who are mourning loved ones and even children, who are confronting grief and those cruel forms of trauma that have forced their way into the psyche and will remain forever, we must nonetheless face up to the difficult challenge of understanding the tragic—this is generally not possible early in the course of treatment or even for the first few years. Astonishingly, however, this understanding comes about one day for certain patients (it even differentiates these patients from others, on both moral and intellectual levels). No one can predict when this will happen, and indeed no one can ensure that it will take place, for nothing is less certain. And yet *time regained* is precisely this: it is the distant memory of what was, but it is also forgetting, making place for something else, something that may or may not be just as great. It is the possibility of joy, like the possibility of an island; it is the capacity to keep this possibility separated from irrevocable grief; it is the subject's ability to traverse the latter. This recalls Nietzsche's references to Dionysus and Zarathustra, who are both figures of the expression "know thyself": the first may be more painful and the second more joyful, but both are figures of metamorphosis, in that they appeal to the multiple and also to an idea of unity that is more creative and less absolute.

I have often tried to explain this Dionysian figure through the concept of the thiasus.[91] Dionysus is one, yet he is not one; he is multiple within himself, but he is also relational, linked to those who accompany him as so many pieces of him, so many sequences of life, so many strangers who will never be him and that he will never be. It is the procession of the shapeless, of youth and old age, the procession we don't want anything to do with, that resists every attempt at normalization, and also every desire to take on this or that form—if not, it would be nothing more than a masquerade. The thiasus allows us to conceive of a subject who is more illusory, more poetic, more humble, and who is not awaiting an aesthetics that would fulfil the needs of his pride. There is something archaic about this thiasus, something fanciful, and yet we sense that it contains a potential freedom, a potential joy in the face of overwhelming pain: the dominated have disappeared, and resentment has finally gone silent.

— 18 —

GREAT HEALTH

Choosing the Open, Choosing the Numinous

We might consider one of the best ways of silencing domination (even if not permanently) as acceding to creation. The person who creates ceases to be dominated: in this sense, he is free, even if his creation serves the ends of institutions or the state, or even of ideologies, because his creation is able to keep pace with the institution, in the sense that it is a temporal act, it creates time, it lasts. And what plays out in the passing of time cannot be determined in advance, regardless of the institution's influence over the creator. Appealing to creation means entering into a passage of time that cannot be controlled; it means loosening the grip of the institution, even if the latter believes it can determine the nature of the work that is creation's outcome—for any authentic work will turn out to be emancipatory. In this sense, choosing the path of the work always means choosing the Open,[92] as Rilke knew; it means choosing that which cannot be tarnished by resentment, that over which resentment has no hold, for the infinite nature of its openness doggedly resists the captivity to which resentment seeks to cede.

The work lets the air in: it creates the opening, the window, the escape that we do not seek to resist because it seems natural, made for us, a dynamics of existence—it is life in its vital purity. "The tragic man affirms even the harshest suffering: he is sufficiently strong, rich, and capable of deifying to do so."[93] The creative force that this affirmation implies thus works against the instinct for revenge—but perhaps what is at stake is the instinct for play, the roll of the dice, not the die of relativism but that of ways out, of possibilities, of metamorphoses, of lives reopened when they had seemed closed off, affected by a yawning gap that is not a wound. To say this—to appeal seriously to the poetry of Nietzsche or Mallarmé, to listen to Deleuze

PART I

discuss the metamorphoses of Dionysus, who knew a thing or two about the *fold*—is not to engage in empty talk. It is simply to read or write what is said in the space of analysis (which, to repeat, is not exclusively that of psychoanalysis): in the space that posits analysis, the outsider, outsiders, oneself, me, the unconscious, the thiasus, the sense of the tragic, verbalization that is aborted and hence prevented, a sublimation that is impossible and indeed unbearable until one day it is achieved without anyone being aware of it—time regained, times regained.

This is health, what Nietzsche called great health. And I also find it in my own clinical work: in the attempt taken up once more (the only viable repetition) by patients to extract themselves from resentment, to force themselves to have capacities, so as finally to feel without having to force themselves to do so, to produce a gesture, an *ethos*, a style—so as to one day simply do this, without wasting time talking about it or being pleased about it, instead taking pleasure in the world, in life, in that which is elsewhere, in a self that is vanishing but still there and that no longer feels its wounds to be so painful.

Let us consider the chapter "The Play of Thought" from Maurice Blanchot's *The Infinite Conversation*, which comes to structure the notion of what he calls the "the limit-experience," namely "the response that man encounters when he has decided to put himself radically in question."[94] Blanchot, the very thinker who posited the structural lack of birth, tells us that man, finally, is "everything," that he is the everything in his project, a project that is inseparable from a society released from its forms of servitude. What, then, is this "everything"? It is precisely "the play of thought," consisting of holes (as Lacan would say) or dice, of rolls of the dice. What is important in this metaphor is the throw and the infinite combinations that result from it, not only the outcome of a single throw. It is the idea of a fate but also of a roll of the dice, a fate from which one might extract oneself—who knows?—through this roll. "*O the dice played / from the depth of the tomb / with fingers of fine night / dice of birds of the sun.*"[95] This sounds like Mallarmé, but it is Blanchot who lets out this biting explanation for poetry, for a leap into chance. What is played is only ever *the very possibility of playing*. There is no other *benefit*, he reminds us; but this *very possibility of playing* the infinite conversation of souls, and this movement is insurrectional, he tells us, positing writing as the moment of insurrection.[96]

This is the difference between rumination and repetition: the latter can found a style. This, of course, recalls Péguy's poetry, in which it is impossible to find the vice of rumination, and equally impossible

50

to negate the presence, in his repetition and in his inimitable stylistic practice, of Nietzsche's *amor fati*, the sense of eternity and the way this sense dances with the individual who is moving beyond the throes of resentment. Bruno Latour has studied the importance of Péguy's repetitive style to show that through it, he invents another space, that of great stability, of the time that plays on its own terms in that it makes sublimation possible: "That which is natural reproduces itself; that which is interesting passes by and does not remain; that which is misleading drones on; that which is essential repeats itself. What is important remains present and is thus ceaselessly taken up so that it does not pass by; above all, it is taken up differently so it does not speak in empty ways. . . . Repetition extracts being from time."[97] Through repetition, through style, we can inhabit a world that is different from the one that surrounds us, a world that links up with the past, with the permanence of the souls who preceded us, whose force continues to rumble on in style. If we were forced to make an insufficient comparison, it would have to do with the link that exists between ritual and repetition: the capacity of rituals to launch us into immanence, with its link to the transcendent. Ritual allows us to inhabit the world. Stylistic repetition allows us to inhabit the world,[98] precisely by creating within it, or elsewhere, a space-time on which the world has no hold.

This is a point that is difficult to overcome in Nietzsche's thought, as Deleuze underlines. For he is right when he calls the spirit of revenge, or indeed resentment, the great motor of modern history. The spirit of revenge seems to have conquered everything: metaphysics, psychology, history.[99] As Deleuze comments: "The spirit of revenge is the genealogical element of *our* thought, the transcendental principle of *our* way of thinking."[100] But must we conclude from this that resentment is the only possible motor of history? Is it still possible to make history outside of resentment? Is this the Nietzschean and Zarathustrian project: making history otherwise, not allowing history to be born within resentment? Is this the path advocated by the concept of the eternal return—is it a new principle of civilization? Hasn't history as we have known it simply been that of resentment? There is no doubt that resentment has been a real force, indeed inherent to the dynamics of history; it also seems conceivable that resentment was not itself "sullied" by a dynamics that is less sullied. But the challenge that we are nonetheless faced with is difficult to confront: how to make history without resentment? The issue is essential, in my view, for it is not a question of negating the existence—and perhaps even the necessity—of resentment, but rather of understanding how to sublimate it, how not to give it the role of leading, on its own, the historical dance. Humanistic civilization is situated in the path of a confrontation with resentment, not to deny it but to get beyond it; this is what separates ethics from history, or from what we have tried to define as humanistic civilization, namely a history that does not content itself with living solely in the wake of resentment. "Man is under house arrest within becoming, man is the slave of the forced labor of temporality."[101] How better than with these words of Jankélévitch to express the obligation of an engagement in history; how better to state that the meaning of the past is found in the future, or that we must remember the future to build the present and to not wallow in discouragement in the face of barbarism? "The sky of values is a torn sky,"[102] he writes elsewhere, and this allows us to console ourselves for having finally renounced the supreme illusion of purity.

— 19 —

CONTINUING TO BE ASTONISHED BY THE WORLD

One of the fundamental "characteristics" of resentment is the fact of no longer being able to see, losing access to a correct view of things, losing the capacity of wonder and more simply of admiration—this is not only a blindness but a disfigurement of everything, as though the subject had put his eyes out, as though he had also lost access to his own capacity for generosity.

In the work of Descartes, generosity is fundamental, and serves to protect the sad passions (anger, envy, jealousy). Article 156 of *The Passions of the Soul* allows us to grasp how this human quality protects us from resentment, configuring the latter as a sort of convergence of envy, hatred, and anger:

> Those who are generous in this way . . . have complete command over their passions. In particular, they have mastery over their desires, and over jealousy and envy, because everything they think sufficiently valuable to be worth pursuing is such that its acquisition depends solely on themselves; over hatred of other people, because they have esteem for everyone; over fear, because of the self-assurance which confidence in their own virtue gives them; and finally over anger, because they have very little esteem for everything that depends on others, and so they never give their enemies any advantage by acknowledging that they are injured by them.[103]

Prior to the description of generosity, a virtue that is at work in the struggle against the disordering of the passions, there is the notion of admiration (article 70), the first of the primitive passions. It is defined as astonishment before rare and extraordinary things, but it also implies the continuation of this astonishment. We can consider

PART I

admiration as being opposed to the double movement of resentment, in that it functions in a similar way: there is an initial arousal, and then an intensification of this arousal in a more conscious form. The dialectic is posited thus: admiration increases our capacity for attention and indeed love, but the psyche that is aroused itself produces an admiration. We know that within admiration it is impossible to dissociate the gaze of the subject from that which is admired. It is possible for us not to admire what is admirable, and to admire what is not admirable. When Descartes appeals to admiration, he imperceptibly links it to generosity, so that it will be deficient to the least possible extent, and will confer upon the subject a more elevated capacity to regulate his own passions.

Deleuze deals with this inability to admire, to respect, and to love in subjects who are enamoured with resentment.[104] I say "enamoured with" because these subjects display something like a perverse ecstasy: where others take delight in admiration, they allow themselves to take delight in resentment—or rather in fanaticism, an overflowing enthusiasm that of course conceals a desire for recognition. Admiration, when coupled with generosity and humility (in its most Cartesian version, in other words), is not fanaticism but a reasonable sentiment: it means learning to look at the world and at others, admiring them in the sense of grasping within them a singularity that allows for a general growth of learning, all of which falls within the realm of an aptitude that is well known in philosophy: the capacity for astonishment (*admiratio*) or for questioning, one that is delivered from the temptation to disparage others. When we admire, we give rise to an awakening in ourselves, we open our cognitive capacities, we make it possible for the mind and the body to move about and thus to act. Deleuze's interesting analysis shows how the man of resentment, in his inability to admire, eventually becomes incapable of respecting anything, not only the object of his disparagement. And this is completely logical: if admiration confers upon the subject a relatively indeterminate capacity for the growth of his mind and his field of action, resentment, on the contrary, leads to a shrinking of the soul that is every bit as indeterminate. "What is most striking in the man of *ressentiment* is not his nastiness but his disgusting malevolence, his capacity for disparagement. Nothing can resist it. He does not even respect his friends or even his enemies. He does not even respect misfortune or its causes."[105] Everything becomes small, even misfortune becomes small, to the extent that it simply becomes the fault of another. Everything is mediocre. And if we believe ourselves to be surrounded by mediocrity, it is logical that

BITTERNESS: WHAT THE MAN OF RESENTMENT EXPERIENCES

we should at some point cease to be able to resist it: its putrefaction ends up reaching the man of resentment, even if he does not grasp the extent of the danger.

A correct sense of self-conservation should lead him to grasp the importance of preserving a zone of putrefaction, if only to reside within it, but even this undertaking seems impossible. Undoubtedly it is nonetheless achieved in one of the political translations of said resentment, namely fascism, which establishes, in opposition to resentment, a sort of protective wall to the illusion of putrefaction, inside of which the new community, having rid itself of its waste, can establish itself. At least, this is the discourse that justifies the necessity of fascism. A regime that is merely populist will often not be able to go beyond perverse attempts to recover admiration; such a regime remains within the register of passive aggression, well known to those who are "perversely mediocre."[106]

It is not easy for anyone to think that his misfortunes should not be taken seriously even if they are serious. It takes a great deal of work, an effort on oneself that is anything but pleasant because it requires getting away, taking distance—like the distance we take when faced with the misfortunes of the world, with which we are all familiar, except that what is at stake here is not so much distance as ignorance, a lack of empathy or consideration—egoism, in short. We believe that we take the misfortunes of the world seriously, but the reality is quite different. We don't take them seriously. So when we take our own misfortunes seriously, it becomes obvious just how ridiculous and irrelevant these misfortunes are. This does not make things any less difficult, for we must still remove this emotional stinger that bores into us.

Once again, it is not a question here of denying this pain, or of suggesting that those who from the outset are removed from this sentiment are of "strong" mind. It is simply a question of insisting on the need for distancing, the ethical and intellectual obligation to not distort one's judgments in any lasting way, and to preserve not only personal health but also the collective health that is linked to democratic sentiments. It is an almost stoic exercise, "aristocratic" in that it appeals to the best part of oneself: if there is any place in which an elitist relationship must be preserved, it is first and foremost with oneself, with the idea of imposing a discipline, a method, and an ethical aim upon oneself. "The aristocrat's respect for the causes of misfortune goes together with an inability to take his own misfortunes seriously."[107] These are Deleuze's words, but they could be Nietzsche's. They echo the style of Jankélévitch, for which the

PART I

"serious" is serious precisely because it implies the responsibility of the subject rather than his disengagement. In this framework, he does not try to withdraw from the misfortunes of the world: confronted with the seriousness of his own misfortunes, he does not try to dramatize or exploit them so as to be more tragic than anyone else. He is able to take the misfortune of the world into account in his actions, and ceases to content himself with feeling [*ressentir*] his own misfortune.

— 20 —

HAPPINESS AND RESENTMENT

A tainted definition of misfortune leads to a tainted definition of happiness. This is the first and most typical shift for the one who does not love, who wants to be loved, and who does not recognize the absurdity of the situation. "He wants to be loved, fed, watered, caressed and put to sleep. He is the impotent, the dyspeptic, the frigid, the insomniac, the slave. . . . He therefore considers it a proof of obvious malice that he is not loved."[108] The dyspeptic is the one who does not know how to digest, who suffers from heartburn—nothing passes through him. Nothing passes, nothing is digested—bad digestion is a classic leitmotif in Nietzsche and in Deleuze, who follows in his wake. He wants to be loved, like the child who fiercely desires this and who, faced with the slightest obstacle, collapses into screams and tears, angry because the other has done something that frustrated him—done something, in other words, that did not take him as an end, that was not addressed to him, that was indifferent.

What is acceptable in a child (because it will eventually be corrected) is much less so in an adult who holds fast to a sentiment of having the "right to": I, who respect nothing and do not respect you, have the right to be respected. This is a sullied definition of happiness that takes into consideration only material proof of the latter, notably proof that goes beyond symbolism, which itself is discredited. "The man of resentment is the man of profit and gain."[109] Those believe that this simplifies things, that it suffices to go along with the man of resentment and give him the material benefits that he expects in order to heal him, are bound to be disappointed. We are dealing here with the vessel of the Danaïdes. A resentment that is fully developed, as we have seen, no longer dissociates a resentment of having and a resentment of being: one cannot heal from the second through the first, even through the possession of something that is seemingly infinite—which nothing ever is. What is given will never be enough.

This is the danger of an unwavering resentment: it is no longer capable of negotiation, exchange, conciliation. It betrays a conception of happiness based on entitlement: a "passive" conception, to take up the terms of Nietzsche and Deleuze. Happiness, Deleuze writes, appears in the form of a "narcotic drug,"[110] in other words an addictive substance that allows one to delude oneself and flee reality, to use joy as an instrument, whenever it is convenient to do so—but this is of course a false joy, one whose pleasure becomes more and more fleeting. For every ethics, happiness—logically—is an effort, inseparable from work undertaken on oneself, from the development of the soul; it is not exempt from suffering; it is a form of consciousness capable of synthesizing discrete elements into a whole (even one with deficiencies) and of affirming itself and life as a whole. The man of resentment does not aim for this rather laborious definition of happiness, difficult to elaborate at a subjective level. He aims for the immediate, for that which can be commanded and (remote) controlled, a happiness on demand, a happiness-object rather than a happiness-subject. In summary, his question is "What can I gain from this happiness" rather than "How can I become a different person?" There is a superb formulation in Deleuze that recalls the incongruity of the one who does not want to admire, but wants to be recognized: "it is he who claims an interest in actions that he does not perform."[111] From here, we arrive at the final link, one that is seemingly counterintuitive, but which, as we have already said, is well known to perverse workings: passivity and the will to entitlement link up with aggressiveness,[112] and the circle closes; the all-the-more passive is henceforth the all-the-more aggressive.

— 21 —

DEFENDING THE STRONG AGAINST THE WEAK

The "spider" is in the room. It is there and nothing can satisfy its voracity. The spider, the tarantula[113]—this is what Nietzsche calls the impossible digestion of our own misfortune . . . or rather of what we judge to be so, for it is astonishing to witness, in clinical work, how the greatest forms of suffering (from a purely objective standpoint) that descend upon us—mourning, separation, illness, abandonment, torture, rape, betrayal, etc.—do not necessarily form the basis of resentment. They fall upon and strike down the subject. He is lying on the ground, lower than the ground, or even elsewhere, not capable of returning to the world, not even capable of resentment—so irrelevant is the latter. Some are able to get through this, but for most, it is a total deportation, a definitive separation, something from outside the world that falls upon them. Disparaging it makes no sense. There is a hole, an immense emptiness, an abyss into which we find ourselves falling. But there is not necessarily a spider there.

Clearly those who have been nourished by the spider of Louise Bourgeois perceive it, as something fearful and possibly as something else as well. We cannot negate the necessity and the value of the art of weaving. Here we might decide to go along with the Nietzschean metaphor to show that the art of weaving cannot be reduced to forming a trap for potential prey. The spider needs the help of the artist to get beyond the aim of his own web, to invent another aim for it. We think here of Tomás Saraceno, for whom the web creates a work of art in which there are no traps: to gaze upon it is simply to admire it, to be astonished by it. "Please don't engage me in a battle of wits," says the man who is enamoured of resentment and who weaves his web so as to remain entangled in it; we find the same way of being and of reacting in the one who is paranoid, in the conspiracy

PART I

theorist, who always takes his stupidity for intelligence precisely because it is a hysterical dynamic of weaving and interpreting signs that always ends up meaning the same thing. Legitimizing resentment is something anyone can do—it is based on rumination.

"One always has to defend the strong against the weak":[114] the maxim is Nietzsche's, and it has given rise to many interpretations, which often have fascistic leanings. Deleuze helps us to form another understanding of weakness, that of resentment, which has a strong presence in Nietzsche and indeed in Hegel, because it arises from the very presuppositions that structure the dialectic of master and slave. To be strong is to be strong in oneself, not necessarily powerful in the real world; it may even mean the opposite, given that resentment is powerful yet betrays a weakness of the soul, that of those who renounce their power to act and instead point the finger at others. The triumph of resentment is seen in the crumbling of the strong and the resulting rise of the mediocre, and we can understand that this crumbling occurs at a personal level, for what comes to be valued by society is not the best of oneself but rather the "vile"—another Nietzschean term that is opposed to the notion of the nobility of the soul. Citations of Nietzsche have often been used in instrumental ways to promote those who are already the strongest, so as to find within these citations a superb justification for everything they lack. "Defending the strong against the weak" does not mean, in any case, defending the politically powerful against the destitute. The equation is more subtle; the combat is first and foremost interior, spiritual. Defending the strong means defending the need to sublimate resentment, whatever the costs; it means affirming the fact that annihilation cannot be the final word in the experience of resentment.

Once again, it is possible to get through this, but if we succumb to it or remain stuck within it indefinitely, we create slaves within ourselves—we submit ourselves to a lethal passion. Resentment is a denaturalization of morality—all the while that it appears as a semblance of the latter—because it separates man from his actions.[115] Of course, not every separation between the individual and his actions can be reduced to resentment; if this were the case, reflection would be nothing more than resentment, and the law would be nothing more than a weapon of the mediocre, which is not the case. To create a mediation is already to symbolize, which makes sublimation possible.

60

— 22 —

PATHOLOGIES OF RESENTMENT

Examining the criteria of the DSM-IV[116] is useful when we need to define resentment in a more clinical way. The text does not clearly define resentment as such, but it is at the core of many disorders, such as "Oppositional Defiant Disorder,"[117] very typical of certain adolescents, characterized by a systematically negative, hostile, and vindictive attitude. The person afflicted by this disorder never admits that he is wrong, aggressively provokes others, has uncontrolled bouts of anger, a pathological bad faith, is overly sensitive, disavows all forms of authority, and disobeys without necessarily under-standing the meaning of this disobedience—in short, he closes himself off within his negative behavior, never questioning or proposing solutions for this behavior. His resentment is permanent and posits him as victim and persecutor at the same time.

Furthermore, these adolescents have often, earlier in their childhood, been more or less diagnosed as having attention problems and hyperactivity. It is interesting to note how the disorder that is exacerbated by resentment can build on what was earlier an attention-deficit disorder, in the sense that the subject does not know how to nourish himself by gazing upon things: he is no longer capable of concentrating on what he is looking at and hence of considering what he sees as spiritual nourishment; his gaze no longer serves as any kind of compensation. On the contrary, what is seen provokes irritability and is identified as "hostile," or at least as putting the identity of the individual in danger: he judges himself to be inferior, or considers himself to be a victim, excluded or discriminated against, not able to benefit from that which others possess. The antagonism that structures the position of resentment is often associated with these disorders of attention, which is logical,

PART I

because concentration, in order to exist, requires a form of consent or receptivity that is properly foreign to the antagonistic posture. Understanding something, becoming knowledgeable, simply being astonished—all these assume a prior attentiveness. The subject who is glancing in every direction cannot easily bring about this attentiveness, even though it would be beneficial and would serve to protect him. We can therefore see why being able to attain a certain quality of attention is essential, for attention is fundamental for many cognitive and social forms of behavior.

Resentment also appears in childhood, and in disorders associated with childhood, whenever there is separation anxiety, an initial inability to confront frustration where one's parents are concerned. This reveals the importance of those aspects of education that, while they will perhaps not prevent resentment from coming about, will nonetheless give the subject the ability to resist its grip and even to get beyond it: being able to separate oneself from one's parents, understanding the meaning of frustration, understanding that this may lead to freedom and not just seeing its drawbacks—all this is key to how one will end up conducting oneself. Education is a teaching of separation, of the ability to one day create an autonomy that, while it is conscious of its dependence on others, is also conscious of its genuine solitude. This subtle game of the taming of distance, of cutting ties, of symbolization, in other words that which permits one to break away from something without completely turning one's back on it, that which allows one to maintain the presence of that which is absent: all this is lacking in resentment. There is an inability to symbolize: one wants the thing and not merely its symbol. One must *possess* it, and only through this possession is reality confirmed. Strictly speaking, a permanent possession is impossible—and this is not even to think about how harmful this idea is for the health of the subject, who must always be mobile, in movement, hence separated, and hence a symbolizing being.

Freud gives this sublimated frustration a name: culture or civilization. "It is impossible to overlook the extent to which civilization is built up upon a renunciation of instinct, how much it presupposes precisely the non-satisfaction (by suppression, repression or some other means?) of powerful instincts. This 'cultural frustration' dominates the large field of social relationships between human beings. As we already know, it is the cause of the hostility against which all civilizations have to struggle."[118] Repressing one's instincts, and understanding that this repression should be seen not as an enslavement but as a liberation. We nonetheless quickly grasp this,

BITTERNESS: WHAT THE MAN OF RESENTMENT EXPERIENCES

for anyone dominated by the drives has a sense that he is not their master—a sense, that is, of his own alienation. But the opposite can also be true, and here education is essential, not to falsify the nature of enslavement but to posit that there is only freedom exists only within a context, namely in a state of constraint, that of conflict with others; in other words, freedom is no way almightiness: it arises when we cease to be alienated with regard to our own drives and those of others. Freedom refers to our capacity to act, to maintain our initiative within an environment that is not exclusively our own. We know, furthermore, that Freud drew up the unconscious in much the same way: the subject is not master in his own house, and he is often unaware of the play of drives that take him for their object.

Hyperactivity, attention deficit, separation anxiety, inability to accept frustration and sublimate it, inability to symbolize: to this portrait of disorders, we must add the classical understanding of schizophrenia, namely schizoaffective disorder (typical of bipolar disorder) and delusions associated with persecution, defined thus by the DSM-IV: "This subtype applies when the central theme of the delusion involves the person's belief that he or she is being conspired against, cheated, spied on, followed, poisoned or drugged, maliciously maligned, harassed, or obstructed in the pursuit of long-term goals. Small slights may be exaggerated and become the focus of a delusional system. The focus of the delusion is often on some injustice that must be remedied by legal action ('querulous paranoia'), and the affected person may engage in repeated attempts to obtain satisfaction by appeal to the courts and other government agencies. Individuals with persecutory delusions are often resentful and angry and may resort to violence against those they believe are hurting them."[119]

We see here the difficulty with which clinicians, but more generally the entire universe of justice, are confronted. Demanding justice is necessary, and is not necessary pathological—this must be said and maintained. But "querulous paranoia," namely this ultra-procedural capacity, conceals a will, or rather a belief, that the law is everything, and will always find in favor of the person who believes himself to have been wronged; in other words, the law here is nothing more than a superego that imposes one's own beliefs upon others (the opposite of the law, in other words), and here we return to Nietzsche's argument that the desire for law is sometimes the outcome of resentment. This procedural madness or mania is foreign to the one who is not driven by resentment: obtaining reparations via the law is virtually impossible for him, in the sense that he does not consider the law to be a

63

PART I

personal conduit for reparations. Demanding justice does not mean taking the law into your own hands. We see here that our relationship with the law is often very tainted, and the fetishization of the law, very common in certain countries, corroborates this. This allows us to understand that this contradiction—whereby one disparages and at the same time demands the law—is at the heart of resentment, which does not perceive the nature of the delusion that consists in desiring what one claims to despise. This does not mean that we should do without the law, but that it is undoubtedly necessary for us to distance ourselves from it and to use it only as an *ultima ratio*.

We find here the internal contradictions of the man of resentment and of his drives of hateloving.[120] These also echo his passive-aggressive personality, which is also very characteristic of negative and oppositional personalities. Once again, we must recall that we can only begin to say that a person is within resentment when an invasive and recurring disorder comes to light, and not because the person has this feeling from time to time. It is fixation that defines psychotic behavior. We must understand passive aggressiveness here in a general and not only an impersonal way. When working, for example, one can be passive aggressive, in other words one can procrastinate; one may be annoyed with oneself for procrastinating and yet still be incapable of starting to work: one experiences the displeasure of one's inaction without believing oneself to be responsible for it, indeed without seeing this reaction as an absence of action. Obstinacy and voluntary inefficiency can also reveal a passive-aggressive attitude. These are the characteristics identified in the DSM-IV. We know that the resistance to oppression can veil this type of "inaction," but only in a very different way: an active resistance can deliberately conceal, procrastinate, and lose interest, but only to clear the way for a different form of interest, one that manifests itself in action rather than in acting out.

Here is a classical clinical example described by the DSM-IV: "When an executive gives a subordinate some material to review for a meeting the next morning, the subordinate may misplace or misfile the material rather than point out that there is insufficient time to do the work. These individuals feel cheated, unappreciated, and misunderstood and chronically complain to others. When difficulties appear, they blame their failures on the behaviours of others. They may be sullen, irritable, impatient, argumentative, cynical, sceptical, and contrary."[121] It is interesting to see here that all direct conflict is avoided, because this would require a form of action, that of countering someone with arguments, possibly by recognizing that

64

BITTERNESS: WHAT THE MAN OF RESENTMENT EXPERIENCES

there is not enough time to undertake an action and thus taking the risk of being seen to be lacking by a potential critic. The subordinate would rather accentuate his shortcomings than confront them, and invents a story about loss: in other words, he seeks the assistance of chance, which is out of his hands, so as to ensure that he cannot be accused of incompetence. This is an extremely common attitude, one that is generally ineffective because it is so easily found out: those who employ this strategy do so constantly, leading the hypothesis of chance to fall apart. Their aggression only increases when they are unmasked, sometimes transforming itself into an accusation of discrimination and hence falling back into resentment and its attitude of victimhood.

It must be understood that what makes the man of resentment so aggressive here is precisely the demand for action—the fact that he is called upon to act by the situation. It is unbearable for him to be brought back to his responsibility—that is, the subjective possibility of constituting himself as an agent. The aggression only grows if he is then asked to perform at a certain level[122] in the act he is supposed to undertake. This is furthermore an important aspect of clinical work in combatting resentment's grip: there must be no initial demands for a result, for the disappointment of the patient who is incapable of achieving said result will become all the more unbearable. It is thus important in an almost behaviorist way to refocus the individual, to put him in a position in which he can act in his own way, regardless of his shortcomings. The demand for performance is perverse, and using it in therapy would be just as perverse. Before determining objectives and end goals for action, it is necessary to return, in a mechanical but life-affirming way, to the road of action—for example, the simple act of walking, of moving about, and of beginning to focus one's attention while doing so.

This is anything but simple: finding the humility required for such an undertaking is already a huge step. And as we have already seen, subjects who are afflicted by resentment are marked by a real loss of humility. We discover by way of these experiences—but is it really a discovery?—that humility is an ability and not a shortcoming: it is a realization of the lack that is inherent to us, and at the same time a refusal to shirk responsibility without falling into the delusion of almightiness, believing that one can vanquish lack. The question of lack is the most important issue arising from birth. To be born is to lack.

— 23 —

HUMANISM OR MISANTHROPY?

I've always thought that I was born too early, but I'm willing to recognize that even if I had been born later, my birth would have turned out to be just as poorly "barred" (to play on the Lacanian sense of the term). It would be better not to be born, as Cioran suggested in *The Trouble with Being Born*. And Blanchot perfectly describes birth's incurable nature: "To be born is, after having had everything, suddenly to lack everything, and first of all being. . . . It is always around lack, and through the exigency of lack, that a presentiment of the infant's history, of what he will be, is formed."[123] Here as well, the dialectic is to be found between what is at play in the formation of the subject and what is at play in history, a history at once personal and undeniably collective. We find in Blanchot's work this originary myth of fullness, this illusion that only lasts an instant—and does the child ever become conscious of it? This is quite simply early childhood: the impossibility of separating, of making a world, and hence the absence of the consciousness of lack—fullness, in other words, but that of total dependency, outside of consciousness, the impossibility of individuation. The exigency of lack will certainly follow (education and culture demand it): this step that goes precisely toward the sublimation of lack, the refusal of its negation and the refusal to not go beyond it.

Perhaps I have only written a single book, for here again I see the triad *imaginatio vera—pretium doloris—vis comica*: lack, the exigency of lack, the difficulty of the path, the fact that the result is unknown; but also the resilience that is brought about by an inventive beginning, an individuation at work; but also the mockery of the entire process, which is one among many, one among too many. But we can't let ourselves remain stuck in misanthropy—we must find

BITTERNESS: WHAT THE MAN OF RESENTMENT EXPERIENCES

ways to escape it. Let's be honest: I don't know if misanthropy is any less humanistic than humanism itself. I'm not so sure, but I have not chosen this path or dared to choose it, for a major contradiction quickly arises within it: one's own life, the non-value of one's own life, which must thus from the outset be made to vanish. Others push this logic—a logic of exterminating the other—to its end, before exterminating themselves; but history has shown that these people who aim in such a pure way for extermination are rare; generally, this aim weakens along the way, and becomes a choice between those who must and those who must not be exterminated. The somewhat haphazard choice of extermination turns out to derive from a very weak humanism, one that doesn't sense its own weaknesses, is self-satisfied, and does not seek to confront its drives. For this reason, in the final analysis, I have chosen the humanism of laughter: not a booming laughter but a vanishing laughter, perhaps only a smile, one that is real but vanishing, which does not weaken but also does not aim for grandeur at any price, for this would tarnish it. Here as well, it is difficult to abandon the dream of fullness, of the immense self, a self capable of satisfaction; it is difficult to abandon this dream without abandoning oneself, without renouncing the need to work on oneself.

— 24 —

FIGHTING RESENTMENT THROUGH ANALYSIS

I have often said it, but it seems to me that the challenge of fighting resentment is most pertinent to analysis. In the cure, many things are verbalized: the question of the origin and our relationship with it, along with family, parents, and the cultural society that we are born into. The subject seeks to understand what he has not understood, what he has even judged to be insignificant, since he finds within this insignificance the key to a possible explanation, or at least part of this explanation. He verbalizes, and through this verbalization, he undoes the threads of reality, hence revealing a share of the "truth"—but this truth is insufficient to finalize "healing." Healing is not only a question of self-repair and of the return to a previous state. Canguilhem said it perfectly: healing is a matter of invention, of producing new norms of life—of creation. At the organic level, the subject puts into place a therapeutic protocol to find his own homeostasis; at the symbolic level, he does the same, in a certain way, except that work on this level turns out to be linked to an even greater degree to a dynamics of creation. To maintain the momentum of this work—to maintain this vital possibility of resilience even though it is precisely this vitalism that is afflicted—it is important to produce a "capacity for truth." This is not a lie or an omission but refers to a manner of speaking, of making oneself understood, and of concerning oneself with the consequence produced by the "truth." Here again, this is not easy, because the subject is the first to interpret everything that is said, by him or by his analyst, in such a way as to validate himself.

This propensity on the part of those suffering from resentment[124] to refuse any interpretation that might pull them out of their stagnation is furthermore very typical: we can explore every nook and cranny

BITTERNESS: WHAT THE MAN OF RESENTMENT EXPERIENCES

of the truth, search for what is most empowering in the enunciation of this truth, but nothing works. The subject resists speech, resists solutions: he has already thought about that, already done that, even though he has generally done nothing for a long time. The subject knows that, has done that, has tried that, and it doesn't work. He doesn't say that he has failed but that "it doesn't work": "I know, I've tried it, it doesn't work." In its more social or collective version, resentment arises from the same attitude: it is a question of finding collective validation for the fact that it doesn't work, not with the aim of trying to find something that does work, but to dismiss what doesn't work and thus to establish it as an object of hatred, so as to project all one's energy onto it, even though it symbolizes a void.

But let us return to the capacity for truth. The surest way of producing it is not to propose an interpretation. Of course, patients are waiting for a "magic" statement, but this is the surest way of failing, because such a statement is not endogenous, not produced by oneself, and will not be recognized as adequate. I do not believe that the analyst and the patient are so separate that every word can be identified with the one who says it. In analysis, everything is linked, co-invented, and co-revealed. It is still important, for all that, to preserve the verbalization of the patient so as to more easily unleash within him the power to act—or at least the feeling that he will be able to act. As such, it is important for him to be the one who is working things through, for him to undergo his own silence and that of the analyst. It is a difficult test, one that at times creates the sentiment of being abandoned once more. The patient is in disarray before his analyst, and must once again confront the analyst's silence, which echoes his own. Hence an approach that is capacity based and not strictly formalist: not everyone is immediately capable of silence, and of transforming this silence in creative ways. The art of this is to produce words that will reestablish the subject's confidence without giving him a specific orientation, and that invites the subject to undergo his silence—to understand that there exist, within this silence, resources for thinking, for refining what he thinks he knows and what he does not know. This minor development of the capacity for truth is necessary so as not to produce misinterpretations—which can then be substituted for the speech of both the analyst and the patient. When resentment is very prevalent, this development is very difficult—indeed, it is jeopardized. I don't believe in allowing resentment to have the final word in analysis; on the contrary, I believe that the persistence of resentment proves that analysis has not taken place, even if the patient was in analysis—that the masquerade persisted within the analysis. This happens often, and brings about an even higher level of difficulty, for it allows the man of resentment to fortify himself: thanks to a pseudo-analysis, he will now be able to give free rein to his resentment, dressing it up in the guise of a different diagnosis.

— 25 —

GIVING VALUE BACK TO TIME

It is not only language that allows for sublimation. There is also experience itself, the ability to create experience, to transform life into proper lived experience. In Maurice Blanchot's work, the two are combined: for him, experience undoubtedly refers to the heart of the work, writing as such, but also writing's tireless hunt for experience, for life, for that which was and that which takes place, for the weakening of life that confines us within the unworking that is proper to every work. Analysis here undoubtedly follows upon education (on the condition that it is lifelong education): in this gaze upon oneself that is mediatized by the world and hence enlarged, one no longer examines oneself in the manner of simply looking at oneself (this would be ridiculous and boring, even if many think that analysis is nothing more than this: looking at oneself); on the contrary, one opens one's gaze, peels the wool back from one's eyes. Because analysis is the antechamber of experience—the possibility of learning or of relearning to experience. And resentment is that which no longer knows how to experience: it is a life in which everything passes before one's eyes, and all that remains is bitterness—all that is left is a lack of satisfaction; the hatred of others dries out the soul and renders all its territories arid; it does the same to our capacity to mediate.

Getting back to experiencing things again seems so simple, and basically it is—but there is a price to pay. Because experiencing requires time—finding time that unfolds, and this unfolding of time plays out first of all in the mind, in the will to stretch out time. And time, as we know, is a rare commodity in our societies. Some people, however, think that they have too much time—namely, adolescents, who feel that they are stuck in their lives and their territory.

PART I

Literature is full of these beings who are finding their way, searching for an escape because empty time is eating them up, leaving them with the feeling that they are rotting in their immobility. Yet it is not so much that they have too much time, but that they don't know what to do with it, for as yet they have not been sufficiently initiated in sublimation, in the exigency of lack.

Undoubtedly we all find ourselves, at one time or another, foolishly confusing boredom with time. We throw accusations at the world, our environments, our families, our lives that in the moment seem pathetic, our lack of freedom, our seeming house arrest—and none of this is false, exactly; it is simply insufficient. But if we do not discover the value of time, and indeed become apprentices to it, resentment will inevitably reveal itself at the end of a journey that was supposed to get us out of our slump. It must not be believed, of course, that escaping resentment means feeling a pleasant fullness. As Nietzsche said, great health in its Dionysian version is no stranger to breaking into pieces. The convalescent always has the taste of exile in his mouth, the feeling of being a permanent runaway, of always running away from his history. It is a matter of assuaging this feeling: success consists in taming it and thereby gaining a bit of peace. Instead of exile, we can nonetheless choose this other pole which is that of experience—but the two are not completely foreign to one another.

Verbalization reactivates damage that we have suffered but at the same time pacifies it: when the feeling of exile is too strong, there is very little that can resist it. There are words, our own words, which have been refined by analysis, and which can at times feel like a refuge. An analytic session can create a home, a habitat. Not only analysis is capable of this: it is one of the deepest truths of writing, of reading, of the work as a general rule. The work must not be confused with "everyday speech,"[125] which, as Blanchot writes, is meaningless and fades away; this is what is most proper to the everyday, the current, to those words that come about incessantly every day, which never stop communicating without anyone really hearing them. Social pleasantries, in short, are not without their interest; they play an important role, notably when we are faced with anxiety; they calm, but only in a fleeting way. A more focused anxiety requires something else: speech that we can interiorize, of which we can become conscious; speech that is undoubtedly more silent, that is drawn out—that is capable of welcoming.

— 26 —

IN THE COUNTER-TRANSFERENCE AND THE ANALYTIC CURE

There is a phenomenon that is not, strictly speaking, that of resentment, but which can leave itself open to the latter, at least if it is channeled: I am speaking of the feeling of strong bitterness that occurs within the analyst when, in seeking to accompany the patient in his work, he in turn becomes the very object—sometimes for a brief moment, sometimes in a chronic way—of said resentment. What emerges then is a confused feeling: wounded by the patient (even if he defends himself), what can play out for the analyst is the awakening of unpleasant emotions, which leave a sort of trace, leaving the analyst stuck between the feeling of knowing exactly what is happening (it is an old lesson that is well known in psychoanalysis), and his obligation, as a therapist, to continue, and indeed to confront this feeling so as to produce something viable for the patient, and no doubt for himself as well. Winnicott defined this moment, which clenches the stomach and constrains the mind, as "hate in the counter-transference."[126]

An autobiographical anecdote, one that has often been commented upon and linked at times to the notion of reparations[127] and at times to "hateful" counter-transference,[128] describes the ambivalence of this feeling in the child Winnicott. He is playing with his sister's wax doll, whose nose he destroys with the help of a mallet, judging the doll to be all the more unbearable in that his father uses it as a ventriloquist's puppet to tease his son, and to sing him a song that *stages him with his sister*: "Rosie said to Donald / I love you / Donald said to Rosie / I don't believe you do." Winnicott then comments on what follows from this:

> I knew the doll had to be altered for the worse, and much of my life has been founded on the undoubted fact that I actually *did* this deed,

PART I

not merely wished it and planned it. I was perhaps somewhat relieved when my father took a series of matches and, warming up the wax nose enough, remoulded it so that the face once more became a face. This early demonstration of the restitutive and reparative act certainly made an impression on me, and perhaps made me able to accept the fact that I myself, dear innocent child, had actually become violent directly with a doll, but indirectly with my good-tempered father who was just then entering my conscious life.[129]

Not being the innocent little being is a discovery we make every day of our lives. In no way innocent as an individual, in no way innocent as an analyst, in no way innocent as a patient, but always shaped by this lack of innocence, able to deny it but not to resolve it. It is at this point that the road toward reparations begins to open up. But the real road toward reparations is not that of repetition: we cannot ceaselessly repeat the lack of innocence, satisfy ourselves with recognizing it, and forgive ourselves by denouncing it. This way of taking cognizance of our non-innocence has all the markings of false modesty: we recognize our insufficiency not by going beyond it but by remaining within it and judging it to be sufficient. This is a point that Deleuze describes well when he invites his reader to beware of the one who describes himself as not meeting the standards of someone else, judging this other to be magnificent and himself to be unworthy. This is the most stylized version of resentment: the grand declaration of inferiority. "We must beware of those who condemn themselves before that which is good or beautiful, claiming not to understand, not to be worthy: their modesty is frightening. What hatred of beauty is hidden in their declarations of inferiority."[130] Recognizing the form of cruelty of which we are capable is a necessary moment, as is the need to surpass it.

The metaphor of the reconstitution of the face is key. It echoes Levinas's conception of ethics, which came later, and which turned on the question of the other's face. Hating the other means refusing him his identity as a subject; it means refusing a face, refusing the dignity of someone other than oneself; it means identifying the other as waste, as refuse—and refuse, of course, is made to throw away. Re-establishing the face is part of a double restoration: that of the subject, who allowed himself to be carried away by hatred, and that of the other, who may have had to endure the subject's moment of madness. This also leads to the understanding that restoration can come about thanks to another—the one through whom part of the vacillation played out. Yet all this is tied in with what Winnicott

BITTERNESS: WHAT THE MAN OF RESENTMENT EXPERIENCES

describes as the movement of the soul: its incipient capacity to take things upon itself, to escape the hateful drive that had taken it in its grasp. We also see here how difficult it is for a patient to put up with his analyst, so even tempered, who has just entered into his conscious life.

Voyenne's commentary on the notion of hatred in counter-transference is enlightening in many regards. First, because it recalls the Freudian truth that sees in counter-transference an obstacle to the functioning of analysis. It is true that counter-transference provides an exceedingly difficult test for the latter. It may be that every analyst dreams of being a neutral and perfectly impartial node onto which everything can flow. But is this possible? If not, we should ask ourselves what the analyst who believes that he can escape the violence of counter-transference is playing at—what kind of analytic illusion he is caught up in. Confronting this question in no way assumes success, but nonetheless displays a certain lucidity on the part of the analyst. Supervision is thus advocated by Freud[131] to permit the analyst to continuously rectify moments of aggression that can arise when counter-transference has not been surpassed.

The archetype of the therapeutic relationship is the one that links a baby to its mother: the support that the latter lavishes upon the former is of the same nature as the support lavished upon the patient by the analyst; I return below to the question of the mother's imaginative development, which in a sense is Winnicott's version of the *imaginatio vera*, as a key element in the construction of the subject and in the emergence of his potential to resist and surpass any future resentment. This imaginative development of the mother is the environment in which the child grows up, the framework of his future individuation. It is not that the analyst is the mother, or that the framework of the analysis is the maternal environment, but once again, there is a familiarity between these two environments. Voyenne employs Winnicott's definition to describe what it is, at the beginning of the process, that makes possible a future subject— namely, the quality of the link between this subject and the maternal (let us say parental) concern of which he is the object: "'I would say that before object relationships the state of affairs is this: that the unit is not the individual, the unit is an environment-individual set-up. The centre of gravity of the being does not start off in the individual. It is in the total set-up.'"[132] It is not a matter substituting the analytic framework for the parent in order to reconstitute this heteronomous center of gravity; as the analyst knows, it is almost certain that this environment—and especially the parent in question—was deficient

75

PART I

during the patient's childhood. Yet the framework constructed for the analytic sessions—the quality of the environment, the relational quality of listening, engaging, being attentive—is essential and fundamental for the functionality of the cure. On the other hand, a deficient framework will produce dysfunction: "The notion of environment . . . brings with it an understanding of the importance of the framework in analysis, and of the counter-transferential potential of the framework's shortcomings."[133] Voyenne then returns to Winnicott to list the fundamental aspects that preserve a correct framework, commenting: "It is by way of deficiencies, or variations to the elements of the framework that have not been sufficiently thought through, that the analyst's repressed aggression and hatred can infiltrate the analysis, at times in insidious ways that are repudiated by the analyst."[134] This is thus how the analyst's resentment infiltrates the analysis: it does not necessarily happen in a direct way, or because the correct mediation of the correct framework (which contains the patient) was not produced. Resentment arises from the breakdown of this proper mediation—the latter is now incapable of erecting dikes to hold resentment back:

> 9. In the analytic situation the analyst is much more reliable than people are in ordinary life; on the whole punctual, free from temper tantrums, free from compulsive falling in love, etc. 10. There is a very clear distinction in the analysis between fact and fantasy, so that the analyst is not hurt by an aggressive dream. 11. An absence of the talion reaction can be counted on. 12. The analyst survives [!].[135]

We see here that the framework of the analytic session preserves both patient and analyst from the violence of their drives of love and hatred. With many patients, the demand for love (in particular from the analyst) is initially immense: the patient interprets everything with reference to this sentiment, and both love and hatred can come about at any moment. And yet many analysts play upon this feeling— do they play upon it or are they played by it?—thus causing distress when the analysis enters into its next phase. The difficulty of analysis is that of the Aristotelian mean, in other words of the most measured and least vindictive reliability that is possible. Reliability in all of its boredom, in a way, which may not have the panache of romantic passion, but which also does not give rise to possible feelings of abandonment. Simply being reliable is of modest difficulty, but it is necessary for combatting alienation in the patient. Simply being reliable is a road that necessarily leads to ingratitude on the part of

BITTERNESS: WHAT THE MAN OF RESENTMENT EXPERIENCES

the patient: the latter may later recognize its benefit, but this is far from certain; the time in which the patient idealizes his analyst does not last—a good thing in the fight against the patient's alienation, but painful for the analyst as it reveals to him his limited value.

Nonetheless, the hatred that an analyst can feel for his patient derives not only from the latter's eventual ingratitude, which is in fact quite reasonable; it can also come about in the analyst who sees his lethal drives awakened by the conscious and unconscious provocations of the patient. Voyenne, commenting on Winnicott, underlines the exhilarating aspect that the spread of hatred can bring about, both for the patient and for the analyst. Undoubtedly the difference between the man of resentment and the one who is able to get through it without remaining its prisoner is to be found here: at stake is the enjoyment of hatred. The one who gets through resentment . . . undoubtedly gets through it because he feels no enjoyment in keeping himself in this state: he derives a real displeasure and indeed guilt from it, which makes it imperative to come out of repression. Conversely, for the one who is used to enjoying hatred—finding within it a vital energy, using his conscious mind to justify it and to disguise it as anger—the challenge is greater, for to cut oneself off from enjoyment can seem senseless. Here we begin to see the contours of an objective for education: teaching the subject, as early as possible, to experience displeasure when he gives free rein to his drives of hatred—in other words, to link the capacity for frustration to a pleasure, that of a certain form of mastery and symbolization: thanks to this capacity for sublimated frustration, I can get out of this situation, I can transform absence into presence, having into being, or the opposite. I can be mobile, I can escape, I can begin to feel the freedom that consists in ceasing to be alienated.

Let us return to the reliability of the analyst, which recalls what it means for a mother to be "good enough"—in other words, the absence of perfection that pushes the developing subject to experience frustration, and above all to build his own road by separating himself, if only on an intellectual or symbolic level. Indeed, the potential of the analytic cure does not become apparent prior to this gesture of separation, which can in no way be reduced to the fact of physical separation; I would even say that a physical separation can lack the truth of symbolizing separation, which is not an argument for not leaving one's analyst—leaving the analyst is not the same as stopping the analysis. For Winnicott, the possibility of this hate in the counter-transference is not a simple shortcoming. The issue is not so much that of a possible reversal—the analyst, of course, has his own way of sublimating this drive—but that of the possibility of a dialectic between the analyst and the patient, through the experience of competing hatreds that are nonetheless mediated by the session. Something happens here that can undoubtedly never happen between two forms of hatred in ordinary, nonmediated life, and it happens precisely because there is a reliable framework. The reliability of the framework and the environment—not the purely formal aspect of the framework, but the demand for quality and the adaptation of the patient's singularity to the specificity of the interrelational dynamic—allows the hatreds to be mediated and to symbolize together what they would not be capable of symbolizing alone. Voyenne sees the main benefit of Winnicott's analysis in this definition of hate in the counter-transference: "His two articles on counter-transference usher in a new conceptualization: there is a zone of common labor between the patient and his analyst. The movements of the drives that are brought out in the session have an impact on both protagonists, which allows for a shared creation which will lead the patient to live within the cure—not simply a repetition of what he has already lived, but also an ability to create the new experiences that are necessary for analytic work to be truly transformative."[136]

Does this mean that we should hope for the analyst's hatred to arise in the counter-transference? By no means. But this allows us to understand how a specific space, an environment, can be a key mediation tool for the liberation of the individual, and how something that appeared to be a shortcoming can later be revealed as empowering. This opens up a form of hope: the confrontation of two individuals besotted with resentment, if they are able to enter into a specific framework, can overturn this resentment and produce an escape valve that is all the more singular for being common. This in no way removes the difficulty of finding such a space, for a subject besotted with resentment feels no obligation to find it, and since he is not looking for it, he is often incapable of recognizing, in this or that space, the opportunity for interior transformation.

— 27 —

TO THE SOURCES OF RESENTMENT, WITH MONTAIGNE

Montaigne, like all the builders of humanism, scatters clues throughout the *Essays* that allow us to think the nature of resentment, human weaknesses, customs, conditioned reflexes, forms of complacency, small acts of cowardice, or larger instances of bitterness. "How the soul discharges its emotions against false objects when lacking real ones":[137] a title (Book I, Essay 4) every term of which outlines an element of said resentment—discharge, emotions, false objects, lack of reality.

In resentment, there is always an overflowing, a drive lacking direction, an error of judgment, the fact of taking the false for the true, a focus on objects (in the knowledge that focusing on an object always serves to alienate). In this chapter, Montaigne describes an ordinary and indeed bland man, filled with bad faith and furthermore conscious of this, not trying to surpass it, perhaps finding within it a certain pleasure or at least a support that allows him to assuage the displeasure brought on by his torments: "A local gentleman of ours who is marvellously subject to gout would answer his doctors quite amusingly when asked to give up salted meats entirely. He would say that he liked to have something to blame when tortured by the onslaughts of that illness: the more he yelled out curses against the saveloy or the tongue or the ham, the more relief he felt."[138] The anecdote may make us smile—we can all recognize ourselves in it. But it is important: it shows that the subject prefers the pleasure of hating an object, the pleasure of grievances and insults, to the obligation of taking upon himself the fact of not giving in to his desire—the obligation of responsibility. Montaigne continues, citing Lucan: "'As winds, unless they come up against dense woods, lose their force and are distended into empty space.'"[139] In other words,

PART I

resentment that does not designate an object to hate, an object to stumble over, cannot be sustained as resentment.

This seems to contradict what Scheler says about the indecision that defines resentment. But not exactly, because resentment is often initially marked by a close focus on the object, which it only begins to detest later. This phase of indecision is important, but it is sometimes accompanied—this is often the case from a collective standpoint—by a strong hatred (often called irrational) of a human or non-human "object" that is furthermore designated as the symbol of this very hatred. A resentment that never found anything to stumble over could be connected with a form of nihilism—an irrevocable withdrawal from all *affectio societatis*. In order for resentment to be politicized and to appear in the public sphere, the man of resentment must abandon the simple interiority of subjective malaise, so as to stigmatize something outside of himself. If this outside is equated with a person, resentment can become incessant in that this person is a living being: in his mobility, he provides an unwavering support (in spite of himself) to the spread of resentment. From this point, the man of resentment is permanently capable of reactivating his resentment simply by contemplating the life of the object of his resentment, independently of the real nature of this person's acts and gestures. Simply seeing the hated object endlessly rekindles the negative energy of the man of resentment, who begins to demand more and more of this energy instead of taking upon himself the analytic labor of combating alienation.

In the chapter devoted to liars, Montaigne evokes the frenzy of Darius: "in order not to forget an insult suffered at the hands of the Athenians he made a page intone three times in his ear as he sat at table: 'Remember the Athenians, Sire.'"[140] We see here that the man of resentment willingly creates this little voice to remind him of humiliation, precisely at the moment when he is meant to relax and enjoy a simple meal. The little voice always comes back, and the individual goes beyond merely putting up with it as if it were a voice foreign to him, a sonorous hallucination. This can happen in particular with cases that lean toward psychosis, such as an exacerbated paranoia, schizophrenia, borderline personality disorder, etc. But psychosis diagnosed as such in no way has a monopoly on resentment, and this is precisely the difficulty, especially for the possibility of living in society. Being anchored in repetition is typical of resentment; this is the case for rumination and also for stubbornness—"stubbornly defending a fort without good reason,"[141] as Montaigne said (even if, admittedly, he said it with regard to someone who, in the manner

80

BITTERNESS: WHAT THE MAN OF RESENTMENT EXPERIENCES

of a zealot, persists in holding out against an opponent who is much stronger). This is not an argument to defend cowardice, but an occasion to recall, in the manner of a good Aristotelian, the importance of the virtue of the mean, and that only this virtue befits reason—in other words, in this instance, the sense of proportionality, the ability to consider a situation in its generality and not from a single point of view that opens onto excess. But as Montaigne was the first to articulate, the notion of the limit or the border between vice and virtue is not always easy to establish.

— II —

FASCISM[142]

The Psychological Sources of Collective Resentment

— 1 —

EXILE, FASCISM, AND RESENTMENT

Adorno, 1

Adorno is a key thinker for understanding the problem of resentment in its individual and collective processes, and for understanding how to resist it—or at least for understanding which personality types can extract themselves from it, even though they may have been wounded or destroyed by it. Adorno himself was able to leave resentment behind: he saw its abyss, perceived its proximity to us all; given his own weariness, the difficulties he underwent in exile, it could easily have destroyed him. But his oeuvre escaped it: his *Minima Moralia: Reflections from Damaged Life* sidelined resentment in favor of the Open in the Rilkean sense; indeed, *The Open* could be an alternative title for *Negative Dialectics*—namely, the form of thought, proper to Adorno, that attempts to make something out of the negative without magically transforming it into positivity or ceding to nihilism: a path constructed in the shadow of vertigo, a path that can indeed cause vertigo but prefers to make peace with the latter rather than inventing a system in which everything has its place and its resolution—which would necessarily be false. The "Fragility of Truth,"[143] as he writes, to distance himself from all notions of Hegelian synthesis—to which he prefers the idea of a musical theory that is capable of composition and improvisation.

> Analogously, instead of reducing philosophy to categories, one would in a sense have to compose it first. Its course must be a ceaseless self-renewal, by its own strength as well as in friction with whatever standard it may have. The crux is what happens in it, not a thesis or a position.[144]

Adorno wrote this text at the end of his life, after his forced exile, after encountering the decrepitude of the world, i.e., Nazism, after

PART II

having to flee to protect his life. But even from a great distance, he sees the disaster, he reaches it, for he knows he has fled—certainly, he had no real alternative, but guilt will always be at the heart of Adorno's oeuvre. As a musician, he knows that the trace of this guilt is audible, that it impregnates music, perhaps even more surely than theory, and it is thus that we should understand negative dialectics, the form of dialectics that cannot justify what has happened, that can simply confront it and produce, in those who remain, enough consciousness and vigilance to hold fast and to combat the horror of what has played out. We understand, furthermore, that whether one confronts a horror that has taken place or the mere threat of such a horror, the result is almost the same: horror radiates outward, beyond the instant that has passed and in advance of the instant to come; horror leaks from every direction, like a malignant water that seeps in, but also like an explosion. The terrible thing about horror is simply that it exists. All doubt ceases when faced with its positive existence. There is no more doubt: horror is right there, irreversibly there. And yet nothing is understood—nothing makes sense. And even if we can make sense of it, searching for this meaning plants the seeds of our despair—we run the enormous risk of taking root in it. Horror wins, it constantly gains more ground than we think. This is undoubtedly the horizon within which negative dialectics is deployed: what is needed to counter this malign potential is another form of the Open, the one that does not delude itself, the one that is able to transform negativity.

With the danger of Nazism becoming clearer, Adorno goes into exile, first in Europe and then in the United States. There, he will encounter no shortage of thinkers who are capable of decrypting what is at work in the all-encompassing resentment that makes identification with the Führer possible, even though a mere glance (and not even a particularly critical one) at him reveals the weakness of his person. But here we come upon a well-known Nietzschean adage, that of the morality of slaves or the vengeance of the weak: "The agitators disavow any pretense to superiority, implying that the leader . . . is one who is as weak as his brethren but who dares to confess his weakness without inhibition, and is consequently going to be transformed into the strong man."[145] Adorno will seek to understand the mechanisms of fascist thinking, above all the decisive reversal that it operates. For fascism, in its acceptance by the masses, functions according to this vengeance of the weak, and specifically with an identification—one that comes about gradually—with the strong man who avenges the weak. This reversal of wounded

FASCISM: THE PSYCHOLOGICAL SOURCES OF COLLECTIVE RESENTMENT

narcissism (a form of narcissistic restoration) is necessary for fascism to establish itself in a more lasting way, and with a violence that it ends up accepting as its own, even though it may once have refused to admit its existence—as is always the case for "weak" defensive and reactive techniques. Adorno also speaks of "repressive egalitarianism,"[146] a notion that is particularly pertinent when we seek to understand the ambivalent relationship to a leader who takes hold of groups—a relationship that posits the leader as an extension of oneself (of this weak self or "false self") that finally allows one to assume all of his drive-related demons without anyone preventing him from doing so. Those who seek a degree of differentiation, a level of individuation, find that this is impossible: they are reprimanded and their actions unleash a high degree of hostility on the part of other group members. The group cannot be escaped. Individuation has no place, not even for the leader, who gives the illusion of being a free individual who has overcome his alienation. He has reached the highest level of reification, has pushed the logic of becoming a thing as far as it can possibly go: he is the maximum implementation of this logic, an almighty figure of regression—yet is never able to gain access to himself. Adorno gives the following definition of fascism, one that resonates with the psychotic reality of the illness of resentment: "a dictatorship by persecution-maniacs, [which] realizes all the persecution fears of its victims."[147]

Resentment is an illness of persecution: ceaselessly believing oneself to be the object of an exterior persecution, feeling that one is the only victim and, within this position, refusing responsibility for oneself as a subject. This illness of persecution tends toward an enjoyment of loathing, for one loathes one's position of submissiveness. But one prefers to believe that this submissiveness is without remainder, the better to overturn it and give free rein to the drive to destroy the other, which appears fully justified. The problem is that there is a remainder. But the man of resentment chooses to delude himself and not see this remainder, for it would offer him the possibility of a solution or an escape—but one that would entail effort: he would have to take responsibility upon himself. It's better to hate than to act, and to communicate this hatred to a group whose members have made the same choice, that of the delusion of a submissiveness without remainder; this unleashes the mechanism of generalized hatred, which produces a form of action constructed solely upon the cruelty of the drives, a form of action that is in no way action but that, once it is adopted by great numbers or quantities of people, produces a qualitative reversal that gives

87

PART II

the illusion of being a true action—even though it is in fact a mass reaction.

In the 1950s, Adorno continued to develop his theories of personality, notably of the personality that may be at the origin of "fascistic *potential*."[148] Several traits converge in this personality, such as "conformity, conventionalism, authoritarian submission, determination by external pressures, thinking in ingroup-outgroup terms, and the like."[149] We find here several of the criteria of the *resentmentist* personality, which equates order with a restoration of its goods and its being; which employs servility to practice authoritarianism without facing the consequences; which brings about its renowned passive aggression; which fantasizes, invents stories, and projects all sorts of false representations with the aim of reinforcing its prejudices and stereotypes; and which settles into a perverse and reified manipulation, incapable from this point of considering the other as a subject (it would find this to be unbearable) or of seeing him as anything other than an instrument.

As others fall into this collective movement of loathing, one must be able to resist and to find resources within oneself. One must invent a *minima moralia*, a morality of fragments—which is a long way from a complete and unperforated, but illusory, *magna moralia*—comprising events, chasms, impasses, ebbs, and flows; by way of these minuscule elements, one must aim for the ocean, for water, air, the open sea, an elsewhere, others who are still alive, a self that is still dignified. "What would happiness be that was not measured by the immeasurable grief at what is? For the world is deeply ailing. He who cautiously adapts to it by this very act shares in its madness, while the eccentric alone would stand his ground and bit it rave no more."[150] We enter morality here by way of a song that Adorno happens to remember, a song from his childhood that had made him happy, "Between the mountain and the deep, deep vale":[151] two rabbits are enjoying themselves on the grass when a hunter suddenly kills them; they fall, play dead, indeed believe that they are dead, realize that they are not, and run off. What moral should we take from this story? One about semblance? Absurdity? Injustice? The stupidity of a carefree attitude? Adorno does not say, and instead simply reminds us of "'the unreality of despair,'"[152] which is totally compatible—alas—with the feeling of certainty that horrible things are taking place, have taken place, will take place: this is existence, it is inseparable form existence, not as its goal but as its unavoidable companion. A few lines of a song, therefore, a little fragment by way of which to enter: we can use this mouse hole as a keyhole, shoot

FASCISM: THE PSYCHOLOGICAL SOURCES OF COLLECTIVE RESENTMENT

for a way out without being sure of anything, for this way out will appear to be unreal, just like the despair for which it seeks to provide an escape.

Adorno's musings on the way of the world might remind us of what Walter Benjamin calls the "loss of experience" by those who no longer know how to transform what they live into experience—a sensible lived experience that would be conscious of itself, thus permitting it to be an object of transmission. Confronting this disturbance in the world, one finds the moral fragments, the stellar fragments; there are also the "dream notes" that Adorno will leave behind like so many unresolved clinical cases, as a way of coming to terms with his unconscious—or more generally as the unconscious of a man who brushes against the misfortunes of the world and builds a path that does not validate them, a clinical description of his dreams that gives every reader the possibility of employing his talent for interpretation: "We were walking . . . on a ridge path. . . . I set about looking for a better path."[153] Adorno, thinker at the cross-roads of a denunciation of resentment, the emergence of fascism, the establishment of the concept of reification, and a consideration of unconscious life (even if he sidelines psychoanalytic interpretation, it is clear that he recognizes the universality of the unconscious); Adorno, caught up in his own disenchantment, undergoing the bitter experience of exile, of the need to think in a foreign language, and of a merely grudging recognition by his colleagues. Nothing is fluid, nothing is easy. Everything is stained. Philip Roth,[154] in his own particular style, could be seen as one of his heirs.

"Every intellectual in emigration is, without exception, mutilated."[155] To moral, existential, and psychological precariousness is added a material one, that of a competition between those who have been humiliated, in which each emigrant is an enemy of the others, whether or not he is a professor. Adorno found himself within "the most shameful and degrading of all situations, that of completing suppliants [who] are thus virtually compelled to show each other their most repulsive sides"[156]—the suppliants in question being intellectuals in emigration. Adorno, who experienced a lack of recognition, a permanent humiliation, the absence of any refuge, and intense competition, could undoubtedly have fallen into resentment. In *Minima Moralia*, he speaks of how exiles are cast into oblivion—how they must leave behind their own value and every-thing that marks them out as different, which is reduced to their intellectual "'background,'"[157] is "reified,"[158] and immediately set aside, forgotten, devalued; in an entry entitled *"To them no thoughts*

PART II

shall be turned," he writes: "The past life of émigrés is, as we know, annulled."[159] All those who have the experience of crossing from one shore to another have learned this lesson at their own cost. From the moment one crosses, one no longer counts for anything, for one no longer possesses anything. Intellectual experience is considered "untransferable," as are no shortage of other forms of status—this is a trick to bring the emigrant down from his perch, to remind him of his sad condition on those rare occasions when he believes himself to have escaped it.

The humiliation is all the greater for the intellectual who prides himself on being universal, on having skills that transcend this or that border and apply to all of humanity. This is undoubtedly a form of vanity, but it is also a demand: that of going beyond his little circle, of thinking in a way that applies to the world and not only his world. For my part, I lacked that courage—the courage of going into exile, of forcing oneself into exile. The circumstances of my life spared me from this, and I did not consider it to be my task to force it upon myself. I might put it this way: I thought that exile might be beneficial, but I worried about the exile of language, which seemed to me even more difficult than physical exile. Adorno did not have the chance to avoid this obstacle. *Minima Moralia* is entirely devoted to describing the torments of the "intellectual in emigration"; it transmits to us a "melancholy science,"[160] the testimony of a *"dialogue intérieur"*[161] which is undoubtedly what permitted him to not succumb to the drive of resentment; the "science" is sad but it remains dialectic; it is interior and does not reject this interiority— quite the contrary. Adorno goes over his life with a fine-tooth comb in *Minima Moralia*, and this life acquires a newfound dignity as a result; it is sublimated without being reified, opening onto something outside of itself instead of enjoying its own mutilation in the manner of a victim who has become persecutor.

Adorno's work lacks humor. It contains the art of the song, the reminiscences of artisans, a sensitivity to all the markers of beauty, even the least significant ones—far from being mocked or denigrated, these markers undertake a work of mediation. Adorno extracts something from every possible occasion. But strangely, humor is mostly absent. It appears between the lines, more specifically in the titles of fragments: it is clear that a title such as *"To them no thoughts shall be turned"* testifies to a strong capacity for derision. But any affirmation of the need for the *vis comica* is absent, as though humor negated negativity—which it in no way does. Humor builds itself on negativity and thus becomes capable of deposing the latter; perhaps

FASCISM: THE PSYCHOLOGICAL SOURCES OF COLLECTIVE RESENTMENT

it allows itself not to take even a tragic negativity seriously—what is at stake in such humor is a strong gesture of "composition." Adorno confides to us his extremely fine sensitivity to the small moments of life, such as the one in which a child takes delight in a couple's visit to his parents: these banal moments are the promise of a different world, of habits that can be broken, of rules that will be annulled on this evening to welcome and to lodge the guests; this might also mean that rules will be relaxed for the child, that he will be admitted to the night for the first time, outside the requirement to sleep. The child beams. Adorno names this entry "Heliotrope," and one could call this a form of humor that turns us unremittingly toward the sun, toward an energetic light, and that liberates "the joy of greatest proximity . . . by wedding it to utmost distance."[162] This game that humor plays with space-time—the art of symbolization, in short—is very familiar to us, and we can all experience it: it is an escape from the instant, one that does not negate the present but does not submit to it either; it is a taking of distance that does not entail detachment, at least not in the pathological sense of the term; this *vis comica* is essential for the minimal upkeep of our psychological health—we do not make enough use of it. We misunderstand its real nature, construing it as a superfluous asset or the gift of a salesperson who makes others laugh without any real awareness, just to amuse them. But this is only a small part of humor, the one that is least interesting and that lends itself least to sublimation: it merely creates a screen. We will return below to the resource with which it provides us in the fight against human resentment.

— 2 —

CAPITALISM, REIFICATION, AND RESENTMENT

Adorno, 2

Let us return to the notion of reification, which is at the heart of the resentmentist process. The notion comes from Marx, who perceived the reifying dimension of capitalism. It is also present in Adorno's work, and is dealt with at length by the Frankfurt School, over the course of several decades and in the work of several authors. Reification is also the offspring of the process of reproducibility (superbly analyzed by Benjamin), so dear to modernity, which standardizes its objects so as to mass produce them and gain the maximum profit from them, while at the same time reducing its manufacturing costs. The entire world is now bound to this logic. Culture itself has been reified, simply by becoming the culture industry. In the work of Georg Lukács,[163] reification is the process of "thingification"[164] of life and of the subject. This is not unlike Weberian rationalization, which aims to "qualify" the quantitative, in other words to disqualify the qualitative so as to overvalue the quantitative, which is henceforth called upon to become a new form of the qualitative by substituting the numerical figure for the power of the name.

We thus see a reductionism at work, one that affects every element of the life of the subject, which comes to be filtered entirely through economic categories, and henceforth attains value only by way of this mutilation at the level of its definition. The world, the subject, and life become "calculable" in the sense of costs and benefits, as though everything could be circumscribed within these categorizations. The world becomes binary: the share of those who are "disqualified" increases as the same rate that this great movement of rationalization gains greater magnitude. Reification is the other name for instrumental rationality, which has been well known since Weber's analysis of the disenchantment of the world fostered by

FASCISM: THE PSYCHOLOGICAL SOURCES OF COLLECTIVE RESENTMENT

modern technology and calculation. Honneth's work takes up reification and suggests an antidote to it in the concept of recognition. For in fact, this is what counterbalances our interdependence, and permits us to not experience our forms of dependence in a disqualifying way. We are all dependent, interdependent; domination can be defined as the fact of rendering this dependence invisible, and placing the other within a regime of non-recognition. Clearly, it becomes easier to live with dependence if the latter is inscribed within a regime of reciprocal interdependencies, in which individual success is impossible without the collective. The ethics of recognition is the framework that allows us to experience these dependencies in a legitimate and valid way that is not disqualifying for individuals. Recognition in this sense is a principle that allows individuals to resist the processes of reification that are at work in the capitalist world. Honneth lays out several different levels of symbolic—and, more specifically, material—recognition. To refuse recognition to someone is to reify him, to place him within a reifying relationship, turning him into a simple object that one can do without or replace; it is to negate the singular value that he has determined in his own process of self-empowerment.

Let us return to Adorno, in whose work we find the dialectical play of reification and resentment. "Capitalist production so confines them, body and soul, that [consumers] fall helpless victims to what is offered them. As naturally as the ruled always took the morality imposed upon them more seriously than did the rulers themselves, the deceived masses are today captivated by the myth of success even more than the successful are. Immovably, they insist on the very ideology which enslaves them."[165] In other words, the strength of capitalist rationalization is its ability to place the individual in a situation in which he falls victim to desires that are not specifically his own; in this situation, he is caught in the well-known mimetic rivalry of psychic laws, desiring what he does not possess, and closing himself off within a regime of permanent frustration that makes him desire that which he believes to be necessary so as to be recognized as a subject. The consumer has allowed himself to be swindled by adopting from the outset a desire that is not necessarily his own, by not questioning it, and by not realizing that he himself is its object of consumption, an object that does not reify in its turn because it remains at the object stage, and hence does not promise him any illusion of recognition.

We see this loop between reification, missed recognition, and resentment once again when Adorno and Horkheimer explain to

PART II

us the way in which the culture industry operates to confine the individual. Where our time is concerned, we can put things in almost the same terms. An astonishing movement of *de-narcissization* is at work in the world of labor: the individual feels himself to be "replaceable," interchangeable, precarious, disposable, and under constant pressure that becomes arbitrary in its very permanence. This phenomenon of de-narcissization works in concert with the other end of the production process—namely, the universe of consumption, which seeks to *re-narcissize* the individual so that he is able to return to work by obeying the same inept rules that take away his singularity. On the one hand, there is a strong psychological decompensation; on the other, there is a compensation in the form of addictive goods that are able to compensate only in a fleeting way, for the subject must be maintained in a state of anxiety to keep coming back to this compensatory and falsely re-narcissizing entertainment.

Already in 1944, Horkheimer and Adorno grasp the perverse nature of these workings and their indubitable effectiveness: "Nevertheless the culture industry remains the entertainment business. Its influence over the consumers is established by entertainment; that will ultimately be broken not by an outright decree, but by the hostility inherent in the principle of entertainment to what is greater than itself. . . . Amusement under late capitalism is the prolongation of work. It is sought after as an escape from the mechanized work process, and to recruit strength in order to be able to cope with it again."[166] The thesis here is somewhat different, but is based on the same presuppositions. People at work are subjected to automation, but the latter is so generalized in the whole of society, touching upon so many of its vital elements, that individuals are no longer capable of experiencing anything but standardized automation, even in their leisure time: "What happens at work, in the factory, or in the office can only be escaped from by approximation to it in one's leisure time. All amusement suffers from this incurable malady. Pleasure hardens into boredom because, if it is to remain pleasure, it must not demand any effort and therefore moves rigorously in the worn grooves of association."[167]

In our time, everyone is liable to experience this decompensation, which for some tends toward depression, to professional exhaustion, or to psychotic disorders and forms of conduct; at an individual level, this gives rise to an enhanced anxiety, and an incapacity to make any form of effort, even during moments of pleasure. Pleasure must now be immediate, abundant, repeated, unprecedented, so as to undertake its compensatory work in an instantaneous manner.

FASCISM: THE PSYCHOLOGICAL SOURCES OF COLLECTIVE RESENTMENT

But instantaneous compensation is in no way resilience: what is at stake here is the difference between addiction and desire, or between the pleasure that annuls itself at the very moment it is experienced and the joy that is capable of exceeding the instant in which it comes about.

— 3 —

KNOWLEDGE AND RESENTMENT

Nathalie Heinich views the work of Norbert Elias (though this is undoubtedly true of the work of many authors) as a marvelous attempt at transformation and sublimation, in the face of the biting reality of resentment. What is said of artistic work can also be said of sociological work as such, in that the latter seeks to explain and hence distance itself from phenomena; its reflections aim to create the capacity for symbolization and for action. "Sociology instead of resentment,"[168] as she puts it in an article that she devotes to Elias. The sociologist critiques not so much the lack of critical thinking in our world as the impossibility of questioning instrumental rationality, which by focusing exclusively on ends not only destroys action but thought itself—the two are inextricably linked in emancipatory conceptions of labor. To combat this, she advocates sociology, knowledge, reason, and analysis; confronting human contradictions and deciphering drives, she argues, can protect us from resentmentist excesses:

> Yes, I think that the work of Elias is a vast and extraordinary endeavor that seeks to sublimate a single problem: that of how to be a Jew within a non-Jewish society, and indeed within an anti-Semitic society. Considered within various contexts, above all that of courtly society, this problem has given rise to the systematic study of the ways a society comes to modify itself due to the efforts of certain groups to change their place within social hierarchies, so as to move from lower to higher places within these hierarchies. It has also given rise to the study of how these changes in social structures affect individual lives, at the most intimate level of experience.[169]

FASCISM: THE PSYCHOLOGICAL SOURCES OF COLLECTIVE RESENTMENT

We return here to the feeling of injustice that chokes the heart of the individual when he feels humiliated, unintegrated, excluded from circles of symbolic recognition; and to the question of how each individual contends with the persistence of social, economic, and cultural determinations. The archetypical example is that of the Jew, but it can be extended to every human being, to every man or woman. The question, in short, of how being excluded from social mobility is an absolute danger for the body and the soul of the individual. There were many occasions on which Elias could have vacillated in his own approach to this issue—when considering, for example, neurotic repression, psychotic denial, or indeed lethal resentment—but he abandoned approaches based on victimhood in favor of sociological work so that others would be able to relate to these problems that initially concerned him, so as to universalize his aims and his quest, and to develop a form of thought that speaks to us all, thereby expanding our world.

> Of course, there were other ways to deal with trauma: repressing it, so that nothing could come out of it apart from neurosis or even psychosis; or transforming it into resentment, anger, perpetual accusations against its perpetrators, or complaints about his own suffering and victimhood. But there is nothing of the sort in Elias's work: neither repression nor resentment, just silence about the Jews within a vast body of work devoted to the fundamental question of what happens when Jews try to integrate into a society that is anti-Semitic from top to bottom—Jews whose difficulties sprout from no other reason than that of being born where they were born.[170]

We return here to the essential categories of the inside and the outside, those very categories that the man of resentment seeks to reject because they bring about feelings of bitterness that cannot be overcome. He thus seeks to erase the border between them and to bring in other categories by gathering together urges that are hostile to them both. Heinich speaks of Elias's "incredible ability to overcome resentment through conceptual work," and shows that he was able to shift the very notion of "domination" toward that of interdependence, a notion that Honneth speaks of in the context of recognition:

> This notion of interdependence, associated with that of the interiorization of constraints, allows us to escape the binary opposition between "individuals" and "society" . . . and to understand . . .

97

PART II

the displacements of psychic, bodily, and emotional determinations between individual and collective dimensions. . . . Resentment implies a focus on "bad" objects. Elias could have devoted his intellectual energy to endlessly fighting his enemies, whatever their names may have been. Instead, he completely abandoned a perspective centred on objects to turn toward what is really at stake when we try to challenge social stratification so as to obtain inclusion within a desired group: relations between individuals.[171]

Resentment does not just entail, as we have seen, a focus on bad objects. It is rather the case that every obsessive focus tends to transform the nature of the object, which can thus be neutralized: it is not merely that the individual desires what he should not desire, but that he distorts the very notion of desire; by alienating himself within the desired object, he desires poorly. The art of desire is a lesson in sublimated frustration, for it cannot be equated to an almightiness, one that is necessarily illusory and hence necessarily cruel (in that it does not go beyond this illusion). Escaping resentment is not only a question of undertaking analytic work that is worthy of the name: it is also a matter of bringing about, between individuals, relationships that are worthy of the name.

As we have seen with Honneth, only the notion of recognition prevents the inevitable interdependence between individuals from being perverted into a form of domination. In Honneth's work, the concept of indivisibility is also linked to this. A lack of recognition makes individuals invisible, which allows us to better understand why resentment has such a need for vindictiveness, as though it sought to make amends for an excess of invisibility that it rightly judges to be illegitimate; to combat this, men of resentment—who have seen their subjecthood and their lives rendered invisible—seek to appear, to be seen, to be heard. This is something that Heinich perceives well, and it is something that Elias exhibits in his work: even though he experienced the violence of exclusion, he does not employ sociology to construct a new position of power that would allow him to exclude others from behind the veneer of science. Such a form of knowledge[172] would play the game of power, enslaving the individual to a "falsified" recognition (in Honneth's sense) that would not be able to protect him against resentment. As for Elias, one of the lessons he learned from his greatest influence, Max Weber, was that of axiological neutrality, which allows one to detach oneself rather than seeking to "settle a score" under the cover of theorizing:

FASCISM: THE PSYCHOLOGICAL SOURCES OF COLLECTIVE RESENTMENT

The famous lesson of Max Weber on axiological neutrality, or the suspension of value judgments, in the exercising of one's functions as a teacher and a researcher: this is a lesson that Elias absorbed magnificently in his well-known opposition between "investment" and "detachment." Clearly, anyone who uses sociology (or any other academic discipline) to "settle a score," as one says—that is, to fight his enemies—would automatically adopt a normative position, in other words a conception of sociology as tool of disqualification, denunciation, or critique. . . . Inversely, anyone using sociology to justify or establish his own social position would probably try to highlight the causes and reasons for actually-existing social stratification, so as to justify it as the only rational way to organize a society.[173]

We must therefore aim for the act of comprehension in its etymological sense, that of "grasping with"—but we must also try to "grasp ourselves with," in other words to be active parties, not to cancel the phenomenon of axiological distance, but so as not to delude ourselves, to see ourselves as above the fray or excluded from it. We must try to be within the fray, within the chaos, history, the present, not in order to profit from it, but simply to be there, to experience this reality, understand something of it, open up the world, open up its "vastness," in a way. We must do everything we can to counter the reverse of this, namely the intellectual and moral closing-off that is proper to resentment. A tension arises here: on the one hand, the expansion of openness, and on the other, the overflowing of resentment; on the one hand, a spreading forth, and on the other, a closing off. We must always ensure that we are at work on this openness—shaping the Open—so as to grasp that which can allow us to assuage our lethal drives.

Here, ethics brings us back to the metacritical universe behind every project that is based on knowledge: the demand for questioning that, while it is inseparable from the scientific regimes of truth production, never arises in a void. Chaos rumbles all around this scientific demand. In this sense, science—the movement, desire, and work that comprise it—is a form of resistance to the drives and passions that form the chaos of the world. Here, it is difficult to dissociate ethics from epistemology, processes of knowledge from processes of resistance. When scientists rightly demand their autonomy from society, we should understand this autonomy as an act of resistance in the face of societal prejudices and demands of all sorts. To think is to aim for impartiality, but it is impossible to bring about this impartiality without clashes and conflicts.

99

— 4 —

CONSTELLATORY WRITING AND STUPOR

Adorno, 3

There is another path, one that is similar to those I have described even if it differs from them: the entry by way of a language without sociological pretentions (even if sociology nourishes social philosophy and, more globally, all attempts at understanding); in other words, entry by way of the work, whether we are speaking of poetry or (since we have been speaking about Adorno) a more *constellatory* writing, one composed of fragments and aphorisms, like so many stars or little nothings, pebbles or seeds—however one wants to describe it. The "constellation" in Adorno's work is that which negative dialectics attempts to think, at the same time as it seeks to employ the constellation as a methodological tool: "Becoming aware of the constellation in which a thing stands is tantamount to deciphering the constellation which, having come to be, it bears within it. . . . Cognition of the object and its constellation is cognition of the process stored in the object."[174] Adorno is not aiming here solely for a cognition or a knowledge of the singular. This is a well-known Hegelian move (even if Adorno denies it): the singular is the road toward the universal, but its thinking does not seek to create a system; rather than seeking to fill in all of its holes, it allows for these perforations, preferring the constellation to the system. There is nothing better or more adequate where this is concerned than fragmentary writing, one that basically consists of the path of this thinking (its meanderings, its incongruities), not because it thinks falsely but because it follows reality, thus accommodating its own phenomenology. We must seek to understand the idea of this constellation, which necessitates the use of aphorisms. Adorno does not simply give free rein to the twists and turns of his thinking: he always chooses the most *constellatory* version of these meanderings;

FASCISM: THE PSYCHOLOGICAL SOURCES OF COLLECTIVE RESENTMENT

what appears is that which is enhanced by the process rather than the process itself. What Adorno constructs is a writing that is pregnant with this movement, a writing that opens without overflowing. An entry in *Minima Moralia* entitled "Memento" sets out the rules for this writing: "No improvement is too small or trivial to be worthwhile. . . . It is part of the technique of writing to be able to discard ideas, even fertile ones, if the construction demands it. Their richness and vigour will benefit other ideas at present repressed."[175]

Adorno's writing, if it at times can appear poetic (in its aphoristic and fragmentary nature), is in no way precious or cozy—it does not reveal a sentimentality. On the contrary, Adorno tends to disappear in the writing, which displays a capacity to sublimate frustration, and which resolutely opposes resentimist overflowing with an entirely different form of expansion, that of the Open, the aura. Adorno turns his writing into that of a *micrological view*. He invents another kind of metaphysics, one that "immigrates into micrology," one that "cannot be a deductive context of judgments about things in being."[176] There is no such context: there is rupture, dissonance, and discontinuity, "the smallest intramundane traits."[177] Such is the "micrological view" with which Adorno concludes: "There is a solidarity between such thinking and metaphysics at the time of its fall."[178] This last citation has been the object of a great deal of commentary, for it is symptomatic of a humanity that, if it is conscious of its own decline and of being trapped within this decline, nonetheless tries to extract itself from it by employing this micrological view, by grasping the tiniest particles that are at once forever isolated from one another and embedded in a whirlwind of relationships whose key they do not possess.

Adorno is also the great thinker of that which comes after Auschwitz, or rather of the fact that Auschwitz marks the end of any possible "after": it destroyed the very illusion of historical progress, ensuring that such progress would forever be marked by horror. The fact that this crime against humanity is inalienable also means that the crime lives on. Certainly, this crime will forever be punishable, and it will always be necessary to take responsibility for it. But far more difficult to bear is that which this responsibility is linked to and implies: the crime lives on. The horror took place, the horror is taking place, the horror will take place. This does not mean that the subject is not responsible, but that his responsibility is forever engaged—that his vigilance can never cease, that the combat will often be lost, and that the proper ethical gesture in the face of this, which should act in favor of civilization, will remain an incessant duel against the "fall"

101

PART II

of the latter. At the very heart of his being, and at the heart of his writing, Adorno experiences the disappearance of symbolic thinking, one that would be able to sustain man and his history. All this has collapsed. He is the writer who affirms that poetry is impossible after Auschwitz,[179] yet whose writing is in no way foreign to poetry. But what he seeks to say is that all writing will from this point on be pregnant with this horrible rumbling, and that every entry into poetry is a fall. This is furthermore the principle that he will position at the heart of his writing: the impossibility, for the author himself, of having any home.

It is by reducing itself, by pushing itself to disappear, that Adorno's writing separates itself from Adorno and becomes the potential site of a universal constellation. Every writer knows that a body of work always opens itself up [*l'oeuvre s'ouvre*]. The writer may very well, at the start of the process of literary creation, be positioned within his writing, where he "sets up house,"[180] but he will eventually have to leave the premises without feeling sorry for himself—and we can recognize in this departure the effort of the one who attempts to work through his resentment (without equating the latter with writing). But we also understand how that which is most beautiful—writing— can succumb to resentment if it allows itself to be submerged in its own overflowing—its "refuse,"[181] Adorno writes. Writing must not be allowed to "drift along idly"; it must separate itself from "the warm atmosphere conducive to growth"[182] and not give in to this irritable comfort. Adorno conceives of writing as an act of resistance to resentment itself. It is true that he describes resentment time and again in all its devastating power; he explains its progress, com-prehends it in the sociological sense of the term, "takes himself with" it without believing that he can remain unscathed; for all this, he never gives into it in his heart of hearts. If he did, he would undoubtedly be incapable of writing, or his writing would not be able to serve as a refuge for others—it would miss its destiny as writing. "For Adorno, art, and poetry alongside it, are refuges at the heart of which it is possible to articulate the opposition between individual and society—'the cleft between what human beings are meant to be and what the order of the world has made of them.' Adorno's fundamental conviction is that literature is 'a protest against a social situation that every individual experiences as hostile, alien, cold, oppressive,' and that historical conditions negatively carve themselves into these aesthetic representations."[183]

Adorno, undoubtedly because his writing confronts the impossible "after Auschwitz" and the danger of a disenchantment that is always

FASCISM: THE PSYCHOLOGICAL SOURCES OF COLLECTIVE RESENTMENT

entrenched deep in the souls of men, turns toward writers such as Beckett, Kafka, Hölderlin, and Eichendorff[184]—authors who grapple with barbaric absurdity, who seem to have given up the combat even though they are nothing more than this combat, who are doomed to failure but persist without grandiloquence or bombast. Adorno calls this stupor,[185] and it is typical of Beckett's *Endgame*: stupor of the world that is regressing, stupor with which Beckett's play begins and ends—which means that we must affirm, in spite of everything, that there is a path between the stupor of the beginning and that of the end: "CLOV *(fixed gaze, tonelessly)*: Finished, it's finished, nearly finished, it must be nearly finished. *(Pause.)* Grain upon grain, one by one, and one day, suddenly, there's a heap, a little heap, the impossible heap. *(Pause.)* I can't be punished any more. *(Pause.)*"[186] This is how *Endgame* opens. Is it an opening? A thousand possible interpretations, all evaluated against a grey horizon, a world no one wants; and yet there are characters who try to haul themselves out, not from their unease but from an inversion of unease into the hatred of the other, one that does not, for all that, fall into an acceptation of this determinism. "Something is taking its course,"[187] says Clov. Hamm: "I'll give you nothing more to eat. . . . I'll give you just enough to keep you from dying. You'll be hungry all the time."[188] Or this as well: "Then there's no reason for it to change," to which Clov responds (but is it a response?): "It may end. *(Pause.)* All life long the same questions, the same answers."[189] It is not a question of elevating Beckett's writing into a morality to be followed. Beckett's writing is a writing that resists without putting this resistance on display, which navigates through absurdity by probing the relational adventure between two characters who remain no less interdependent for the fact that they are no longer able to provide anything to one another. This is a way of defining the relational poverty that is sometimes established between individuals who are gripped by resentment: they are no longer a resource for themselves, they are no longer a resource for others. They drift along idly, and Beckett's writing, which does not seek to mask this with any pomp, is all the more terrible in that it leaves us standing alone before this barrenness. We experience the absence of resources, and we experience this sad chessboard before us: a ridiculous chessboard on which everything is small, and yet everything—so beautiful is the destitution of Beckett's absurdity—is capable of opening up.

— 5 —

THE INSINCERITY OF SOME, THE CLEVERNESS OF OTHERS

The man of resentment experiences the latter as a just form of anger that is indissociable from indignation: it is the simple translation of a discontent of which he is the victim. For some, this is related to authenticity. Indeed, men of resentment often present themselves as being of the people. This concern for authenticity is symptomatic. Such men are certain of being within their rights, certain of belonging to the "true" people, protected by their "status" of victim: they set themselves within this victimhood, which is perceived as something owed to them and that they never question. They claim to speak the truth, accusing others of being liars and imposters; they claim to represent the side of the genuine. Adorno saw this perfectly well while studying the phenomenon of antisemitism, which, as I have said, rests in large part upon resentment. There is no such thing as sincere antisemitism, as Horkheimer and Adorno argue: "Anger is discharged on defenceless victims. And since the victims are inter-changeable according to circumstances—gypsies, Jews, Protestants, Catholics, and so on—any one of them may take the place of the murderers, with the same blind lust for blood, should they be invested with the title of the norm."[190] It is thus impossible to simply attribute resentment to this or that group, for it is in constant movement, cutting across all those who allow their drives and their frenzy for victimhood to boil over—all those, in other words, who believe themselves to merely be victims, in no way responsible, completely subject to rules drawn up by others.

In order to understand the nature of the impulse toward victimhood, it is essential to think about the absence of sincerity that is proper to it. Those in whom this impulse is at work at first seem entirely sincere. But they cease to be so the moment they claim to be victims, at which

FASCISM: THE PSYCHOLOGICAL SOURCES OF COLLECTIVE RESENTMENT

point the impulse exhibits a will to oppression and vengeance, even though this is unavowed—in other words, it becomes ideology. Resentment, as we have said, is always just one step removed from lethal fixations. Everyone deals with resentment, everyone boils over with it from time to time, but not everyone comes to see himself as its permanent victim. There is an entire world between experiencing forms of bitterness, humiliation, and indignity that are real but not seen as permanent, and the fact of considering oneself a universal victim, turning this into a status, seeking to make this acrimony visible and even to theorize it, and always being on the point of reacting and indeed boiling over.

The transgressions that arise from this are also linked to insincerity, because the hatred of others is dialectically linked to the hatred of oneself, at least when resentment is present—resentment in the sense of jealousy, envy, the projection of destroyed ideals, the feeling of not being recognized for one's true worth, and feelings of injustice: all this leads the individual to undervalue himself, which he inverts by projecting it onto another who is judged to have taken his place. For this reason, men of resentment hate what they call, in a pejorative manner, "intellectualism"—the form of intelligence that sees through their lack of sincerity, and views their supposed "authenticity" as a sham. Convinced of their authenticity, they reject all approaches that claim to be scientific. They systematically disparage all sociological work, refusing it the very objectivity that they themselves are lacking: since their alienation has led them to exist solely within their impulses, they cannot imagine that anyone can be exempt from alienation—or that anyone who, having fallen prey to alienation, might attempt to escape it.

For this reason, Adorno also denounces those who are "too clever,"[191] who believe that they are sheltered from outpourings of resentment because the latter, since it is not rational, can only be counterproductive for those who feel it. These people believe themselves to be knowledgeable, but they don't put in the effort required to truly understand people at both conscious and unconscious levels. "One of the lessons which Hitler has taught us is that it is better not to be too clever. The Jews put forward all kinds of well-founded arguments to show that he could not come to power when his rise was clear for all to see."[192] The "too clever" are also guilty of a blindness of which they are unaware, lacking at once humility and perspicacity; in Adorno's words, they are characterized by a "clever superiority."[193] Resentment proliferates in the space between

105

PART II

those subjected to the impulse of resentment and those who, besotted
with their clever superiority, lack the capacity for expansion; like a
contagion, it captures those who were already dreaming of submitting
themselves to it.

— 6 —

FASCISM AS EMOTIONAL PLAGUE

Wilhelm Reich, 1

In order to grasp the nature of collective resentment—above all how it comes about, the way "the mass" chooses a leader, the way this mass is responsible rather than simply following blindly—we must turn to Wilhelm Reich's 1933 book *The Mass Psychology of Fascism*. Reich turns on its head the traditional image of the great leader directing the crowds; he confronts arguments that derive from a rather caricatural understanding of Hegel—in whose thought, admittedly, the cunning of Reason makes instrumental use of great men, along with their great passions, and creates the course of history through the mediation of a complex dialectic between the event and the singular being. Reich is interesting because he takes the responsibility of the mass into account—the responsibility that is masked by the mass's claim to be "apolitical." Thanks to him, we can understand more easily how—little by little, in a latent but definitive way—individuals constitute themselves in a body whose parts are linked only by resentment; how this abject and deformed body seeks out and identifies a leader so as to legitimize lethal drives, giving free reign to the rumination that had already been eating away at this body for some time. The mass needs to choose, indeed to elect, the leader, this "other," to allow itself to unveil the ugly element that it had been afraid to display. "Hitler not only established his power from the very beginning with masses of people who were until then essentially non-political; he also accomplished his last step to victory in March of 1933 in a 'legal' manner, by mobilizing no less than five million non-voters, that is to say, non-political people."[194] Reich shows that this supposed apoliticism is in no way neutrality or indifference, but rather a certain form of latency, that of the dissimulation of a personal resentment that bides its time without realizing

PART II

it is doing so (this is what it means to ruminate), that increases its discontent instead of increasing its action, and that willingly (whether consciously or unconsciously) shirks its personal responsibility. The "mass" comes to light from the moment the subjects who constitute it relinquish their subjecthood, spitefully renounce responsibility for their own lives, define themselves as victims, and eventually turn themselves into persecutors to reestablish justice.

> The more a man who belongs to the broad working masses is non-political, the more susceptible he is to the ideology of political reaction. To be non-political is not, as one might suppose, evidence of a passive psychic condition, but of a highly active attitude, a *defense* against the awareness of social responsibility.[195]

Apoliticism is an ideology that doesn't admit to being one, an ideology of the short term, the lack of personal convictions and social consciousness. What is at stake within it is in no way "distance," but the good old retreat of the individual, which Tocqueville already grasped very well when he defined the democratic selfishness[196] that turns the individual into a pathetic and vindictive weathercock. "In the case of the average intellectual 'who wants nothing to do with politics,' it can easily be shown that immediate economic interests and fears related to his social position, which is dependent upon public opinion, lie at the basis of his noninvolvement. These fears cause him to make the most grotesque sacrifices with respect to his knowledge and convictions."[197]

Reich, however, goes even further, by explaining that this "apoliticism" betrays not only a short-term ideology, one that turns its back on the common to focus on its own immediate advantages (and also to keep the cost of his engagement low, for this relatively cowardly individual is well aware of the danger of public acts, at least those undertaken by a minority), but also "sexual conflicts."[198] This thesis is not new; it falls within the purview of Freudian considerations of the individual's libidinal investment, and is thus a matter of sexuality not in a restricted sense, but from the standpoint of an idea of vital and sexual energy, that of an investment of desire into the world—a *desire for the world*, in other words—that can thus fall prey to frustration if it is not fully appreciated.

The symbol of this vital and sexual energy, or of this energy that is on the one hand individual and biological, and on the other that of the collective or the nation, is the swastika, about which Reich argues the following: if the swastika can represent a wheel that

108

FASCISM: THE PSYCHOLOGICAL SOURCES OF COLLECTIVE RESENTMENT

carries along with it everything in its path, violently planting itself in the earth, it can also be interpreted as the alliance of masculine and feminine principles. "*Thus the swastika was originally a sexual symbol.* In the course of time it assumed various meanings including that of a millwheel, the symbol of work. . . . Here fertility is sexually represented as the sexual act of Mother-Earth with God-Father"; referring to two images of swastikas that he reproduces in his text, Reich observes that "they are the schematic but nonetheless clearly recognizable representations of two interlocked human figures. The swastika on the left represents a *sexual act* lying down; the one on the right, a sexual act in standing position."[199]

The symbol of the swastika sought to encapsulate, in a single design, the unconscious aspirations of man, whether they arise from his sexual or mystical economy. But instead of doing so in the interests of an individual emancipation, it served the interests of a dogmatic and fascist ideology, incessantly seeking to substitute man's original and vital satisfaction with a fantasmatic satisfaction, one that is artificial and submissive and that is being updated in the contemporary world. Hitler, as Reich recalls,[200] often repeated that it is useless to approach the mass with arguments or with logical and scientific reasoning; he claimed that proofs and erudition had to be set aside in favor of symbols (notably sexual ones) and binary racial beliefs that presupposed an ideal of purity. "*The creed of the 'soul' and its 'purity' is the creed of asexuality,* of 'sexual purity.' Basically, it is a symptom of the sexual repression and sexual shyness brought about by a patriarchal authoritarian society."[201] And Reich adds that we do a disservice to freedom if we simply content ourselves to laugh at this creed and label it foolish, for the force of stupidity is immense, and its effectiveness is difficult to combat.[202]

The ethics of responsibility requires us to try to understand why this "mystification" of feelings is more effective than appeals to intelligence and scientific proof. Reich argues that the exhilaration to which the swastika gave rise allowed people to finally remove sexual repression, and to do so with the full authorization of the father, without any risk of being punished—on the contrary, the father authorized the punishment of others, which allowed the perpetrators to avoid the self-harm that can come about when sexual repression is maintained for too long.

It is undoubtedly at this point in Reich's work that one sees the potential for a dialectic (one that is admittedly complex and non-linear) between the psychological health of individuals and the constitution of the mass, between private life and what has been

109

PART II

called the history of nations. "One has to know the hidden life of these five million indecisive, 'non-political,' socially-suppressed men and women to understand the role that private life, that is to say essentially sexual life, plays quietly and subterraneanly in the hubbub of social life."[203] We once more find sexual life, not in the sense of mere sexual relations between individuals (though this plays an important role) but in the sense of an expansion of energy, one that is oriented toward an objective, one whose destination is the world and those who inhabit it—and which thus produces an immense potential for frustration.

Reich employs several notions to think about this, such as emotional plague, character analysis, moralistic resistance, and orgone energy. So many terms that are considered nonscientific because they are difficult to prove, except by way of singular and nonreproducible clinical workings, but which present us with archetypes on the basis of which we can elaborate a more general analysis of the human psyche, and of the way these human psyches come together in a particularly malleable form—one that, to our eyes, does not look as much like an indistinct mass as it did to Reich in the 1930s. Still, we could learn a lot about contemporary social groupings by examining them from the standpoint of Reich's concepts. He was perfectly aware of how unscientific these concepts were. The social life of apolitical people, he argues, "is not to be grasped statistically; nor, for that matter, are we partisans of the sham exactness offered by statistics, which bypass the real facts of life, while Hitler conquers power with his negation of statistics and by making use of the dregs of sexual misery."[204]

— 7 —

THE FASCISM WITHIN ME

Wilhelm Reich, 2

Reich employs the word "character" to name the various protections (walls, borders, barriers) that the ego constitutes to form itself. They are necessary for the subject, but the way they are constituted produces a certain type of resistance or defense with regard to the world and to others. The task of education is thus to produce the correct psychic defenses, those that permit the subject to grow and not to regress, to move toward the world (retreat can be a relation to the world as long as the subject chooses it—as long as it is not combined with an unavowed resentment) and to others. There is more than one way of living with others: our relationships with people allow us an infinite exploration of their presence, which can in no way be reduced to simple physical proximity. The aim of the "character structure"[205] of a being is to avoid displeasure. We could also speak of the thymus homeostasis that is dealt with from Alfred Adler to other more contemporary doctors, such as Grimaldi,[206] even if this notion is different from character structure. It is nonetheless true that these different authors share a single task, that of analyzing that which expands in the individual, or on the contrary that which is blocked, when he begins to relate to his emotions, and notably those of sadness. In Reich's work, sexual economy is that which is understood by everyone in a very straightforward way. The banality of this thesis can frighten us, he admits, since we like to understand the world through complex theories. But his clinical experience, even if it is slanted, affords him a very realistic view of human behavior:

> An apolitical man is a man who is absorbed in sexual conflicts. To want to make him conscious of his social responsibility by excluding sexuality, as was the case until now, is absolutely hopeless. Moreover,

PART II

it is the surest way of delivering him into the hands of political reaction, which makes no bones about exploiting the consequences of his sexual misery. . . . A neglect or denial of these facts constitutes an inexcusable reactionary support of the domination of Middle Ages' mentality and economic slavery.[207]

With this argument, Reich shows how, by systematically neglecting a psychoanalytic approach to explaining human behavior (by claiming that it is not scientific), we in fact produce unflagging support for the maintenance of this behavior in a form of resistance that prevents the patient from arriving at a concept of change based on action, leading him instead to an acting out whose foundation is resentment. Reich employs the notion of "emotional plague" to define the type of social situation arrived at by the mass of individuals who are not able to expand their *orgonotic* energy—whose orgonotic energy, in other words, is repressed, which notably occurs beginning in early childhood and adolescence, eventually maintaining the adult subject in a pseudo-infantile position—a position of submissiveness—at the very moment that he should become "capable of freedom."[208] This notion of the capacity for freedom is also employed by Reich to speak of the idea that "the masses are incapable of freedom,"[209] all the while that he recognizes that this is not "natural"[210] and therefore not irrevocable.

The capacity for freedom should thus be the object of the education and care given to succeeding generations (if this care and education have not already been developed in families and, beyond the circle of the family, in society), who will thereby be able to extract themselves from repetition that is at first neurotic but soon turns psychotic. Certainly, dealing with some forms of trauma and resentment requires several generations. But to this point, we have been very careful to differentiate trauma and resentment, as the place of the subject's responsibility is not the same in these two cases. As we have seen, the principle of individuation is defined within resentment as the very dynamic of resistance, and it is therefore quite logical for education—the aim of which is to accompany the emergence of the principle of individuation in the subject—to seek to end the generational transmission of said resentment if the latter has been inherited from past generations. In Freud's work, culture is defined precisely as the sublimation of lethal drives, and the task of civilization from one generation to the next is to wrest transmission from resentment.

"As was thoroughly demonstrated by sex-economic sociology, with the help of clinical experience, *the mechanism that makes*

FASCISM: THE PSYCHOLOGICAL SOURCES OF COLLECTIVE RESENTMENT

masses of people incapable of freedom is the social suppression of genital sexuality in small children, adolescents, and adults. This social suppression is not part of the natural order of things. It developed as a part of patriarchy and, therefore, is capable of being eliminated, fundamentally speaking."[211] Anyone reading these lines understands that Reich is no admirer of patriarchal society, or of a Name of the Father understood in a caricatural and authoritarian way. On the contrary, Reich recalls that it is within patriarchal society that one finds the conditioning that will later allow for the consolidation of resentment, and that will lead the individual to support a pseudo-leader who gives him an illusion of the protection that he believes is necessary, since he has long been incapable of liberty. This "need for protection on the part of the masses"[212] should be directly linked to the libidinal economy of each of the individuals who make up these masses; it leads these individuals not only to choose a leader they believe will protect them, but also to identify with him even when he denigrates them in private. "The more helpless the 'mass-individual' has become, owing to his upbringing, the more pronounced is his identification with the führer."[213] It is thus not the leader's charisma, his intelligence, or his sense of history that give him his power over the masses; it is rather those individuals who, having been rendered idiotic by their patriarchal education and their voluntary servitude (nothing has changed since La Boétie), seek to be led by the person who will give them the illusion of infantile protection that they need on an emotional level. Certainly, the charisma of the leader can aid in and reinforce this rapture, but it is not necessary; history, furthermore, shows that such leaders have often been uncharismatic men. Indeed, it is this very lack of charisma that has often been posited as a "charismatic mystery" to explain his ascendency; in fact, what is key is not him but the masses who shirk their responsibility and turn their backs on their education.

> In addition to this, however, the intensive identification with the führer had a decisive effect, for it concealed one's real status as an insignificant member of the masses. Notwithstanding his vassalage, every National Socialist felt himself to be a "little Hitler." Now, however, we want to turn our attention to the characterological basis of these attitudes. We must seek out the dynamic functions that, while they themselves are determined by education and the social atmosphere as a whole, remold human structures to such an extent that tendencies of a reactionary-irrational nature are capable of taking shape in them; to such an extent that, completely enveloped in their

113

PART II

identification with the "führer," the masses are immune to the insult heaped upon them by the label "inferior."[214]

The mechanism is unstoppable: individuals have deliberately subjugated themselves in choosing a person who, though mediocre, opened to them an art of reverse stigmatization, and produced a resentment that puts forth the illusion of being an activity. Now that he has been chosen, it is his turn to confirm that the mass is nothing more than a mass—that there are no subjects within this mass—and to assume the fiction of the protective Father, even though this fiction is essentially manifested in the suppression of those who have been designated by the men of resentment as troublemakers, as those who have made these men feel like victims. The individual believes in "the exalting idea of belonging to a master race and having a brilliant führer," when in reality "he has sunk to a position of insignificant, blind allegiance."[215] No leader can lead free men by the nose, but anyone can do so with enslaved men. Such a statement may seem binary, too simple, but it is in fact not so far from the truth. Reich explains this once again with a magisterial formulation: man, he writes, "abandoned the possibility of comprehending himself."[216] This is a true plea for analysis, whether psychoanalytical, philosophical, or other. The renunciation of self-comprehension evokes the renunciation of the faculty of judging and thinking for oneself, which is the biggest obstacle to the coming of Enlightenment.

> For centuries man has not only denied the existence of a soul; what is worse is that he repudiated every attempt to comprehend sensations and psychic experiences. At the same time, however, he devised mystical conceptions which embodied his emotional life. Those who questioned his mystical conceptions of life were persecuted and punished with death, whether it was the "saints," "racial purity," or the "state" that was questioned. In this way man developed mechanistic, mechanical, and mystical conceptions of his organization at one and the same time. Thus, his understanding of biology remained far behind his dexterity in constructing machines, and he abandoned the possibility of comprehending himself. The machine he had created sufficed to explain the performances of his organism.[217]

Reich's hypothesis, which strangely resonates in our own times, has to do with the management of our emotions through technical means, for want of being analyzed and directed through noetic and ethical work. Man has renounced self-understanding, and he has

FASCISM: THE PSYCHOLOGICAL SOURCES OF COLLECTIVE RESENTMENT

delegated the treatment of his anxiety and his feelings of emptiness, and the care of his soul, to machines; he has invented entertainment (as Pascal would have said) so as to shirk the responsibility of confronting infinite nothingness. The technical and the mystical (in the sense of dogmatic mystification and *mythologizing*), furthermore, go hand in hand: they are two types of *getting things done*, two instruments in the service of the management of anxiety (specifically, that of nothingness), two ways of envisioning dogmatism (a technical way that is more gentle, a religious way that is more violent), two ways of creating entertainment.

It is thus interesting to show that entertainment has no lasting hold on resentment. It is effective only in a momentary and superficial way. It can even reinforce or deepen resentment when it ends, as for those who experience decompensation. An example is the addiction that is brought about by immersive technologies of information and communication, technologies that make uninterrupted use of images, sounds, and everything that can bring about an artificial reproduction of emotions without contending with the true substance and indeed the darkness of the latter so as to produce a sublimation (what Aristotle would have called a catharsis). It is not that catharsis is incompatible with current technologies, but it is not their primary aim: their objective is to make a profit within a logic of consumption and accumulation. A logic, as we have seen, that seeks to re-narcissize the individual—the very individual who, in the real universe (that of work and of capitalist society whose general rule is that of deregulation), was confronted with a de-narcissization.

Furthermore, the civilizational undertaking that takes shape in Reich's observations is not only an attempt to understand why most individuals organize their lives in a way that prevents self-comprehension (the increase of a rather vindictive narcissism that we are witnessing today at a societal level is symptomatic of this abandonment of self-analysis),[218] that leads them to think that the subject of *the care of the self* is not a subject; it is also an attempt to get beyond the situation in which denial becomes a mode of organization for society. The political question that comes about here is that of understanding why society, even though it has established the principles of law that underlie the state, nonetheless tirelessly resists putting these principles into general practice. In fact, to say "society" is to speak in terms that are too general in the sense that this "society" that "makes" history, with all its progressive advancements, is rarely made up of a majority: it is the fruit of the few who ceaselessly mobilize themselves and bring about, at a specific

115

PART II

moment, the confirmation of others, who in fact do not consent (in the sense of having reflected on this consent) but rather "follow."

We understand why the general characterological incapacity for freedom on the part of masses of people has never been a subject of public debate. This fact is too dark, too depressing, and too unpopular to be discussed openly. It demands that the overwhelming majority subject themselves to a self-criticism, which is sure to prove embarrassing, and to undertake an enormous reorientation in their total approach to life. It demands that the responsibility for all social events be shifted from minorities and islands of society to the overwhelming majority, on whose work society is dependent. This working majority has never managed the affairs of society.[219]

Reich may be imagining here a successful Marxism (in imagining a proletarian mass achieving the collective emancipation that they have dreamt of), but today we understand that the "great number" of people—the crowd, the mass—has a very specific way of reflecting on itself: it is unlikely that this mass would be able to envision a real emancipation that is not simply that of the individuals that comprise it. The law-based state [*l'État de droit*] is without a doubt the political framework of the most effective combination of, on the one hand, the constitution of individuals as a collective entity, and on the other, the constitution that restricts itself solely to individual emancipation. But Reich remains an heir of this twentieth-century form of thinking that believed democracy to be compatible with the masses. Today, we know different: the disasters of history have reminded us of the tyranny and indeed of the totalitarian frenzy of the majority; they have reminded us of the need to invent another form of collective emancipation, one that does not (not in all of its aspects, in any case) pander to the masses. All discussions of "good government," the one that would be the most virtuous for democracy, must leave more room for questions that precede the inauguration of said government, which must be as limited as possible, having recourse to rules and regulations only as a last resort—all the while leaving open the possibility of intervention. Questions concerning education and care (in the broad sense, including health and social solidarity) are imperative for producing a capacity for liberty in individuals, an individuation that resonates with efforts to consolidate and strengthen the law-based state. "A general capacity for freedom can be acquired only in the daily struggle for the free formation of life."[220]

116

FASCISM: THE PSYCHOLOGICAL SOURCES OF COLLECTIVE RESENTMENT

This daily struggle for the free formation of life is the very object of education and of care, from childhood to adulthood; it is an incessant struggle, for the task is exhausting, always subject to new pressures that derive from reification and servitude. Freud analyzed these three professions (governing, educating, caring) in *Analysis Terminable and Interminable* (1937), and in the years since, many authors have disparaged his interpretation, noting that Freud does not use the term "to care," but a more specific and a more technical one, "to analyze."[221] In this text that reads almost like a testament, Freud opens his introduction by recalling that analysis is "a time-consuming business,"[222] and that a large number of analysts, and undoubtedly also of patients, have dreamed that neurosis could be "got rid of"[223] in its entirety, in less time than it took to even utter the words. A paragon of these analysts was Otto Rank, whose thesis—which is not unrelated to one of the possible titles of this book, *Here Lies Mother*—Freud recalls. Indeed, in his *Trauma of Birth* (published in 1924), Rank argues that the act of birth is the true source of neurosis. Per Freud's characterization: "He supposed that the true source of neurosis was the act of birth, since this involves the possibility of a child's 'primal fixation' to his mother not being surmounted but persisting as a 'primal repression.' Rank hoped that if this primal trauma were dealt with by a subsequent analysis the whole neurosis would be got rid of. Thus this one small piece of analytic work would save the necessity for all the rest."[224] The thesis is audacious, Freud writes, especially in its idea, indeed its fantasy, to heal in this way the whole neurosis of the subject, and this in record time. Even if Freud repudiates the thesis, the fact remains that it contains an essential test for the constitution of a subjectivity equipped with a capacity for freedom. When he turns to the question of healing from neurosis, Freud employs an expression that seems more feasible, and which might be thought to echo what Canguilhem writes on the topic of a new pedagogy of healing, especially in the case of chronic illnesses. Freud explains that "permanently disposing of an instinctual demand"[225] does not entail the disappearance of the instinct or the drive, but rather its "taming."[226] The same goes for the resentmentist drive: this never disappears, or at least its affects of rancor, jealousy, envy, fear, anger, and the refusal arising from frustration often work together; it remains no less true that the subject who resists his resentment is not the one who has never known resentment, but the one who is able to tame it. Such is analytical work: learning this art of the taming of the drives and, in a certain way, using the time of the session—and beyond, of course, for analysis stretches beyond the

PART II

limits of the session—to practice what has been learned, to bring to life the conflict between one's own drives.

Freud, who is apt to employ vivid imagery in his texts, uses a very clear formulation to explain the necessity of periodically awakening the subject's drives so as to help him to get beyond them. "The warning that we should let sleeping dogs lie, which we have so often heard in connection with our efforts to explore the psychical underworld, is peculiarly inapposite when applied to the conditions of mental life. For if the instincts are causing disturbances, it is a proof that the dogs are not sleeping."[227] Furthermore, it happens quite often that people who suffer from resentment, while they certainly dwell on this resentment, at the same time refuse to analyze it in greater depth, as though it were a question of protecting themselves against the "dogs" who might turn on them. Here we see the functioning of a vicious circle, for it is the very people who most need to grasp the nature of the conflicts between their drives who refuse to do so, out of fear of "awakening" the dogs who are in fact attacking them with their full force. Freud also explains that the refusal to heal is not the exclusive domain of the resentmentist subject, or rather that the inertia of the patient is relatively common, in the sense that patients are very quickly satisfied by any improvement in analysis. They often explain that they have nothing more to say, that they no longer see any important reason for their analysis, that they are bored—all the while thanking their analyst for the care they have been given. As Freud says: "Analytic experience has taught us that the better is always the enemy of the good and that in every phase of the patient's recovery we have to fight against his inertia, which is ready to be content with an incomplete solution."[228]

For my part, I don't believe that neuroses can be "got rid of." But nor do I think that the patient's questions about whether the analysis should proceed are worthless and invalid; nor do I think that it is wrong to consider the possibility of stopping, or of continuing elsewhere or in a different way. It is true that analysis is interminable, but it is also true that people have to experience their thresholds in different ways, so as to see how these thresholds might be integrated into the psychic web, allowing the latter to evolve. The time for "digestion," to return to Nietzsche's term, is absolutely necessary— which in no way prevents the patient from returning to analysis, whether occasionally or in a more prolonged and regular way, should he so desire. Freud believes that there are two reasons for resistance in analysis, which in a way are responsible for the "interminable" character of the cure, in the sense that the subject is never

FASCISM: THE PSYCHOLOGICAL SOURCES OF COLLECTIVE RESENTMENT

able, strictly speaking, to get beyond them. In both cases, what is at stake is a "'repudiation of femininity'": so long as the male subject refuses to get beyond his "'masculine protest,'"[229] and so long as the female subject continues to aspire to the possession of a male genital organ, the subject, in the most universal sense of the term, will not heal from neurosis. This thesis is extremely interesting, and I would like to propose here an entirely personal interpretation of it, in the sense that I bring it into dialogue with my expression "here lies mother." It is clear that Freud in no way says this, but his reflection helps us to define "here lies mother" in a more extensive way. In fact, this expression describes the subject's necessary separation from the parents, the father, indeed the Name of the Father, indeed the demand for infinite protection, as well as the flip side of this: the hero in all his virile caricature. In short: the opposite of lack, of humility; the desire for omnipotence, the illusion of fulfilment and of being fulfilled.

Analyzing, educating, governing: these are the three terms that we must henceforth develop to a greater degree, taking into account that the first and the second create the conditions of possibility for the effectiveness of the third. One of the most interesting points of Freud's text, which is not without echo in the work of Reich, is the way it recalls that one of the main stumbling blocks in progress toward a cure is the denial of the feminine on the part of a man or of a woman—in other words, the caricatural desire for all that a phallus might represent in the social sphere. "Viewed with respect to a man's character, *'fascism' is the basic emotional attitude of the suppressed man of our authoritarian machine civilization and its mechanistic-mystical conception of life. It is the mechanistic-mystical character of modern man that produces fascist parties, and not vice versa."*[230] Drawing out the medical and physiological metaphor, Reich reminds us that it is sadly easier to prevent an illness, and thus to orient ourselves toward its prevention (to educate and to care), than to correct it (to govern). This should be the aim of government: to work collectively on the means to get rid of government, even if the latter should ultimately retain its sovereign powers of arbitration.

Now the genuine democratic revolutionary movement can have no other task than to guide (*not* "lead" from the top!) the human masses that have become apathetic, incapable of discrimination, biopathic and slavish as the result of the suppression of their vital life over thousands of years; to guide them in such a way that they sense every

PART II

suppression immediately and learn to shake it off *promptly, finally, and irrevocably*. It is easier to prevent a neurosis than it is to cure it. It is easier to keep an organism healthy than it is to rid it of an infirmity. It is also easier to keep a social organism free of dictatorial institutions than it is to eliminate such institutions.[231]

Reich is still relatively optimistic in the way that he speaks of neurosis—a neurosis that is undoubtedly severe. But this remains an illness with which it is possible to negotiate, indeed that it is possible, in the long run, to sublimate, even if it is very often incurable. By contrast, psychosis is not a terrain on which sublimation and negotiation are possible. Psychosis—the psychotic and phobic tendencies of individuals—have multiplied beneath the pressure of the reification that prevails today, first as techniques of defense, and later as signs of a generally unconscious yet virtually irrevocable mutilation, one that invents a new psychotic "norm" of life so as to avoid the wounds that arise from the reifying dynamics of society. Reich, as we have seen, speaks of a "mechanistic-mystical character," and this vocabulary works quite well for today's psychotics—for those who are schizophrenic, borderline, or perverse narcissists, in that their behavior often attires itself in the most convoluted, verbose, and sophistic forms of speech, or in a psychological rigidity that might recall that of fundamentalist religious movements.

In Reich's work, there is a deep correlation—indeed, a causality—between, on the one hand, the consent of servitude and the inability to be psychologically and intellectually independent, which thus produces an incapacity for freedom, and on the other hand, the patriarchal weight that descends upon our social and personal lives, which quickly becomes inseparable from religious or mystical temptation. This temptation comes to appear as the only possible path for a falsified sublimation, in the sense that "mystical experience puts [one] in a state of vegetative excitation, which never culminates in natural orgastic gratification,"[232] only a fantasy of gratification. This is furthermore not so far removed, as we have noted, from the process of bringing forth a fantasized satisfaction instead of a real one. Reich is very much the heir of Marx, according to whom religion has the effect of opium on the masses, alienating their cognitive, neurological, and emotional systems. He is also a true humanist in the sense that he in no way believes that the masses are inherently incapable of freedom: it is the aim of democratic government to work toward their social disalienation, in the knowledge that the psychological path of disalienation is also

FASCISM: THE PSYCHOLOGICAL SOURCES OF COLLECTIVE RESENTMENT

individual. Reich believes in the responsibility of man and in his ability to find the path toward his "natural morality,"[233] or what he calls "biologic and natural self-regulation," itself linked to "natural work-democracy" or "cosmic orgone."[234] These different notions in Reich's work are not cut off from one another, but are in fact completely interdependent.

There are few authors whose work contains such an interweaving of psychiatric, psychoanalytic, political, and psychological theses. For Reich, it is only the alliance of the different phenomena that can eradicate human slavery, or indeed "enslavement to authority" (read: authoritarianism), "social irresponsibility," or "pleasure anxiety."[235] If the individual abandons all attempts to locate his original vital energy, to become a subject, and to resist the infantile temptation of patriarchy; if the individual replaces real satisfaction with a fantasized and indeed mystical satisfaction, one that punishes those who embark upon the adventure of emancipation; and if the individual cedes to the anxiety he feels when confronted by nothingness, then he ends up bearing "fascism *in himself,*"[236] which quite logically turns, in its more collective version, into political fascism, embodied by a falsely charismatic leader who allows the individual to live a cut-rate version of his repressed ideal of omnipotence. Reich's explanation seems all too simplistic, and yet a simple clinical examination shows that he is far from being wrong, and that the mechanisms that reinforce voluntary enslavement are not irreversible, as long as the individual combats them.

> *The biological rigidity of the present generation can no longer be eliminated, but the living forces that are still operative in it can attain space to develop in a better way. However, new human beings are born every day, and in the course of thirty years the human race will have been biologically renewed; it will come into the world without any trace of fascist distortion.* It is a question of the conditions under which and in which this new generation will be born; will they be conditions safeguarding freedom or will they be authoritarian?[237]

It is thus easier to sacrifice a generation than to help it to move toward an intellectual and sexual liberation: a rather sad pronouncement, for in the guise of an eternal renewal that opens possibilities, it unblinkingly postpones success until the future, thus liberating us all from the guilt of having not lived up to the moment. What does it matter? Tomorrow it will become possible—structurally possible—for a

PART II

generation to emerge that is not contaminated by this psychological "fascism." What do our current failings matter if there is always tomorrow? We can all, of course, see the limit of this reasoning, in the figure of the shrewd individual who yet again shrugs off his responsibility to other humans and other centuries.

— 8 —

HISTORIANS' READINGS, CONTEMPORARY PSYCHES

Fascism in action[238] definitely existed, and it will exist again, for it designates a psychological rather than a historical situation, one that takes "'a return to the past . . . as its ideal'";[239] this ideal can poison all those who are not capable of transforming the torments of their own time into something different, all those who have surreptitiously set up within themselves a frenzy of persecution—a frenzy that corresponds to their inability to produce transformative action in the world, and which is all the more odious in that it perceives the clamor for social justice but keeps it at arm's length for singularly base reasons. It is awful to witness magnificent and essential ideas ensnared by the pettiness of wounded souls who have given up on trying to heal themselves in favor of a strength based on victimhood. It is awful to see the symbol of "an axe encased in a bundle of rods,"[240] which originally conveyed the great solidarity of men, serving the interests of subjects who no longer want to be subjects, and who are ripe for vile behavior.

If the work of Robert O. Paxton is interesting, it is not only because he, along with a few others, helped to open our eyes about French history—to leave behind a "rose-colored" vision of this history that brings together de Gaulle and the communists in the image of a heroic France. The 1960s struck the first blows against this mystification, this fabrication of honor; the coup de grâce came in the 1970s, in the work of Marcel Ophüls (*The Sorrow and the Pity*) and of course that of Paxton (*Vichy France*).

The French masses[241] and their ambivalent behavior were never really close to de Gaulle's heart, even if he always sought to preserve the image of an eternal France, unwavering in its ideals and its resistance to the enemy. The following words of General de Gaulle

123

PART II

give an idea of the low regard in which he held his compatriots: "They [the French] are not very interesting, it's a fact. The fact is that each of them secretly acquiesced to the armistice. . . . An insignificant number of them joined me. I'll say it again: an insignificant number."[242] De Gaulle never stopped doing this: not ruminating on French shortcomings, but positing the country as having been, in large part, responsible for his misfortunes. Of course, he also unceasingly recalled the merits of an elite minority, a tiny handful of those who were not spineless. De Gaulle suggests that the three thousand French who volunteered to serve in the 2nd Armoured Division comprised the extent of the French nation in 1944. Pierre Laborie is more generous than Paxton, even though he speaks in a similar vein: the 1980s and 1990s, he suggests, were years of a tripartite France, that of a soft belly of the wait-and-see masses separating two extremes, collaborators and resistance fighters. Laborie goes further than Paxton in his analysis of this wait-and-see attitude, which in fact included several different types of behavior: the French may not have been overtly courageous, but the resistance nonetheless implicitly benefited from the strong "non-consent" of the French toward the Germans. It is also true that the nature of the relations between Pétain and the French considerably delayed awareness on the part of the population: it is amazing to see how feelings that could be qualified as anglophile, Gaullist, anti-German, and respectful of Pétain were able to coexist. Laborie became the historian of this behavior, which is extremely instructive for understanding the meanderings of the soul during moments at which History wobbles, and for comprehending the difficulty of simultaneously thinking and experiencing historical events.

Furthermore, historians are never historians solely of their own eras. Their importance lies in the fact that the silhouette of the contemporary era is implicit in their historical work. And we thus understand how resentment goes hand in hand with modernity, not only with the past. Paxton, following the example of Reich, did not allow himself to be fooled by the fascist indoctrination that consists in making people believe that the fascist leader is the one who guides the crowds, the one who converts the pristine and innocent masses so that they might receive the mark of the leader and bring forth history. On the contrary, he devoted his work as a historian to deciphering the behavior of individuals, their lived experience, their feelings of having come down in the world, their budding resentment. "Early fascist movements exploited the protests of the victims of rapid industrialization and globalization—modernization's losers, using, to

124

FASCISM: THE PSYCHOLOGICAL SOURCES OF COLLECTIVE RESENTMENT

be sure, the most modern styles and techniques of propaganda."[243] Our contemporary experience resonates with what Paxton writes here: everything is in place for a "new" version of the same old regressive tune, one with just enough novelty to make us believe that it hasn't been heard before, when in fact it should be entirely recognizable.

> The image of the all-powerful dictator personalizes fascism, and creates the false impression that we can understand it fully by scrutinizing the leader alone. This image, whose power lingers today, is the last triumph of fascist propagandists. It offers an alibi to nations that approved or tolerated fascist leaders, and diverts attention from the persons, groups, and institutions who helped him.[244]

Paxton was also able to show that fascism is in no way the anticapitalist movement that it claims to be. It constructs itself in this way,[245] against capitalism, by denouncing the latter's injustice, its unequal divisions of wealth, and indeed its egotistical bourgeois ideal and the illusion of its supposed meritocracy. But once fascism attains power, it lines up behind capitalism, choosing the path of conservation rather than that of revolution, and pointing its arrows at socialist-leaning movements, judging them to be too internationalist. What fascism repudiates where capitalism is concerned is not property and accumulation, but individualist liberalism, inasmuch as the latter allows the individual to emancipate himself from the community or the nation. Fascism cannot bear the idea of an individual separating himself off to focus on his own lot as if he were not indebted to the collective, even if the latter is in no way "socialist" but rather an identity-based community. "Once in power, fascist regimes confiscated property only from political opponents, foreigners, or Jews."[246] This is reminiscent of Reich's warning concerning the apolitical man. Paxton also denounces the opportunism, very typical of fascist regimes, that authorizes them to excoriate the bourgeoisie while adopting its practices, and that allowed them to be "the first European 'catch-all' parties of 'engagement,'"[247] and to use any disengagement as the basis of a politics of hostility with regard to everything outside it.

Paxton's method has always consisted of not allowing himself to be fooled by the idea of the greatness of fascism—its great speeches, its great programs—and instead to calmly return, time and again, to its concrete actions, which were always driven by the interests of its major players and by short-termism. We are very far here from the magisterial political philosophy that fascism pretends to claim for itself. In comparison, contemporary populist movements are unabashedly down to earth, shunning grand speeches and openly describing themselves as "misologists," shamelessly practicing the Newspeak that denounces political correctness—a denunciation that is as old as the world, whose provocations are purely regressive and contain nothing new. They testify ineloquently to the characteristic mediocrity of fascist movements, which once adorned themselves with a very real aesthetic that very effectively re-narcissized the man of resentment—this is what Paxton calls "mass ceremonies of affirmation and conformity,"[248] which of course gave rise to the ultimate sensorial and aesthetic experience of war. "Fascism's deliberate replacement of reasoned debate with immediate sensual experience transformed politics, as the exiled German cultural critic Walter Benjamin was the first to point out, into aesthetics. And the ultimate fascist aesthetic experience, Benjamin warned in 1936, was war."[249]

War pushes to its extreme something that is true of every political event by its very nature—namely, the fact of being an instrument of narcissistic reassurance for those who use it. The need for this reassurance is the starting point for the warmonger who convinces himself of the decisive role of the event and of the leader, attributing a cathartic power to this leader for whom there is a before and an after, this leader who appears to finally attain reparations for the people at the very moment that he plunges headlong into the darkness of a dead end whose strategic value is not immediately apparent. You want to know the meaning of all this? There is none, responded Mussolini. There is no program, no reasoning (not even a specious one); there is only whatever we care to rip apart so as to avenge the honor of those who felt humiliated. "A few months before he became prime minister of Italy, he [Mussolini] replied truculently to a critic who demanded to know what his program was: 'The democrats of *Il Mondo* want to know our program? It is to break the bones of the democrats of *Il Mondo*.'"[250] These words could easily be taken from a populist speech from our own time rather than a declaration from 1920.

Still, we should avoid the error of confusing fascism with populism. One of the real differences between the two phenomena brings us back to fascism's inscription within a "military" ideal. The new man of fascism is not the man whose buying power has been jeopardized. He is the man who, aware of the nation's potential decay, chooses to make instrumental use of this decay—to dramatize it so as to justify the recourse to violence against those judged to be complicit

FASCISM: THE PSYCHOLOGICAL SOURCES OF COLLECTIVE RESENTMENT

in this decay. And what better to do so than to use legitimate force—namely, that of the army. This, in any case, was Mussolini's strategy. "The fascist militarization of politics abolishes this distinction from the moment it affirms that the citizen and the soldier are identical, thus creating the properly fascist ideal of the citizen soldier, by which it understands that all individual and collective life must be organized according to the principles and the values of its fundamentalist conception of politics."[251] There is no such assimilation in populist discourse, which is much more conciliatory toward "bourgeois" ideals, even if, like fascism, it denigrates these ideals. Populism does not have the same relationship with violence, above all with the myth of regenerative violence,[252] that is found in the fascist universe, which is undoubtedly far more besotted with the notion of purity. Violence certainly exists in the populist universe, but it is less organized, less militarized: it arises from a stampede of impulses or drives. In populist societies, there is no belief in having to undergo "the experience of war" to come forth as a nation; on the contrary, they are only bellicose if they know they will not have to pay the price for being so, whether in their flesh or in their material and affective existence.

A few similarities remain, however, even if they belong to the realm of parody. Take the case of rhetoric, which, even if it is largely impoverished in our time (social networks bear witness to this), remains largely the same. An example is the following remark by the leader of the United States, addressed to the leader of North Korea: "North Korean Leader Kim Jong Un just stated that the 'Nuclear Button is on his desk at all times.' Will someone from his depleted and food starved regime please inform him that I too have a Nuclear Button, but it is a much bigger & more powerful one than his, and my Button works!"[253] Everything is here: vindictiveness, sexual allusion, virile style, readiness to employ strength as a preventative measure, a statement that is so pared down as to be comical—all to flatter the common man's need for reparations and reassurance in the face of his loss of symbolic and material recognition.

Furthermore, the current era is in no way safe from a renewed imagining of war as an aesthetic and spectacular experience. This was the case of the first Iraq War, which was meant to prove the mastery of American power—its ruthless surgical ability to strike its targets with lethal force—by way of an uninterrupted television broadcasting of "aerial strikes" that created a new genre of continuous information, one that is structurally spectacular, market-oriented, and indissociable from cultural and economic imperialism.

PART II

This is all the more true today due to the rise of social networks that allow anyone to express resentment without paying the price (anonymity and weak regulation ensure this, at least temporarily), justified by populist leaders who do so in the same caricatural way as their citizens. This new landscape creates an extraordinary echo chamber for the potentially deadly mediocrity of those who carry their hatred around on their shoulders. The proliferation of hateful words is not a new phenomenon—every dark period of History has had its swell of nauseating and deadly recriminations. But the amplification that we are seeing today cannot be passed over in silence on the grounds that there is basically nothing new in it. What is different is the fact that today it never stops: hateful pronouncements are made continuously, on every subject, from the most serious to the most foolish.

What we have here is the "Two Minutes Hate" predicted by Orwell,[254] but in a decentralized form that allows each person to spew out his bile and then to calmly return to his inaction and his incompetence, undoubtedly so as to await the more "institutional" form of authorization that a new populist leader might bring. We are very far here from the spectacular aesthetics of war. And yet what is played out in this permanent bile is the barbaric truth of war—that of the liberation of resentful drives, of the unregulated compulsion to pillage and to extort civilians. Of course, the material effects are not the same. But the outpouring of hatred is just as venomous: it seeks to defile, an aim with which war crimes are perfectly familiar.

In small doses, the phenomenon is judged to be insignificant, a sort of Dionysian celebration that is nothing to be proud of, but about which nothing can be done: we just have to let the mediocrity play out, just as children only learn from making mistakes. Resentment needs some sort of escape valve, we say—as if this could protect us from its invasive power. But this doesn't protect us at all. On the contrary, it is a sure sign of resentment's progression. It is not enough to forbid it—though it is necessary to do so, for its ability to defile public space has devastating consequences for the latter. Resentment is on the move, embedded in hearts and entrenched in speeches, ready to make its demands. The aesthetics of violence continues to be attractive for the alienated and the subjugated, precisely because it gives them the illusion of a return to power and promises an end to repression. The technique is well known to fascist regimes, and has always been employed in effective yet frugal ways—if it is used too often, it becomes blurry, thus revealing the true nature of fascism: its conservative and non-revolutionary aspect. Violence must be

FASCISM: THE PSYCHOLOGICAL SOURCES OF COLLECTIVE RESENTMENT

legible and justifiable; it must therefore be targeted and made highly symbolic, so as to make people believe in its justice all the more. "It was the genius of fascism to wager that many an orderly bourgeois (or even bourgeoise) would take some vicarious satisfaction in a carefully selective violence, directed only against 'terrorists' and 'enemies of the people.'"[255]

Today, the targets have changed, but the procedures have remained similar: constant waves of people converging on social media to harass this or that person in a very specific way, sometimes for months and months, again without ever stopping, forcing the target to flee the network so as to keep some measure of psychological health and not completely succumb to the overwhelming surge. Once again, it is not a question here of comparing what is incomparable—namely, comparing the situation of the 1940s with that of today. Everything has changed—states and individuals as well. Yet the workings of our conditioned reflexes remain similar in many respects: our psychological functioning continues to be structured by the same old laws.

— 9 —

LIFE AS CREATION

The Open Is Salvation

Happily, the laws of the psyche are not the only ones available to us to explain the human universe: the psyche does not hold the keys to the secrets of the individual and of history. Let us wager that social, economic, cultural, and/or psychological determinism will never win the game of comprehending a being and a society. It is nonetheless true that an "ill" psyche—one beset by an overly strong neurosis or a psychosis—brings about many phenomena that have immense negative repercussions for the subject and his environment. This peculiarity cannot be denied. It in no way expresses the truth of the subject; indeed, it expresses precisely the contrary: how the subject allows himself to be overrun by that which is foreign to him and takes pleasure in doing so, how he allows himself to be fooled. But sadly, in the long run, this can become the subject's truth. Understanding the subject's precise manner of giving up on self-comprehension is decisive for grasping the way he imagines freedom, and develops a dynamic, existentialist, and humanist "truth."

I have always thought that the truth, in its non-dynamic aspect, is essentially lethal: it comprises man's finitude, the dusty side of his existence. I'm not sure that I'm able to live with this truth, which troubles me and drives me to despair. The part of the truth that interests me is the one that has to do with the work—an artistic work, or one that belongs more generally to the order of subjectification (childbirth, love, sharing, the discovery of the world and of others, engagement, contemplation, spirituality, etc.). This axiom of mine, which consists in positing that the truth lies in that infinitesimal part of it that is eternal and nowhere else, means that I am a Platonic or a Plotinian thinker and that I always will be. This is the only durability that speaks to me, and that is able to attire itself in

FASCISM: THE PSYCHOLOGICAL SOURCES OF COLLECTIVE RESENTMENT

this idea of "truth" in the sense of something that persists beyond the moment at which it is uttered, and will still hold meaning in the time to come. We must always remember the future if we are to give meaning to our humanism. All the rest is froth, though it is not false, and indeed comprises the truth for some—historians, for example. The truth of our failures, of our persistent illness, of our inability not to repeat, is an essential truth that is narrated by historical facts—the history that shows us the extent to which the lessons of history are never learned. In the face of this dead sun, we require the clarity of a different truth, a clarity that knows that another, hitherto unseen, aspect of the truth exists.

Analytic work exists to help the subject to grasp the creative element contained within his truth. To grasp, in other words, his pact with the Open—a Rilkean notion that has never been far from my mind ever since my first publications. When I discovered it, I felt like I was finally able to breathe. And yet in the sensitivity that it invoked, it was more powerful than my ways of thinking, which were more abstract, more theoretical, more calmly Platonic. There was something of the animal, of nature, of the living, of the sky, and of mountains in this Open—and also of death. There was the painful poetry of Rilke, his elegies; there was this entire great century of misfortune and of romanticism that would be that of the two world wars, and the catastrophe that preceded them in its initial tremors—as though this, as well, rumbled in the helplessness of the Open, the one that presides over humans and leads them to ruin. "With all its eyes the natural world looks out/into the Open."[256] I devoted an entire chapter to these words in my book *Métaphysique de l'imagination*,[257] where they form a path on which I try to understand individuation and its encounter with the real, with that which lies beyond Kantian synthesis. The name of the next chapter in this book might be read as an explanatory maxim for Rilke's poetry: "The Imagination of Death and the Calm Gaze of the Animal."

If I had to make a link, today, between this previous book and the "here lies bitterness" of this one, I would do so by echoing the great poet's "Open." Literature and poetry are higher than all else: they give themselves over to the world and to its eternal evanescence—that of the sublime, of time that is longer than even its own duration, of the nature that does not exist without the hand of man and that nonetheless surpasses man. I, who am not a poet, stand at a distance from this magnificent violence, which I view as too intense for this ridiculous body that is my own; I keep my distance, incapable of experiencing so many emotions without becoming nauseous; I

PART II

keep my distance so that I can write—so that I can write texts that, while they may be inadequate, attempt to explain, for those who feel the distance between themselves and the world and experience this distance as a breach of their being, how despite everything we can keep going in this world, outside of resentment and even of bitterness, and without prostrating ourselves before the absence of meaning. The Open. The Open. When I first read this, near the end of my adolescence, I understood it as a salvation—my own, perhaps. Some who read this will be amazed that a person who does not believe in God can care about the salvation of her soul. But what is the soul if not a magnificent fiction (perhaps the inversion of the fiction of God), an idea that man makes for himself so as not to be made up solely of matter? As I have often written, the only way to prove something of the existence of the soul is through the lives of others, and what they retain of us. The salvation in all of this tormented me from an early age, even though I have no appetite for human reality. I was born a man in spite of myself; if I had been able to choose, I would have fled immediately—I would have remained dust or become something that flies, even if only a little. No, nothing: I would have preferred the nothing that fools itself into believing it is everything—this would have been a more graceful flourish. There is something reassuring about knowing that Rilke, and so many others, went down this same road: it is like a trace of shared humanity, a common weakness that is not shameful.

— 10 —

THE HYDRA

Let us return to the "insignificant number." For one—a single man, all alone—is enough to save all the others: this is the dream put forth by religions, as though it were something we should desire. The idea of man already suffices to save all men, to keep them steady in their hope, and above all steady before the assault of resentment. "As long as we don't ask ourselves: hope for what? Hope in what? I hope . . . as long as I don't depend too heavily on the direct or indirect object."[258] Hope only works if it is not entirely self-interested. The Open against resentment, once and for all. But things aren't quite so easy in our everyday lives: we must often force ourselves to go beyond mere ideas. The "insignificant number" is necessary, we need it, and if we could just increase it, we would take one more step toward a truly dignified civilization. The flipside of the Open, in a very concrete yet no less metaphorical way, is indeed the "epoxy" of enmity[259] of which Paxton speaks: "an amalgam of two very different agents, fascist dynamism and conservative order, bonded by shared enmity toward liberalism and the Left."[260] To explain fascism, Paxton brings together several theses that conflict with one another: an economic argument, a psychoanalytical argument, and a form of metaphysical argument. This is not a problem from my standpoint, though it may be difficult for such an approach to coexist with anxiety that cannot be assuaged through work on the self.

Let us take the economic argument. This is a traditional argument that brings us back to a context of crisis and of the humiliation of the "small," or to the fragmentation and atomization that can increase in a society when it begins to grow at several different speeds, thus shattering the very idea of a common world. The psychoanalytical argument focuses on the personality of the Führer, but it very quickly

PART II

turns to the more interesting question of public opinion—in other words, the fact that the Germans (and their consorts) projected onto the Führer a role that he was able to fulfil successfully. Paxton invokes Ernst Bloch and his splendid theory of the "noncontemporaneity"[261] of souls, in the sense that people do not necessarily inhabit the same now. But here again, is there anything harmful in this? It is a metaphysical, ethical, and psychoanalytical truth that we do not live in the same now, and that over the course of our lives we will discover ways of experiencing the time of the world in completely new ways. And thus, while it is possible that our inability to inhabit a single now can give rise to strong anxiety and feelings of abandonment, it is in no way certain (it is indeed very rare) that this should lead us to tip into fascism. One does not find in fascism the grandiose experience of metaphysical emptiness: one finds only complacent panic in the face of a limited present, a non-metaphysical "now"—the quantitative now of a comfort that we believe is our due.

The temptation that most of us grab hold of is terrible—at least, it is if it always gets the last word—for it keeps us from being able to extract ourselves from the present time and from reification. We always need to keep one foot outside of the quantitative now if we don't want to take the risk of seeing both feet sink into resentment. This sinking into the quantitative now produces the necessary context for accepting the unacceptable, for it gives rise to a sort of "hysterical blindness"[262] that leads us to focus only on ourselves and our survival, and makes it impossible for us to orient ourselves toward others. From here, the individual loses his visual acuity, in the sense of being able to see, to cast his gaze in a truly careful way: the individual becomes incapable of recognizing the face of the other. The other is wiped away. A "reified" being can only produce reification; the sight of anything else becomes unbearable for him, giving rise either to a barbaric reactivation of hatred that he ends up taking out on others, or to a self-hatred that is properly unliveable. For it is true that resentment remains a rampart (even if a squalid one) against his own depression: the man of resentment is discouraged and depressed, but this depression feeds on vengeance, and locates daily but limited forms of compensation that are in no way durable, which he consumes with enjoyment for want of being able to criticize them. Resentment, all the while that it rots his being, keeps the individual at whom it gnaws in perfect physical shape, conserving him in its bitter juice. It has the power of formalin. Resentment is thus a form of low-cost self-conservation: the "weakness of the soul" on which it is constructed requires little effort from the subject—nothing more than

FASCISM: THE PSYCHOLOGICAL SOURCES OF COLLECTIVE RESENTMENT

a complacency of victimhood. Resentment blends well with what Christophe Dejours calls lazy akrasia, or, when it is more virulent, sthenic akrasia. The first is evidence of a split in the ego, one that is rather banal, close to cowardice or egotism; the second, of a more odious and vindictive zeal. Lazy akrasia prefers silence to polemic; it prefers the absence of engagement to responsibility.

Let us take the extreme case of the final solution. The Nazis very quickly realized that the main problems of the process of destruction "were not administrative but psychological":[263]

> The very conception of the drastic Final Solution was dependent on the ability of the perpetrators to cope with weighty psychological obstacles and impediments. The psychological blocks differed from the administrative difficulties in one important respect. An administrative problem could be solved and eliminated, but the psychological difficulties had to be dealt with continuously. . . . Commanders in the field were ever watchful for symptoms of psychological disintegration. In the fall of 1941 Higher SS and Police Leader Russia Center von dem Bach shook Himmler with the remark: "Look at the eyes of the men of this Kommando, how deeply shaken they are. These men are finished . . . for the rest of their lives. What kind of followers are we training here? Either neurotics or savages. . .![264]

We see here how resentment can be a lesser evil, where strategies of defense are concerned, allowing one to avoid psychological disintegration, and to continue committing vile acts without paying any psychological price—and also without undertaking the difficult task of resisting through alternative action.[265] From this moment, resentment becomes the most certain ally of fascism and of every great form of totalitarian reification, turning men's cowardice into a very regular and effective mechanism, unshakable and indignant without having anything to do with one's personal will. Of course, there exist some individuals with ideological resolve—fundamentalists, in other words—but they are few and far between, and would be easy to counter if the cowardly masses were not absent. These individuals can even give the impression of sublimating their resentment, which strictly speaking should be impossible. But so great is the denial that marks their psychosis that it becomes possible for them. Unless they are simply able to lie almost perfectly, having attained such a false selfhood that they are no longer able to distinguish the truth from bad faith. They cloak themselves in virtue, giving evil the appearance of a superior good.

135

PART II

Let us take Himmler, who declares in 1943 that the Nazis have taken "'the riches which they [the Jews] owned'":[266]

"I have given strict orders, which Obergruppenführer Pohl has carried out, that this wealth should naturally . . . be delivered to the Reich. We have taken nothing. Individuals who have transgressed are being punished in accordance with an order which I gave. . . . A number of SS men—not many—have transgressed against that order, and they will be condemned to death mercilessly. . . . We don't want in the end, just because we have exterminated a germ, to be infected by that germ. . . . We have not been damaged in the innermost of our being, our soul, our character."[267]

In his claim to be nothing and to have taken nothing for himself, to be incorruptible, Himmler remains, at least in this statement, a vestige of individuation, and merely studying his personality does not allow us to grasp the vacuity and the banality of the process of resentment. But let us recall Paxton's method: let us leave the speeches aside and focus on actions. Himmler's private diaries, which were found in the military archives in Russia, depict a being who is resolutely psychotic and cruel, who takes enjoyment in this cruelty, who is ready to participate in acts of violence[268] but not to undergo the difficult work of owning up to these acts in any systematic way. No, it all remained for him a form of entertainment, wedged in between innumerable meetings and dinners,[269] demonstrating Himmler's complete "social" alienation and also his psychological alienation, displayed in his unconcealed enjoyment of cruelty and also in the moment he almost fainted—the psychopath, after all, also has his sensitivity. The slide toward psychopathy marks the end of any possible individuation.

Hannah Arendt, along with a few others, was able to highlight the mechanism of deresponsibilization and deindividuation that allowed for the advent, in successive steps, of the Final Solution. By showing these workings, she in no way cleared the names of those who were responsible, but rather revealed the simulacrum of deresponsibilization that they enacted, which is a central part of the process of denial and revisionism. As Raul Hilberg writes: "The destruction of the Jews was not centralized. No agency had been set up to deal with Jewish affairs and no fund was set aside for the destruction process. The anti-Jewish work was carried out in the civil service, the military, business, and the party. All components of German organized life were drawn into this undertaking. Every agency was a contributor;

136

FASCISM: THE PSYCHOLOGICAL SOURCES OF COLLECTIVE RESENTMENT

every specialization was utilized; and every stratum of society was represented in the envelopment of the victims."[270]

Such is indeed the definition of resentment: a movement that progressively envelops its victims; a shapeless plasticity that becomes all the more effective in giving the illusion that it no longer has a body or a head, when in fact it is a hydra with hundreds of thousands of heads. This monster is apposite here because it employs, at the same time, elements that we believe to be opposed to one another: individuals and masses. She is a quite effective embodiment of the dialectic between the quantitative and the qualitative, which at the start are separate but soon become permeable to one another over the course of the process. Doing away with the hydra thus requires eliminating some of its heads, which may lead to stopping the dialectic between the quantitative and the qualitative in its tracks—no one can know in advance. Cutting off all or even a majority of these heads is not necessary—one must simply target a learned few, including those that are judged to be authoritative. It will do us well to understand which few—which combination—so as to protect ourselves from the toxic vicissitudes of these large groups.

— III —

THE SEA

A World Opened to Man

— 1 —

DISCLOSURE, ACCORDING TO FANON

What is the antidote to resentment?

Any number of paths open up from the moment the subject seizes upon this question and allows his engagement, his personal involvement, and his innermost being to live within it. When I discovered the Rilkean Open, and the ways of weaving it into my own writing, this became a "possibility" for resisting bitterness, or more simply for resisting the melancholy that had already found a place within me. I could say the same for my discovery of Mallarmé, especially the fragments that make up *For Anatole's Tomb*[271]—this seeming breathlessness in the work of one who is a master of sounds and of vertiginous syntax in his verse; it is impossible not to hear in this tomb a shortness and indeed an exhaustion of breath, and at the same time an "other" force that cannot be reduced to this, in spite of everything, and that transmits itself to the reader. Writers carry this force within themselves so that others don't have to. They carry our renewal all the while that they wear themselves out in battling their own exhaustion.

Another illustration of the way style can spurn us on, this time taken from philosophy—the phrase of Jankélévitch that continues to resonate: there is no need to be tragic—it is enough to be serious. There is no need to add anything to this; there is no need to believe that it is more difficult than it is. It is indeed difficult, all the more so for the fact that, as we forge the paths we take in life, we at the same time bear the weight of a painful and deficient collective history; in addition to our own inadequacy, we must also bear the inadequacy that others assign to us. Women know this well. Everyone knows, but let's not relativize: women know it, and so do all those whom society considers to be "inferior," "untouchable," "impure," all those who

PART III

have every reason to feel resentful, for they have a share of justice on their side. These people must fight against resentment and go beyond it, for themselves and for those who will follow them, so as to reverse the course of history—to not hang their heads yet again, this time in the face of their own alienation and their own persecution frenzy.

There are many authors who have walked this combative and creative path. I have chosen to walk in the footsteps of Frantz Fanon, but other authors would be just as relevant. The immense Fanon: psychiatrist and thinker of postcolonialism, so brilliant and so terribly young—forever young, because he left us at such an early age. In his preface to the French edition of Fanon's collected works, Achille Mbembe returns to the "three clinics of the real"[272] that not only founded Fanon's thought, but his existence and his exemplarity. Three clinics of the real—Nazism, colonialism, and the encounter with Metropolitan France—that seem irreducible to one another given their different historical contexts, but that, in the work of Fanon, weave together a being: Fanon himself, his resistance, and his sublimation. Mbembe is right to say that there is in Fanon's work an "injunction to care," and to care especially for those who, like him, found themselves caught within the diktats of these three vain and lethal regimes. The injunction to care is capable of founding a morality, an ethics that deposes reification, certainly by fighting against it, but also by invalidating, little by little, its theoretical and legal bases—and as such, going one step further in the clinic of the real. Caring means caring to the end, or at least attempting to do so; it means creating a new order of things for the individual. In Fanon's case, caring means denouncing the brutality of colonialism and Nazism, revealing their absolute violence, and treating them as crimes—crimes against humanity, including the most imprescriptible ones, the Shoah and slavery. It means opening the future by way of the imprescriptible.

Jankélévitch has shown how this "imprescriptible"[273] is essential for the foundation of a state of law, in the sense that the latter forms a regulative idea for democratic justice, stipulating that this justice will be responsible in ways that those of other regimes are not: it will bear responsibility for history so as to "repair" it, or in other words undertake historiographical and critical work on its own chronology and the events that traverse it, like the one that preceded its own constitution. A state that can claim to be truly based in law takes upon itself a true relationship with historical truth, confronts the black holes of history, and does not content itself with official history. It chooses the difficult teaching of a "scientific" history that

142

THE SEA: A WORLD OPENED TO MAN

is based on facts, and that ceaselessly deconstructs the rewriting of these facts by interested parties. These quarrels between historians are at the heart of the democratic process. What is at stake in Fanon's work is "the struggle and the future that we must work for, whatever the costs. The aim of this struggle is to produce life, to overturn the hierarchies created by those who got used to defeating others even though they were in the wrong; in this struggle, absolute violence serves to detoxify and to institute the new. This struggle . . . aims first and foremost to destroy that which destroys, amputates, dismembers, blinds, and provokes fear and anger—that which turns people into things."[274] Fanon bravely combats resentment because he is able to *open himself to grievances*[275] without resolving himself to them. Rather than using these grievances as grounds for a double jeopardy, he *cares* for them, opting for an empowering form of care that builds resilience for those who have been wounded so that "a new human subject" might be constructed from the "mortar of blood and anger."[276]

Fighting against resentment is not pleasurable: it gives us pain at the same time as we fight against other painful realities. Fighting against these realities does not immediately protect us from them. A certain amount of time must pass before we cease to have the feeling of betraying our own cause in freeing ourselves from our own suffering. The path of emancipation requires us to recognize our suffering, but more than this, it requires us to separate ourselves from this suffering, to leave it behind, not to forget it but to build something new, for we must learn—this should be the lesson of a relatively healthy neurosis—not to repeat, not to take up residence in the repetition of pain; we must thereby renounce that which was ourselves, in part, but only in part. We must convince ourselves that this wasn't the self, which is in fact destined for openness, for the future. "Free of the burden of race, rid of the attributes of the thing," writes Mbembe of Fanon, through whose work we come to understand that at the basis of the history of racialization lies reification.

Fanon tirelessly hunts down those forms of social and psychological alienation brought about by colonialism, an alienation that gives rise to madness in the reified subject, transforming him into a hostage of his own suffering. As Mbembe writes: "In colonial situations, the work of racism aims, above all, to abolish all separation between the internal ego and the external gaze, so as to anesthetize the senses and transform the body of the one who has been colonised into a thing whose stiffness recalls that of a corpse."[277] This work—which joins together historiography and care, philosophy and psychoanalysis,

143

PART III

and which enables individuals and peoples to create their own paths through the world, to extract themselves from paternalism and from thingification—is referred to by Fanon as the "disclosure"[278] of the world, as if to echo the opposite of this term, foreclosure; the latter imprisons the subject and then turns him into his own perfect jailer. Disclosure, on the contrary, is an exit from this dramatic emotional magma that produces identities that are captive to their "cultures." The term is perfect for describing the interlacing of collective and individual histories, and for working out how the pathologies of subjects are necessarily implicated in this history they experience. Psychodynamics remains the truth of individual pathology: the latter may very well have its own genetic dispositions, but the fact remains that the sociocultural, economic, institutional, and familial context is decisive in orienting and indeed in correcting these dispositions. In this regard, contemporary clinical practice demonstrates how immigration, forced exile, mass displacements of populations in danger, and indeed all sorts of undesired displacements all reinforce certain types of post-traumatic pathology and psychosis that are inherent to exile, and to which it is possible to add the specific pathologies of certain cultures that are still influenced by religion, hallucinatory ravings, and superstition.

"Disclosure" echoes (and at the same time deposes) the "logic of the enclosure,"[279] whereby those who belong to minority groups are separated, rounded up, and divided, falling into a second-class citizenship. They must become "healthy" once more: this is what is at stake for every man, and in this case for every black man. Only one thing matters: "to liberate the black man from himself."[280] Fanon says this early in his 1952 book *Black Skin, White Masks*, making reference to Aimé Césaire, another great man of the colonial and post-colonial humanist liberation, who bears a universal lesson: "*I am talking about millions of men in whom fear has been cunningly instilled, who have been taught to have an inferiority complex, to tremble, kneel, despair, and behave like flunkeys.*"[281] It is to them that Césaire and Fanon address themselves: those who have been forced to become "lackeys" because of the color of their skin, their cultural or social origins, their sex; those who were taught to kneel, which is the very opposite of teaching in that it aims to transmit the very opposite of the critical spirit, of the sharpness that keeps the mind alert and the body standing. Early in his introduction, Fanon writes a sentence that might harm those who have already been wounded in having been refused ontological status as Blacks: "Running the risk of angering my black brothers, I shall say that a Black is not a man."[282] Every

THE SEA: A WORLD OPENED TO MAN

person is a human being, regardless of his color, and yet the person who allows himself to be defined solely by his color risks leaving himself open (without necessarily being aware of it) to reification. This is a very universalist take, one that has been widely criticized in colonial and postcolonial studies, and the debate around it will go on forever, because black demands and universalist demands can work hand in hand or, conversely, oppose one another. What Fanon says is liable to wound because it does not flatter the individual's identity; on the contrary, it invites him to sublimate this identity from the outset—not to deny it or even to repress it, but to sublimate it, so as to situate himself beyond and elsewhere, to be in the world and to construct the world. "We are aiming at nothing less than to liberate the black man from himself."[283] The black man must concern himself not with the black man but with the man. "The white man is locked in his whiteness. The black man in his blackness."[284]

It is to this liberation from his own community that Fanon invites the reader. He seeks, behind the specificity of a culture, a sex, or a history, the contour of university, not to glorify the disembodied, but to open the future of the world to every individual: "We shall show no pity for the former colonial governors or missionaries. In our view, an individual who loves Blacks is as 'sick' as someone who abhors them. Conversely, the black man who strives to whiten his race is as wretched as the one who preaches hatred of the white man."[285] Black and White are both slaves, the first to his supposed "inferiority," the second to his supposed "superiority": both are slaves of a "neurosis"[286] transmitted from one generation to the next, confirmed by the individual failings of every subject who gives up on creating a subjectivity worthy of the name. And a sort of reflective neurosis thus takes shape for all those who are incapable of "escaping [their] race":[287] each involves himself in the neurosis of the other to maintain his own.

The description of resentment in Fanon's work is more clinical, following upon the work of Eugène Minkowski, and recalling what it has in common with the "negative-aggressive" type (passive-aggressive, per today's terminology) who often develops an obsession with the past, with his frustrations and his failures, thus paralyzing "his enthusiasm for living."[288] Prior to the politicization of resentment at a collective level—at which point the sheer number of people reassures the false subject and incites him to become more vindictive, precisely because he can hide behind others rather than bearing the consequences of his vindictiveness all alone—the man of resentment practices a form of introversion, dissimulation, and hypocrisy typical

145

PART III

of someone who is submissive (not that hypocrisy is necessarily a corollary of submissiveness) and locks himself away within his contradictions: he despises others and at the same time trusts them to change the situation. "His withdrawal into himself does not allow him to have any positive experience that would compensate for the past. Consequently, the lack of self-esteem and therefore of affective security is virtually total, resulting in an overwhelming feeling of helplessness toward life and people as well as a complete rejection of any feeling of responsibility. Others have betrayed and thwarted him, and yet it is only from these others that he expects any improvement of his lot."[289] Here Fanon cites Germaine Guex to close the portrait of this man who is eaten away by a "lack of self-esteem," which acts in the manner of an obsession, producing within him a "painful . . . feeling of exclusion" that consigns him to a permanent affective insecurity and a fear of abandonment, keeping him within a logic of repetition and leading him to "unconsciously do everything that's needed to bring about the anticipated catastrophe."[290]

Guex's diagnosis recalls the insatiable and unquenchable need for reparations, also discussed by Scheler, that makes the man of resentment a prisoner of his illness, and that obliges those of us who work in preventative care to do everything in our power—individually, collectively, and institutionally—to prevent him from falling into a state in which he is beyond repair, precisely because he will never consider his claims for reparations to be closed. The subject thus brings about the perpetuation of his own lack of success: he is capable of producing only the conditions of his failure, embroiled as he is in his severe neurosis (in the best of cases) or, even more frequently, already trapped by resentmentist psychosis. It is here that the work of the writer and the poet is so decisive, for it allows us, by way of its style, to escape ourselves, to recognize the extent of our mutilation, and to move toward a scarring over by way of the genius of a stylization.

"There is not in the world one single poor lynched bastard, one poor tortured man, in whom I am not also murdered and humiliated."[291] These words are again from Césaire, and they open the fourth chapter of *Black Skin*. Césaire tells it like it is: he is the humiliated one, the assassinated one. He bears within himself the stain that descends upon those who are born within a culture that history arbitrarily judges to be "inferior." I'm not saying that every aspect of cultures should be relativized and non-hierarchized. On the contrary: every culture has an obligation to establish connections with the universal and with critical thinking, and to develop its freedom of

THE SEA: A WORLD OPENED TO MAN

thought in a close relationship with science. There are entire aspects of every culture that are shameful, and these aspects must be closely scrutinized and reformed. But it is not my aim to discuss this here. I'm talking about the universal condition of the one who is mistreated by others for no good reason but the delusional neuroses of the perpetrators, neuroses that are projected onto the other, whether with good or bad intentions—and which end up determining the future of entire groups. Césaire takes this burden upon himself and becomes the one who is mistreated, the "poor man." But the moment he writes "poor man" is the moment these words cease to have any hold on him. This is the force of style: speak, and you will escape; speak, and you will no longer be spoken by the other, but on the contrary take control of your life, your existence, your own existence and that of others, in the sense that your existence will inspire others, carry them along: this is what it means to take control of language in the face of colonialism, which sets out to dispossess people of language. It is Césaire, this splendid writer, who takes the language of the other and makes of it a universal language, in order to speak evil and to go beyond it. Through his writing, he recognizes the "humiliated" man, names him, legitimates him, mends him, frees him. Of course, poetry isn't enough, but action will take over what began as a poetic event.

In the chapter entitled "The Black Man and Language," Fanon turns to the condescension of the colonizers when they come upon the "Black," immediately speaking to him in "pidgin," as though they have forgotten that he has a language, a culture, a country, a dignity. Fanon notes that he is labeled an idealist "for speaking to the 'towelheads' in correct French," when in fact "it is the others"— those who do not do so—"who are the bastards."[292] Another example: "You're sitting in a café in Rouen or Strasbourg and you have the misfortune to be spotted by an old drunk. He makes a beeline for your table: 'You African? Dakar, Rufisque, whorehouse, women, coffee, mangoes, bananas . . .' You get up and leave; you are greeted with a hail of insults: 'You didn't play the big shot like that in your jungle, filthy nigger!'"[293] So when Fanon writes simply that "man is propelled toward the world and his kind,"[294] it is a powerful slap—invisible but eternal—that he delivers to the head of the idiot, a magisterial and silent slap, that of style and of emancipation through style. Where is the resentment here? Undoubtedly it is to be found in the one who believes himself to be "superior" but who is plainly pathetic.

147

— 2 —

THE UNIVERSAL AT THE RISK OF THE IMPERSONAL

It's the 1950s, but it's also our own time. Fanon arrives in France and discovers that he is "an object among other objects,"[295] ceaselessly reified by the gaze and the behavior of others. But he refuses any and all "affective tetanisation."[296] He enters into a struggle not against others but against himself and his own propensity for victimhood: no, they won't have my skin a second time; the combat is just beginning. Fanon took the tangent of writing and of militant action: "I wanted to be a man, and nothing but a man. There were some who wanted to equate me with my ancestors, enslaved and lynched: I decided that I would accept this. I considered this internal kinship from the universal level of the intellect—I was the grandson of slaves the same way President Lebrun was the grandson of peasants who had been exploited and worked to the bone."[297] *Accepting via the universal level of the intellect*: this tells us all we need to know in order to understand the possibility of escaping resentment, a victory over oneself and others. This is how it's done: you move to the universal level, precisely the level that is refused to you. But let us not be fooled about the nature of this refusal, which is rarely conscious: often, all we see in front of us is drunkenness. The true adversary is rare, and his contempt is always tricky to oppose. But even this contempt is powerless in the face of the one who takes upon himself the task of accepting the *internal kinship* that joins us all together—all of us who are humiliated, all of us who are born again.

I have often been accused of not being a "feminist," of not doing enough to tie my work to gender studies, of not practicing inclusive writing, of having a very weak—let's say non-existent—reflex when it comes to writing pronouns in the feminine. But for me, feminism is inseparable from humanism. I understand very well the paths of those

THE SEA: A WORLD OPENED TO MAN

women who created a feminism of conquest, which is essential; I even feel that I am carrying its banner as an inheritance, and responding to the tasks it has set out. There is no minor object in any struggle, even if we all have the right to choose our battles. I do not disdain inclusive writing or feminine pronouns, but I come from another world, one that is based on the value of universalism. That's just how it is. And thinkers of gender studies have also been important in my journey, since I know that identity is in large part a social fiction, and I'm familiar with how society assigns us all a certain place. Black, Jewish, Muslim, woman. You here, you there. Let's be honest for a moment. In all sincerity, I don't know what it means to be a woman. History teaches me that it's far from being a panacea in this world—that it is at best an error, a lack, and at worst a tragedy, something that must be made to disappear or be possessed, a sort of great golden pebble swapped from one man to another. I have no compassion for these men, caught as they are in the trap of their frenzy. I keep my distance from them so as to avoid as best I can their idiotic fury, their danger. Happily, there are many people who are not like this: those who are men or women by accident, with whom I walk the path of humanism, who agree to teach me no end of things without condescension, who gratify me with their love, their friendship, or their respect, and who perhaps first saw me as a woman but ended up forgetting, or at least considering it unimportant. I, in any case, don't know what it means, and in any case it is a very unimportant subject when compared with many others—when compared with what Mallarmé called "a capacity possessed by the spiritual Universe to see itself," or what he calls the "impersonal."[298] When you read poets, you discover the extent to which respect for a person—man, woman, black, white, x—is often also the site of a profound acknowledgment of the impersonal, as though this great history of individuation had something to do with that of disappearance. On May 14, 1867, Mallarmé writes to Cazalis: "I am now impersonal and no longer the Stéphane that you know,—but a capacity possessed by the spiritual Universe to see itself and develop itself, through what was once me."[299] This is a declaration of depersonalization, as I argued in *Mallarmé et la parole de l'imâm*. I'm sure that Fanon could have claimed this declaration as his own.

I tasted this freedom of impersonality when I was very young, like the light falling upon me, like the warm sun upon me. I saw that "being a woman" makes no sense, just like "being a man"—indeed, "being a woman" makes even less sense, since a man can always be fooled by the false equivalence between being a man and

149

PART III

being a human. The truth is, you only have to be a tad smarter than those around you to see through the trick very quickly. By contrast, the stupidity of others easily creates a "world" unto itself: there is enough room in the cave for those within this little world who believe they are encountering the universal, who believe they are coming face to face with humanity. Indeed, the problem is not that they believe this, but that they claim to be the only ones able to deceive themselves thus, and that they refer to this deception as the truth. If only this great illusion could include those who saw through it.

Let us not think that it is easy, even for someone as talented as Fanon, to get beyond resentment. The difficulty here explains why people feel like giving up hope, why they grow tired of the world, why they procrastinate. "Yet with all my being, I refuse to accept this amputation," writes Fanon in the chapter entitled "The Lived Experience of the Black Man." "I feel my soul as vast as the world, truly a soul as deep as the deepest of rivers; my chest has the power to expand to infinity."[300] There are many individuals whose very being gives them pain, pain from feeling the depth of the world and from being denigrated by their peers. We could pity these people, we could even say that they are right, but this would be to forget the tricks resentment uses to propagate its evil. In this last instance, the individual is responsible—or at least, he has to believe himself to be so and to behave as though he were so: this is a far better regulative fiction than that of deresponsibilization. It is not a matter of positing oneself as guilty, or of allowing others to denigrate one's self-worth. It is a matter of understanding that when all is said and done, the subject remains a subject by refusing "amputation," incessant denigration—a denigration that is sure of itself and whose stupidity is mechanical, systematic, effective, and at times institutional. Stepping into the universal does not mean fleeing what you are. Depersonalization is personalization. Is this a contradiction? No, it is simply a paradox, as Jankélévitch's moral philosophy teaches us. For if the universal were a deliberate erasure of the person, it would simply be repression, denial; it would be a shadow of itself, a tool of cultural imperialism. The universal welcomes into its midst all singularities, as long as they are prepared to embark upon the adventure of sublimation.

> How come I have barely opened my eyes they had blindfolded, and they already want to drown me in the universal? . . . I need to lose myself in my negritude and see the ashes, the segregation, the repression, the rapes, the discrimination, and the boycotts. We

THE SEA: A WORLD OPENED TO MAN

need to touch with our finger all the wounds that score our black livery.[301]

In analysis, there are often different moments of verbalization, with no predefined order. Sometimes the cycle recommences as one reminisces about pain. No session is ever closed: yes, there is a journey, and it is possible to speak of an evolution, but there will always remain something incurable: there will always be stumbling blocks, stops and starts, bruises, residues; this is where the patient must once again become a weaver of sorts, so as not to give in to the acrimony that takes up all his attention, to his real and justifiable bitterness.

We all have reasons to suffer from our shortcomings and from the injustices that we have endured. Fanon aspires to the universal—simply to be a man—but he'd also like to throw himself headlong into his "negritude," as if this negritude were a kind of elemental ocean, an ocean for us all—a universal. And it is one. I would also like to lose myself in this negritude as if it were my own, and indeed an apprenticeship with Fanon makes it possible to understand the extent of the *internal kinship* between us all.

If literature carries within itself the truth of humanity, it is because, by way of style, we can all experience this negritude—whether our own is buried or visible—as a reality of man and of woman: the great oceanic pain that comes from lacking, from being nothing, from being *the last of the wretched*. Like Fanon, I have walked this road: "Continuing my catalog of reality, endeavouring to determine the moment of symbolic crystallization, I found myself quite naturally at the doors of Jungian psychology."[302] These very doors were my inspiration for the notion of individuation, and by extension that of irreplaceability—I sought to rework both of these notions so as to do away with an impoverished form of individualism that does not allow us to think the links between individuals and the creation of a common world in Hannah Arendt's sense: namely, the state that is based on law.

Sometimes in analysis, patients seem to stamp their feet in frustration: they feel like they are treading water, because they have understood a great deal, but still feel trapped in the cycle of resentment. They come to the session wanting to leave all of their acrimony, their jealousy, and their envy on the couch when they leave; they say they want to get rid of it and that they have to leave it somewhere; they apologize, they get annoyed with their analyst, they cry out to him, irritated by this often silent mirror whom they scrutinize for the slightest glance, the slightest sigh.

151

PART III

Fanon, because he was a psychiatrist (he could have been an excellent psychoanalyst if time had given him the chance), is very good at describing the behavior of these individuals during their sessions, especially the particularities of those who experience themselves as "blacks"—the way this leads to alienation, in the sense that they always try to compare themselves, to denigrate themselves or to assert their own self-worth. This is exhausting, in that the comparisons they make during the session never end. They might end later, if the cure is able to undertake its life-saving work. But in the initial stages, the individual who feels himself to be black does not even possess the unconscious that would be necessary to escape from this alienation, for the collective unconscious within which he is immersed—he, the colonized one, he, the man from the Caribbean—is not unified with the personal cerebral structure of said Caribbean man, but instead falls within the domain of the "impulsive cultural imposition"[303] according to which being black necessarily means being on the dark side, the foreign side, the side of evil, the side without light. You have to be black to think like this, to dare to harm yourself to this degree, to believe that your lack of radiance comes from the fact that you are black. This is so unreal, so false, that it might seem like nonsense. How can someone think this of himself? It doesn't make sense, we say—all those of us who are not physically black. But our ability to say this falls away as soon as we examine those forms of collective and individual unconscious that display a few of the secrets of collective and individual neuroses. As soon as we do this, an all-embracing human stupidity reveals itself to us, that of men who play at hating one another: "In the collective unconscious of *Homo occidentalis* the black man—or, if you prefer, the color black—symbolizes evil, sin, wretchedness, death, war, and famine. Every bird of prey is black. In Martinique, which is a European country in its collective unconscious, when a jet-black person pays you a visit, the reaction is: 'What misfortune does he bring?'"[304]

Those who bear the burden of a "bad" birth or what they believe to be a bad birth, or those who have been convinced that their birth is indeed bad, are innumerable, and their numbers continue to grow. This damage that they do to themselves, and that they have internalized to the point that they seek to justify it, must be mended. But mending it is anything but easy, and it is indeed unlikely. The strategy I have tried most often in my work as an analyst is that of creating something different: a potential future truth that will not be confiscated by the reality of alienation. All those who have been

THE SEA: A WORLD OPENED TO MAN

judged by society to be outside the norms of respectability have done this damage to themselves, and they have all felt its pain, a pain that is sometimes brief and sometimes lasts forever: I'm speaking of women, of foreigners, of men who love men, of women who love women, of men who experience themselves only as "sons" and who are not recognized by their fathers or loved by their mothers. The list is infinite, and the dignity of these people is enormous: their analytic work is so respectable that we analysts wish we were far more gifted, so as to better serve them in this grandiose undertaking of sublimation. This history of damaged singularities, which runs alongside official history, is also real history: the history of individuals in motion, who build freedom and combat alienation, alone and with allies that they have chosen.

> The black man is comparison. . . . He . . . is always dependent on the presence of "the Other." The question is always whether he is less intelligent than I, blacker than I, or less good than I. Every self-positioning or self-fixation maintains a relationship of dependency on the collapse of the other.[305]

This is true for every man of resentment. The mechanism at work here is at once tortuous, regular, and panoptical: the subject understands himself only through what René Girard has called mimetic rivalry, in the eye of the other, in comparison with the other; above all, he links his value to that of the other, and his reassurance to the denigration of the other. If the other—who is experienced solely as an adversary, a rival, a competitor—does not "collapse," then he risks his own collapse, for the man of resentment is an infantile and indeed a nonexistent "ego" with febrile emotional intelligence: he cannot envision a world in which singularities can coexist. If something is given to someone, it is because it has been taken away from him; he is the victim of the entire arrangement. He cannot admire others. He is capable only of being jealous, of envying, and this in turn brings about his own psychological collapse. But he doesn't care, for as his illness develops, he becomes more and more impervious to it. Being dependent on "the collapse of the other": this is what brings about the illness of resentment, and we can speak in more general terms, broaden it to include the historico-social environment of the individual: to be resentful is to be dependent on the collapse of the world, on a general decline. The man of resentment persuades himself that the world is in decline so as to finally allow his own resentment to blossom, and to enjoy his victimization without any shame.

PART III

Contrary to this dependence on the collapse of the other, Fanon pleads in favor of man—simply man, neither white nor black, and this man is him, him as well, him with, him in spite of. "I am a man, and I have to rework the world's past from the very beginning."[306] This past is the history that precedes us, the history of peoples, that of the struggle of freedom everywhere in the world to develop a more common history, that of humanist civilization (of the progress of humanity toward perfection, as Condorcet might say), this story that belongs to the domain of literature as much as that of the real, as much to desire and to the will as to certain facts: yes, this history is "written," wished for, desired, oriented in a specific way; it is "true" in the sense that it is constructed, that it tries to be more than it is, that it tries to create a fertile ground for a greater future, and to not be too shameful for the law-based state that is to come. Fanon does not want to be assigned only to collective history, to this history and to no other—as though the memory of men could be divided and shared out like land. Fanon invents the only viable morality for Blacks, a morality destined for everyone, a morality that does "not want to be the victim of the Ruse of a black world."[307]

I know that there are other ways of resorting wounded pride. But legitimate though they may be, they do not possess the durability of the universalist method. Post-colonial studies, cultural studies, and subaltern studies are essential, for they teach us how to deconstruct the mainstream version of history. We should be able to do this without them, but this is rarely possible. Their contribution is therefore key. But like every current of thought, they must ensure that they remain critical of themselves, so that they do not reproduce binarisms and fall into the very essentialism that they often seek to combat. As such, they must reassert their necessary pact with the notion of the universal. Diversity is a test for the credibility of universality, but universality is also a test for the credibility of diversity.

— 3 —

CARING FOR THE COLONIZED

"I must constantly remind myself that the real *leap* consists of introducing invention into life."[308] Everyone should cherish this citation, for it is a window opening onto a tiny sliver of the horizon, a lifeline allowing us to escape the resentmentist bottleneck. "In the world I am heading for, I am endlessly creating myself."[309]

We find this vitalist creation of the self by way of the self in the work of Bergson; long before him, we find it in the ancient idea of sculpting oneself, which was linked (and rightly so) to the surrounding world, the city, and the cosmos—though the meaning here differs in that the place of the "ego" is still non-existent in antiquity. The paradox we must grasp here is that of how the idea of invention is compatible with that of heritage. We are all depositories of what came before, of the interminable past that structures our neuroses to such a great degree; we are the heirs of these other lives, these multiple lives, and we search for what they can transmit to us, sometimes in spite of themselves. "I am not a slave to the slavery that dehumanized my ancestors."[310] If we had to set down just one humanist truth, it would be this one: nothing—neither the past nor a blocked-off future—must ever imprison a being (neither others nor oneself) through its unsuitability for freedom, to use Wilhelm Reich's expression. We must protect the humanism that protects men from their shortcomings and their "morbid infatuation";[311] we must "care" for them so that they will want to continue to "search." "There are from one end of the world to the other men who are searching."[312] Some will be amazed that "searching" is at stake here, and even more amazed that "searching" is, in a way, an outcome of the care that is given to beings. And yet "searching" remains one of the main challenges of existence, a way of articulating desire and action. This is what

PART III

"searching" means: putting an intelligence and a will into motion; attempting to go beyond mere theorizing in order to experiment.

For the analyst that I am, giving care is also a way of allowing the patient—who has often lost his desire for things and for life—to get himself back to searching, to empower him such that he begins to imagine new possibilities, to imagine writing a new chapter of his life, without being a slave to collective neurosis. Ronald Laing[313] speaks of knots in which we are ensnared: the familial nexus in the first instance, the knot made up of the neuroses of others, of those who preceded us; but also the cultural nexus, the great knot of collective neurosis and also of bilateral neurosis (if I can put it this way), for we are all implicated in large circles but also in one-on-one relationships that are more intimate, and that generate conflicts. The "ego" is often son or daughter of, husband or wife of, brother or sister of, etc. All of which gives neuroses a chance to fork, to split into two: nexuses thus become sorts of fractals that form folds—Deleuze and Leibniz may be the great thinkers of this, but individuals often have trouble interpreting them. Caring for individuals means giving them access to these folds, and above all to their creative and interpretive powers. The end of repetition begins here, in this possibility of loosening knots, leaving them behind (for they are unsolvable), cutting them.

It is important not to remain too long in the vicinity of certain rifts, for they can pull us in just like an abyss, making us giddy with their sheer breadth. We must not believe that we are stronger than we really are. When we stand before our neuroses, we must remain humble—courageous, yes, but humble all the same. Certain battles are best avoided, not to fall to our knees, but so that we might engage in others that we are more likely to win. Of course, it is in no way a matter of abandoning battles that appear too complicated, that seem to be already lost: if this were the case, there would be no history, no beginning, nothing but repetition. This wise mixture of battles that we fight and battles that we set aside (though not forever) is that of the free man trying his hand at individuation, sparing himself from exertion all the while that he does precisely the opposite. Nothing is written in advance; finding someone who can help you create a way out is not easy. There are lovers, there are friends, and there are those who care for a living.

We would have to go through no shortage of criteria to explain the ethics of the carer—the ethics of psychoanalysis, as Lacan would have said: personal limits, the distance that must be established, how much empathy to give, the level of self-involvement, and, more broadly, the institutional ethics within which the carer works, and also the

THE SEA: A WORLD OPENED TO MAN

institutional organization, which allows or hinders said ethics. Care is something that is proven, not decreed in advance. Taking Algeria as his example, Fanon revisits the question of the links between medicine—if it is practiced by colonizers, competent or not—and local populations, links that are difficult and indeed impossible. It would be nice if medicine could erect an autonomous territory that was sheltered from social and cultural forms of alienation and above all from violence and prejudice, but no such *sheltered zone* exists. "At no time, in a non-colonial society, does the patient mistrust his doctor."[314] These words recall something we too often forget: all medicine is political, in that its exercise depends on the conditions of possibility put forth by a political regime. This does not mean that there are no individual doctors worthy of the name, practicing scientifically and ethically respectable medicine, but that medicine as such—as a public politics of care—does not exist without a state based on the rule of law. Giving care—if we want this care to be lasting and effective—requires going beyond the individual technique of this or that carer; it requires, above all, figuring out which "institutional"[315] circle the care is part of. For consent to care also depends on global and institutional consent. Clearly, no one who is colonized can accept the care—technically sound and relevant though it may be—of a doctor who is part of colonial domination, even in spite of himself. Fanon neatly demonstrates the extent to which caring and governing are in a certain way indivisible, in that the absence of a democratic government that respects the rights of individuals renders impossible the delivery of care whose beneficial nature would be above suspicion. Care cannot cope with suspicion: its basis lies in the patient's trust in the person and the institutional system that care for him, not just in technical competence.

This fact is difficult to deconstruct, for what the man of resentment needs—at least the one who is on the edge of resentment, who still has one foot outside of it, who might possibly still be healed—is care. But like everyone who suffers from psychosis or from a severe neurosis, he does not consent to this care, already arguing that he does not need it, or that the doctor is not worthy of his trust. As such, transference does not work, trust is not given, consent is not clarified, and everything gets shut down. Fanon refers to this as "active diminishments," or as "gashes in the existence of the colonized"—in other words, everything that turns the lives of the colonized into "something resembling an incomplete death."[316] The colonized subject who refuses the care that he desperately needs condemns himself. The man of resentment is prey to the same mechanism. Colonial domination

157

PART III

ends up disrupting all the relations between the colonized subject and his own culture,[317] as Fanon says. To this we could add his relations with his own body as well, since the relationship we establish with ourselves is always mediated by culture.

Let us recall the issue of nosocomial diseases, which are always a concern for institutions of care, given the dangers a lack of hygiene presents for the ill. Jean Oury argues that psychological nosocomial diseases also exist—managerial harassment, for instance—that serve to destroy the positive atmosphere one might find in a care community. But beyond institutional dysfunction, there is also a more cultural dysfunction: that of the political and socioeconomic regime within which care is to be found. It is obvious that colonialism gives rise to both psychological and physical nosocomial illnesses; it is undeniable that it structurally impedes the delivery of care. As such, to care is to engage in resistance, whether official or unofficial: it means demonstrating one's separation from this all-encompassing contamination; it means becoming a border in and of oneself to protect the patient from a worsening of his state. Fanon is certainly not the first to have told this tragic story of the marriage between totalitarianism and medicine: how the latter destroys the bodies of individuals to make the former even more effective. The advent of the state of law after the Second World War served precisely to intertwine the system of laws and rights with the right to health, as manifested in the universality of social security in France; but it also brought about a qualitative and protective threshold of medical values, setting down the rules of scientific and medical integrity. As such, theoretically, the values and principles of a state that is based on law serve to protect the bodies of individuals.

This is a very concrete example that shows, in its positive aspect, that every law-based state presents itself as a biopolitical regime. But at the same time, this biopolitical regime must be in the service of the bodies of individuals and their freedom. This is the entire problem, for behind the good intentions lie dormant (but restless) intentions that are more conservative and restrictive. As a result, many people in the liberal tradition seek, and rightly so, to produce a theory of limited government, one that leaves the bodies of citizens outside of its prerogatives. On paper, this is a good solution—but only on paper, for once again the absence of state or institutional regulation does not mean the absence of other forms of interference on the bodies of men and women. As such, politics must be resolute all the while that its impact must be seen to be minimal: it must try to produce a positive impact on individual bodies, according to guidelines defined

158

THE SEA: A WORLD OPENED TO MAN

by representative bodies or by citizens themselves, through acts of participative democracy or civil disobedience. We can all relate to Fanon's description of the interaction between doctor and colonized subject (which basically amounts to a series of misunderstandings), for it echoes well-known experiences in which it becomes impossible to give care—the moment, in other words, at which the surrounding framework comes to be skewed by relations of force and domination. Things are quite similar for the man of resentment, who often lives like a "colonized" subject in his own home: like a denigrated and humiliated being, stripped of his rights—someone who has come down in the world. For this reason, literature on colonialism offers valuable resources for understanding the mechanisms of resentment: the same ambivalence characterizes the resentmentist ego and the colonized subject with regard to the very idea of being cared for.

— 4 —

THE DECOLONIZATION OF BEING

Fanon is a key author for those who seek to understand the link between resentment and history, between the characterological structure of a being and the cultural history, both recent and ancestral, of a people. He is also key for understanding how an "ego" or an "I" who has every reason to experience resentment—whose collective history is painful, and who is still caught in the trap of cultural domination—can be stronger than these constraints and escape them, be it through works, reflection, philosophical and activist creation, or a collective engagement that is in fact already the individual engagement of an "ego" who is out of the reach of resentment. Out of its reach, and hence not imprisoned by it: being fully aware of it, not denying its force and even, at times, its justification, yet never giving in to its temptation. This very difficult tension can be felt in Fanon's expansive yet taut style, which is at times almost poetic, and which is very "medical" in its description of the illnesses of the colonized. If only the events of his personal life had allowed him to keep going. But it was not to be: he died at 36, struck down by myeloid leukemia. During the last year of his life, having already been diagnosed with his deadly illness, he wrote *The Wretched of the Earth*. It is 1960. And the thesis put forth by Fanon is affirmed once and for all: the most dangerous colonization is the one that descends upon a human being, the one to which this being yields inside of himself; it is not exterior, politico-economic colonization, but the more metaphysical and ethical one that is found within the soul. As Alice Cherki writes in her preface to the 2002 French edition of *The Wretched of the Earth*: "His analysis insists on the consequences of enslavement not only for peoples but also for subjects: the conditions of their liberation, which is above all a liberation of the individual, a 'decolonization of being.'"[318]

THE SEA: A WORLD OPENED TO MAN

Resentment is a colonization of being. Sublimating it produces a decolonization of being, which is the only viable dynamic for bringing forth a subject and an aptitude for freedom. Fanon never stops describing the inacceptable violence that descends upon colonized peoples, and showing how this violence transforms beings, often forcing them into a vile alternative between taking action against themselves or against others. Violence never leaves any choice, producing only a forced choice whereby the subject always ends up being its prisoner, enslaved once more. In his preface to the 1961 edition of *The Wretched of the Earth*, Jean-Paul Sartre also discusses the *demolishment* that is the colonial enterprise: a cultural demolishment, in that the colonists seek to negate the language of the other, make it disappear, and refuse it any linguistic legitimacy that would be worthy of the name:

> Colonial violence not only aims at keeping these enslaved men at a respectful distance, it also seeks to dehumanize them. No effort is spared to demolish their traditions, to substitute our language for theirs, and to destroy their culture without giving them ours. We exhaust them into a mindless state.[319]

Sartre also depicts the double bind of the one who has long endured the violence of domination on the outside, but who, little by little, has come to be contaminated by it on the interior.

> [The colonized] are trapped between our guns, which are pointing at them, and those frightening instincts, those murderous impulses, that emerge from the bottom of their hearts and that they don't always recognize. For it is not first of all *their* violence, it is ours, on the rebound, that grows and tears them apart. . . . This repressed rage, never managing to explode, goes round in circles and wreaks havoc on the oppressed themselves.[320]

The correct diagnosis is difficult in that this violence is justified and legitimate, and yet this legitimacy is not enough to validate violence as a therapeutic tool for the individual who is undergoing or experiencing this violence. For it will inevitably be turned against him, whether he is aware of this or not, and whether he aspires to this reversal or not. The "frightening instincts" and "murderous impulses," when liberated, do not give rise to a viable history for the individual, and even less for the collective. All they engender, in the long run, is "common debasement."[321] Debasement is an evil that is

PART III

described nicely by someone who is a great representative of critical theory, an heir to the Frankfurt School and its theories of reification, Axel Honneth, when he outlines the contours of the contemporary neoliberal society that gives rise to a generalized contempt. Debasement is the evil that rots resentful souls, and this leaves them incapable of bringing forth an ethics of recognition, for they argue that they themselves have suffered an absence of recognition—which is indeed true.

But developing a recognition of others is a new stage that the simple absence of recognition cannot invalidate. He who embarks upon the path of individuation will at some point have to pass through this ethics of recognition, even if it means inventing it from scratch, through sublimation, if he has not seen even a trace of it in his own life. For there is also literature in life: reading can lead to being recognized, as can the arts, if only through aesthetic sentiments. The experience of beauty is an ethics of recognition in all but name. And when humans fail, when they are incapable of giving us even a small amount of the recognition that we all need so badly, then we must take hold of lives past and ally ourselves with the dead—the great artists who preceded us and who often went unrecognized. We must ally ourselves with culture to escape the disaster of organized debasement.

It is true that there are times at which only violence can quell violence; in other words, as Sartre writes in his preface, the violence of the guns of the colonized can quiet the violence of the colonizer. True. But is it merely a question of "violence"? This is anything but certain, as much as violence sometimes also belongs to the domain of legitimate defense. The fact remains that if violence turns out, in the medium and long term, to be nothing but pure violence, it will end up also destroying the colonized. Violence is never a lasting process of construction. It is the power of destruction: it may destroy evil, which is totally legitimate and sometimes necessary, but it possesses no dynamic of edification, no capacity for removing resentment. Violence is tautological: it engenders only itself. It is repetition. It is the mechanical and lethal force of repetition.

Sartre, as the offspring of an idealism the explosive force of whose origins he was never subjected to, believes in an almost romantic way in this idea of a violence that will eventually be able to demolish "colonial darkness."[322] The style of this formulation is ruthless, as is often the case with Sartre: it rings true, and one might almost be reading the haughty and arrogant prose of *Dirty Hands*: "a fighter's weapon is his humanity. For in the first phase of the revolt killing is

THE SEA: A WORLD OPENED TO MAN

a necessity: killing a European is killing two birds with one stone, eliminating in one go oppressor and oppressed: leaving one man dead and the other man free."[323] But in fact, what remains after this killing is a man who rediscovers his capacity for freedom, but who is not yet free, for he will now have to back this freedom with the construction of a subject who to this point was nonexistent, and who is at the mercy of a wounded unconscious and of a consciousness that is no less miserable, tasked with the construction of a common world for which violence alone will not suffice.

The violence of hatred alone does not allow us to leave the darkness behind; on the contrary, it inaugurates a posttraumatic phenomenon that imprisons the subject and makes him ill. Fanon, as a clinician and a psychiatrist, knows this perfectly well, and it is undoubtedly for this reason that, despite his militant activism, he does not call for widespread violence; above all, he takes up the task of creating a form of "care" that will allow all those involved to escape this violence.

All the same, I understand that Fanon's philosophy is not quite this clear, and that there is a real ambivalence regarding his position on the use of violence. By declaring himself to be "Algerian," and by adopting a sort of new identity with the name "Ibrahim," Fanon shows his ability to be radical and paradigmatic. Becoming another, even if it means making a link with what you have always been, is a total sublimation, that of a hardliner or a revolutionary. It is radical in its construction, in the way it brings about a new subject, in its link to the future. But it does not lead to destruction. Of course, Fanon could have been more conciliatory with regard to the violence of others, that of the colonized. But when it came to himself, he was always guided by his doctor's ethos, in spite of everything. With Fanon's change of identity, we are in fact approaching the "care of the self," in the sense that this self is the object of a new sculpting.

What must be understood here is that the act of "caring," whether it concerns oneself or others, is political, in that it allows for the construction of a new life, and in that no one is ignorant of the need to bring politics and care together: the truth of politics is to be found in this solidarity that is still to be born, which allows all our individualities to blossom. Care is thus a political engagement, and not a superfluous act, or an act that can be equated to charity or compassion. To care is to enable future life, both individual and collective; it means rejecting the irreversibility that can bring about a violence that cannot be opposed.

— 5 —

RESTORING CREATIVITY

Here again, what Fanon says about colonization, and then about its contrary, decolonization, can also be said of resentment and of getting beyond it. The man of resentment suffers from colonization within himself. He is no longer an actor; he is simply a "spectator crushed to a nonessential state."[324] In other words, the nonessential eats away at him and will eventually kill him. Being eaten away by the nonessential while believing that in fact you are right, that you possess the meaning of justice—this is what this unreasonable feeling tricks you into thinking. When he takes this false axiom as his foundation, the individual is incapable of clear and objective reasoning: he cannot develop a form of critical thinking that would bear witness to the independence of his faculty of judgment. I have sought to maintain the expression *ci-gît l'amer*—here lies, at once, bitterness, the mother, and the sea—throughout this book as an echo of the territory of our soul, which is inseparable from the very real territory of the society in which we live, as well as that of the family, or more precisely childhood, this territory that saw us grow and experience our first painful emotions. This territory is the one on which we must bury so as to eventually bear fruit; it is the one on which we must find the right measure of repression—leaving things aside without abandoning them, advancing without negating—the ability, in summary, to set down roots without becoming prisoners of belonging. Fanon often explains that a gain in personality, which should be understood as individuation, is the corollary of the loss of belonging:[325] each one of us experiences separation so as to finally be—to finally exist as a man, and not only as this or that, this woman, this Black, this other.

Once again, this is a paradox that Jankélévitch could have explained: the fact that our territoriality makes use of both belonging

THE SEA: A WORLD OPENED TO MAN

and unbelonging, connections and disconnections. Often we must set down roots to understand that it is also possible to be citizens of the world; we must first draw up the borders of our own space-time, here and now, to liberate ourselves from these borders, and to grasp the fact that we all belong to a beyond of these borders. Something must inhabit, something must remain—*here lies*—for the individual to expand into an elsewhere, and for the world to open as a horizon. "Here lies bitterness": for me, these words refer back to a long process that began with my book *Métaphysique de l'imagination*, which approaches the writings of Henry Corbin, Hölderlin, and Derrida, especially the magnificent text the latter dedicated to Blanchot, *Demeure*. In Henry Corbin's thought, the island, the sea, and the ocean are essential motifs for understanding the "imaginal world"[326] as he defines it to bring forth the soul. The *imaginal sea*[327] is a watery territory between the visible and the invisible, *twin* of the imaginal world in a certain sense, that offers the soul other types of sensual and metaphysical experiments. When I write "here lies the sea" I refer to this oceanic element, both a starting point and an end point, on which souls in search of themselves sail. I refer, also, to these lines from Hölderlin that continue to resound: "But it is the sea / That takes and gives remembrance, / And love no less keeps eyes attentively fixed, / But what is lasting the poets provide."[328] Here we find the indestructible link between real territoriality (the one that precedes all emplacement in the world) and a non-geographic sea—a cognitive and psychological sea, once again a territory of the soul, that returns memory or takes it away, and gives to those who understand it, and are not afraid to discover it, a capacity for poetry.

It is a question of inhabiting the world as a poet, as Heidegger (who never inhabited it as a poet) said precisely. A bitterness that has been turned into an imaginal sea is the opposite of the "disturbing experiences"[329] of which Fanon speaks when he describes the types of entertainment that descend upon colonized youth. One could say the same of today's youth, which is often abandoned to the market-oriented universe of distraction (parents cannot always be there to counterbalance this assault of temptation), which can turn out to be devastating when education is lacking. I am not saying that young people with an immigrant background, who live in underprivileged neighborhoods, are colonized: the comparison is completely implausible, even if many people lend weight to this diagnosis and to a resentment that would follow from it. But it is simply not the case: the colonization of being goes beyond the borders between neighborhoods and ethnic groups. Every child who is left alone in front of

165

PART III

a certain type of entertainment can become a colonized subject in his soul, without necessarily becoming aware of this. We can add today that such "disturbing experiences" are also addictive: they compensate for other experiences in a false way, and create no lasting stability in the ego. On the contrary, a feeling similar to apathy takes hold of this ego: there is no shortage of young people today, slumped behind their screens, who little by little lose all appetite for involvement in the surrounding world. And in his description of these disturbing experiences, Fanon walks in the footsteps of Reich (without naming him), because like Reich his diagnosis arises from a focus not on a person but on people: he speaks of the responsibility of individuals, of the masses formed by the absence of subjects.

> Our greatest task is to constantly understand what is happening in our own countries. We must not cultivate the spirit of the exceptional or look for the hero, another form of leader. We must elevate the people, expand their minds, equip them, differentiate them, and humanize them.[330]

The duty is clear: it is the task of each person to develop the conditions of possibility of a responsibility, to act in the world, without this person necessarily being exceptional. It is not a matter of being exceptional. It is a matter, on the contrary, of developing educational and work-related standards, the effectiveness of which lies in the expansion of minds—in an increase in aesthetic and existential experiences that allow the mind to "grow." Caring and educating, once again, are tasks that must be seen as essential for the act of governing. Fanon's analysis is reminiscent of Reich's words on democracy at work:

> Once again we turn to the obsession that we would like to see shared by every African politician—the need to shed light on the people's effort, to rehabilitate work, and rid it of its historical opacity. To be responsible in an underdeveloped country is to know that everything finally rests on educating the masses, on elevating their minds, on what we all too quickly call politicization.[331]

This truth in no way applies only to underdeveloped countries. It is the truth of every state that is based on the rule of law: the demand to constitute a public and individual form of rationality. We know this, of course, but we continue to delude ourselves on the question of good government by restricting this question to that of political

166

government, in the sense of the machine that executes the political power of a president and a group of ministers. But the question of good government opens onto a much longer cycle than that of a presidential term. It is not only that of the executive moment, but situates itself well upstream from this—in education and care. There are many of us who are working to bring about the ability to think good government, to create the conditions for its legitimacy and effectiveness, precisely by way of education and care given to individuals—to the very people who will elect this government, in the restricted, representative sense of the term. This question is inseparable from geopolitics, especially in a time of globalization in which all national sovereignty is shared, to the degree that it is inscribed within multilateral frameworks, jostling and at times colliding with the "capacity-giving" arrangements of neighboring countries.

My remarks here should not be misinterpreted: I am not trying to paint Fanon as a fanciful peace-lover. One finds in his work the idea of a legitimate use of violence, a violence that is inseparable from the great movement of liberation of a nation and of men. In Fanon's work, freedom is defined as "disalienation." But in the face of a process of alienation that is equivalent to the "cultural negation"[332] of a nation (a colonized nation, for example), in the face of what he calls "cultural obliteration,"[333] in the face of this unliveable negativity, the violence of retaliation remains a possibility, sometimes even the only possibility. As a last resort, violence can be legitimate. The first manifestations of it can even be a sign of health, a rejection of everything unacceptable that is being carried out. But after this initial moment of reaction, violence must reinvent itself in a sublimated form, one that can create something new.

The difficulties are all the greater, however, in that processes of colonial alienation serve to empty individuals of their culture, and precisely of their strength, of the resources that could help them resist the oppressor and create new norms for life. The pages on which Fanon describes the culture of the colonized cast an acerbic critical gaze on this culture, defining it as "shriveled, increasingly inert, and increasingly hollow,"[334] undoubtedly because violence has given way to the resentment that begins to eat away at this culture from inside.

After one or two centuries of exploitation the national cultural landscape has radically shriveled. It has become an inventory of behavioral patterns, traditional costumes, and miscellaneous customs. Little movement can be seen. There is no real creativity, no ebullience.

PART III

Poverty, national oppression, and cultural repression are one and the same.[335]

In short, a colonized culture becomes a caricature of itself; and in any case, if it were anything else, it would undoubtedly be destroyed by the occupier. Of course, secret attempts are made to save the culture, and secrecy will save no shortage of people on an individual level. However, underground movements are less good at educating a greater number of individuals, and at constituting a stock of resources that can enable their emancipation. Which leads Fanon to say that it is not possible to employ the national struggle for independence as the only foundation for putting into place real cultural independence. Nascent independence will necessarily be "haunted"[336] by what it was for years; it will be a ghost of itself. Being reborn from the ashes takes time, and requires the sublimation of the critical act—an act that is notably critical with regard to the burgeoning nationalist frenzy that, while it cloaks itself in all sorts of virtues, is often purely reactive.

— 6 —

THE THERAPY OF DECOLONIZATION

In order to care for the colonized and their illnesses, Fanon embraces the method of François Tosquelles, a method connected with the heyday of the Saint-Alban Psychiatric Hospital, and which was the origin of the institutional psychotherapy dear to Jean Oury, itself very close to social therapy and ethnopsychiatry[337] (the latter being Fanon's specific contribution to it). Taking a psychodynamic approach, Fanon champions the links between psychiatry and sociology, subjectivity and history, and what he calls "'sociogeny,'"[338] a genetics that is continually offset by sociology to explain how history "'is only the systematic valorization of collective complexes.'"[339] Laing, Lacan, Foucault, and others will take up this understanding of madness as social, as always being embedded within a relational knot. Seeking to care for individuals without at the same time seeking to care for the institution that cares for them, or the society that surrounds them, has little meaning in Fanon's understanding (in this, he is the heir of Tosquelles). We have said it often, but Fanon, as much as he is a psychiatrist, also acts politically—on the individual, the institution, and society. He "cares"—this is what is at issue for him medically and politically, both at once.

Fanon will participate in the emergence of a new kind of establishment, as was the case of Saint-Alban for Tosquelles, La Borde for Oury, Kingsley Hall for Laing, etc. The considerations that all these thinkers undertook regarding establishments are decisive for proper care, even though these establishments sometimes lose their way. Despite this, it is clear that new forms of therapy, and rich and paradigmatic reflections, emerge in these establishments; these reflections and practices revolutionize our ways of thinking about and undertaking care. Fanon's establishment was Blida-Joinville,[340]

169

the hospital in which he experimented with the techniques of social therapy, which sought to open the institution to the world, and to introduce certain activities and roles for those involved. For all that, Fanon never fell into the extremist view that seeks to erase all differences between world and hospital. Such an approach would be both wrong and deceptive; it would also be undesirable from a therapeutic standpoint. Later, Fanon would continue to develop his approach at the Charles-Nicolle Hospital in Tunis.[341] He identifies the same dysfunctions in psychiatric institutions as in the colonialist state: both impose alienation, dissolve the cultural identity of individuals, and thingify beings, classifying them so as to diminish and subjugate them.[342] Fanon's thesis anticipates the way these issues are dealt with in academia, but its importance goes beyond this. The thesis informs the way we describe the behavioral and psychological disturbances of the colonized or the "indigenous," but above all, it informs a political and intellectual strategy of disalienation.

This undertaking is multifaceted, as is always the case with Fanon. This will lead some in academia to treat his work with hostility and to level accusations at him, even though his works are of a rare intensity and precision. "Philosophy being the risk that the mind takes to assume its dignity":[343] Fanon addressed this remark to one of the members of his doctoral thesis committee. Philosophy, for him, is not a posture one takes on at university: it is a matter of existential, ethical, and political import. One notes the solemn tone of his grandiloquent and sincere remark, which shows that Fanon's very life as a man is at stake when he thinks and when he becomes a psychiatrist—that thinking, working, and living are not easily separable for him, even if he has his heart set on escaping the ways these activities are usually determined. But this vigilance is the sign of his ever-present concern in the face of several different reifications, such as that of his own individual and collective history, and that of the institution, often just as sectarian as the others.

In the editorials that he wrote for the internal journal of the Saint-Alban Psychiatric Hospital, his style is just as clinical as it is terribly personal, so much so that it is difficult to know who is hiding behind the "I" of his pronouncements. Who is speaking? Fanon, the psychiatrist? Definitely. But Fanon, the man? Fanon, the Black who is aware of the need to escape this particular identity, even if to do so he must take it on completely? Who is speaking? Fanon, in the name of certain patients who do not have the strength to express themselves? In his editorial of December 26, 1952,[344] he seemingly paints the portrait of a weary man, an individual who might

THE SEA: A WORLD OPENED TO MAN

fall—who knows?—into resentment. It is impossible to know; all we know is that this man experiences himself as someone "forgotten," someone who has waited his whole life for something that has never come, and who finds himself still wearily waiting at the age of forty, without the world ever having responded to his wait. Who is Fanon speaking of? Himself? He has not yet reached his forties—he will die before he can do so. Is he speaking of what he could have become—namely, someone forgotten—if he hadn't been able to "sublimate" the collectively sinister fate that was his own?

In another editorial, dated March 6, 1953, he recalls that man must be able to travel through time: to assume the continuity of the past, the present, and the future; in short, to have memory and the hope for a future. The psychological health of the person who is not able to manage all three dimensions[345] will undoubtedly be more vulnerable than that of others. For my part, I prefer to speak of the three dimensions of time—*chronos, aion,* and *kairos*—that strike me as the most precise when it comes to the dialectic of time and the subject: namely, how the subject endangers his individuation, and hence the entire endeavor of the disalienation or the decolonization of his being, if he is no longer capable of practicing the three temporal dimensions that allow him to embed himself within the world, memory, and the work. A subject who cannot manage the three dimensions can feel "restrained" in his ability to be a subject, which leads to suffering. The threat of resentment can come about in the breakdown of a dialectical time, namely *chronos:* linearity, history, continuity, that which precedes and follows me, the possibility of perceiving accumulation—how one stone follows another. This embeddedness within time is necessary, but if it excludes other forms of time, it imprisons the subject within a feeling of being crushed by time, for the time that passes, that flies by, is stronger than him. Hence *aion*—the feeling of suspense and of eternity—is necessary: a bit of time in its pure state, as Proust emphasizes. *Aion* is another possible name for sublimation: a standstill or a stoppage, not in the sense of prevention, but in the sense of mastery and fullness. The subject here holds firm, breathes, takes advantage of an inalterable present that makes him feel as though he were going beyond his finitude, or the finitude of others. Finally, there is *kairos,* the instant to be grasped, the possible, the right of each of us to make a beginning, to make history: the action of the subject giving rise to a before and an after, however difficult to distinguish they may be. Making an attempt at *kairos,* as a right and a duty of the subject: as soon as the subject gives up on this attempt, something darkens within him. As we have already seen, the man

171

PART III

of resentment is precisely the man who no longer connects himself with these three dimensions: his present is judged to be unacceptable, proof of the injustice that he endures; his future becomes nonexistent; and his past often harks back to a fantasmatic and illusory nostalgia that has nothing to do with the more factual idea of memory, which, even if it is always a story, remains a lived experience, one that can be used to constitute a foundation or a base for the subject.

This, perhaps, is the difference between resentment and the bitterness that risks turning into resentment, but perhaps goes no further than this risk. The illness of bitterness is indeed oppressive, but it does not always manifest itself politically as hatred of the other. Rather, it marks a form of depression on the part of the subject who experiences it. Those who go into exile as adults know this bitterness well, above all when they have the impression—rightly so—of having been forced to abandon, in addition to their country, their status and the social recognition that they were accorded. Elsewhere, they were professors, doctors, lawyers, engineers; here, they are forced to requalify (their credentials are not recognized) at the very moment that they find themselves in extremely vulnerable psychological, affective, economic, and familial situations. They manage by thinking about the past, but they do so too often. This past is essential to remind them of who they are, but it is also lethal in that it reminds them that they are no longer this person—at least externally, socially. This link to the past, which structurally is completely necessary for the subject, becomes a non-ally, a weakening. But nor does disconnecting from the past give rise to any care. The individual is stuck in a time that no longer exists, neither as *chronos*, *aion*, or *kairos*. As though he were no longer embedded in time—which is of course impossible, and which gives rise in him to a feeling of unreality, making his illness all the more insidious. As a result, the subject devitalizes himself little by little. He does not fall into a more hostile resentment. He drowns in bitterness without being able to make anything of this *amer*, this "bitter."

It is precisely at this point that it is still possible to transform *l'amer en mer*—the bitter into a sea; that it is still possible to separate (per the logic of *la mère*, the mother), to leave behind the self-image that one believed oneself to be, to abandon the need for a self-image, to get out in front of the work so as to undertake it. Some are able to do this from time to time. They write, for instance, and in doing so they escape for a moment. But bitterness often resumes, and with it discouragement. It would almost be necessary not to leave them alone for a second, or at least not for a long time—those who are

172

THE SEA: A WORLD OPENED TO MAN

under the pressure of an exile that is always there, reminding them that time is passing, that they have not sublimated their finitude, and that elsewhere, they held all the cards necessary to achieve just such a sublimation. These are the ones who have truly been wounded, in cruel and effective ways, and who deserve all of our attention, so long as it is still possible to accompany them on this territory of the sea.

But it is never easy having to reinvent your life in your fifties or beyond: it is as though there were an invisible wall, a border beyond which everything comes to seem not exactly impossible, but belated and thus no longer capable of giving the illusion of eternity. There is nothing new about this: for young people, eternity has always been an illusion. But beyond the midpoint of life, it becomes more difficult to maintain this illusion. The soul thus bends beneath the weight of the lack of illusions: this lack is healthy and mature, but the soul does not have the means to confront this new maturity. My task is therefore to bring these people toward a path on which they have the potential to invent their lives after the age of fifty. It is wrong to think that this undertaking is the luxury of those who can allow themselves to question their lives—in other words, those who do not have to worry about mere survival. In fact, we rarely see these people in private practices: we see them far more often in community health centers, where illness is omnipresent. Elsewhere, in the sessions of a private practice, we find people from all walks of life: natives and immigrants, locals and exiles, rich and poor, men and women—all of them touched in different ways by bitterness; all of them wanting to avoid giving in to it, but without necessarily knowing what to do in order not to sink into this feeling. They are all exhausted by this bitterness and, as such, incapable of bringing about another form of vitality. And yet they are the first to recognize that they still have a long road ahead of them—between thirty and fifty years. Wanting to make them smile a little, I tell them that they are going to have to "get to work," to occupy themselves, and thus that the best thing would be to find an occupation or a form of work that gives them meaning as subjects. When they smile at this, their faces and their general outlook become more luminous; but when they think about finding work that satisfies their desires, their smiles fade, and their anguish in the face of the immense depths that constitute the non-knowledge of self grows.

— 7 —

A DETOUR BY WAY OF CIORAN

I have always thought that literature, art, and the brilliance of humanistic study were a possible exit for all those who endure bitterness—that aesthetic experiences formed a possible escape route. I know it's not this easy—that the effort demanded by humanistic study is intense, and that those who are afflicted by bitterness do not have the appetite for such an effort, or for anything at all. As for the reading of those who have sublimated bitterness, the experience is not at all straightforward, for it is a double-edged sword: it entails a multiplication and an intensification of a difficulty that already seems bottomless.

Let's take the example of Cioran. It is impossible to describe better than he did the weariness that takes hold of all beings—a bitterness and indeed a nihilism, a way of being forever abandoned by life, but at the same time a poetic capacity that comes to contradict this abandonment. *The Trouble with Being Born* is a brilliant formulation for expressing the vanity of this history—of our history, a history that is so small, so minuscule, and that nonetheless suffocates us. Truly, no one can deny the trouble with being born. To add another layer to the sadness, the feeling of abandonment, we need only read the aphorisms of *Tears and Saints*:

> Everything has already existed. That's why life seems to me like an undulation without substance. History does not repeat itself; yet it seems as if our lives are caught in the reflections of a past world, whose delayed echoes we prolong.[346]

Cioran's feat here is amazing. He narrates bitterness, the absence of any taste for life and for meaning—ennui, the absence of desire.

THE SEA: A WORLD OPENED TO MAN

But to express this bitterness, he speaks of an undulation without substance, of reflections, of a flow that seems already to be that of the sea, even if he does not wish to validate it as such. The sea is an undulation with substance, a magisterial undulation. But for those of us who read Cioran, even if we are caught up in bitterness, the poetry of these words cannot leave us unscathed: there is something here of the great sublimating capacity of the creator that saves us even though it does not save him. And Cioran is precisely this writer: deft when it comes to saving us, inept when it comes to saving himself. There is no greater delight, he writes, than the idea of maintaining ourselves in "pure possibility"[347]: here is the illness that can come to afflict souls that are too sensitive, that fall into melancholy because they close off the great unreal world of possibilities—this world that is in a way that of childhood—and because they undergo the incessant experience of mourning and of renouncement, the heights of disappointment, with the task of making something of them, all the while that they discover that they are nothing. Cioran invents the "catastrophe of birth"[348] from which no one truly returns and which, in a certain way, is the deep foundation of the resentment that can end up destroying us. It is not only a matter of our elementary finitude, but also of the nothingness that constitutes us—we who are so much and indeed too much. "'Après moi le déluge' is the unavowed motto of every person: if we admit that others survive us, it is in the hope that they will be punished for it."[349]

Such is Cioran's antihumanist, or let us say misanthropic, vision of man: a being whose selfishness is only equaled by his mediocrity, his absence of scope, the way he folds back upon his minuscule ego. The pettiness of man, if this is to be believed, renders impossible any escape from resentment: the latter is his destiny.

Or perhaps we must read between the lines and believe, all the same—Cioran himself is proof of this—that there are certain beings who, by way of their style, escape from resentmentist torpor. And sometimes even with a biting humor. This is the case with Cioran. We never really know the tone of his diatribe: Is it melancholic? Resentmentist? Good-natured? Ironic? Every depressing viewpoint is likely precisely because it is depressing.[350] We forgive Cioran his lack of perceptual elaboration precisely because he has style, and because he can boast of being an antimodern—in other words, a form of expression that has learned to navigate the swells of modernity without succumbing to its charm, all the while maintaining a strong individuation. For no one can doubt the "I" of Cioran, even if he reduces it incessantly. When he speaks of the Cabbala, he is once

175

PART III

more in no way complacent as regards man; yet the humor that he displays, a black humor, is the indisputable trace of the very subject that he disdains:

> *Tsimtsum.* This silly-sounding word designates a major concept of the Cabbala. For the world to exist, God, who was everything and everywhere, consented to shrink, to leave a vacant space not inhabited by Himself: it is in this "hold" that the world occurred. Thus we occupy the wasteland He conceded to us out of pity or whim. For us to exist, He contracted. . . . If only He had had the good sense and the good taste to remain *whole!*[351]

In short, a God who does not escape his own shortcomings. Cioran did not opt for an easy path: he sought out contact with revulsion— the one that we experience with regard to ourselves and others—and tried to sublimate it. In the face of the "catastrophe of birth," he enacts the sublime method of passing from one origin to another. Indeed, we see here a possible kinship between melancholy, bitterness, and nostalgia—the latter in the sense of the pain linked to our initial nest. "Instead of clinging to the fact of being born, as good sense bids, I take the risk, I turn back, I retrogress increasingly toward some unknown beginning, I move from origin to origin."[352] We can almost see here the painful description of the Freudian cure, which invites the patient to take up the confrontation with the beginning—or the beginnings, since there are many in life. The patient sometimes resists this, thinking that it will lead him to bring about nothing more than a form of ineffective regression. In fact, moving "from origin to origin" is not the right method, for there is no origin that is definitively first. In this realm of history, there is no irreducible stability, something that can finally be said to have caused everything, or the nothing that we are. "The emphasis on birth is no more than the craving for the insoluble carried to the point of insanity."[353] Cioran is thus well aware of the impasse, and the very notion of insanity links up with that of health, showing the extent to which choosing this path means choosing illness. Such is also the illness that eats away at the one who has fallen into resentment, in that he bears witness to a "craving for the impasse,"[354] defined as an "obsession with birth,"[355] which in fact signifies the obsession with nonsolution—this rejection, very characteristic of psychotics, of a way out.

In Cioran's work, caring is not at issue. Since healing has no meaning, care seems to be emptied of all substance. And yet what brings about care for others, and care for himself, is his style. Cioran

THE SEA: A WORLD OPENED TO MAN

gives his readers a way of walking through walls, a path that allows us—we readers—to create an exit, even if this is anything but easy, because we are sometimes invaded by discouragement when we read him. And yet through his style, he remains an aesthetic and therapeutic resource. Style can sometimes be ethical, in that it invites us to a sublimation. There is a moralistic element to Cioran's work: he is a sort of La Rochefoucauld of the modern world, just as tough, just as funny, just as sad. Behind the terrifying style, there is a certain integrity, even though Cioran has no illusions about himself, knowing all too well his own vices and shortcomings. And yet not all of us are capable of abandoning ourselves to "the thirst for desolation."[356] To do this, you need to have style: a lifestyle that leaves no doubt as to your status as an individual, even if this means being a bastard; it can also mean being a saint. Those who don't have style, and who cannot control their lethal compulsions, won't come across as bastards—they'll simply be the same pathetic people they always were. "Lack of training in the selection of sadness has led to modern man's inability to resist himself."[357] In other words: lamenting your lot in life, regardless of how just the lamentation may be, is shameful, proof of a lack of social competence and of a general gracelessness. "The selection of sadness": a ruthless way of saying that not all forms of melancholy are equal, and that there are some sorrows that an individual must be able to set aside in order not to be ridiculous. Cioran expresses this ethical truth through style, for he would never permit himself to come across as a moralist. The same goes for Fanon, who takes up Césaire's words on the matter and also provides his own. He certainly had style, and knew how to "care" for his style, which allowed him, by way of literature, to find a way out of patriarchal society. But he also knew, in a more concrete and matter-of-fact way, how to bring care to others, by giving close attention to the humblest around him.

— 8 —

FANON THE THERAPIST

By reading Fanon's editorials from the internal journal of his hospital, we discover his method of caring: how he organizes the time of his patients, or at least suggests this organization to them, trying to enable them by way of time. When someone is ill, whether afflicted by psychological disturbances or simply discouraged, one of the first consequences is the disorganization of time. No longer knowing how to cope with the time that unfolds before you, becoming incapable of doing anything, apathetic, sinking into this inertia, taking refuge in it so as to do yourself harm. There is something almost mechanical, ritualistic, that must be done here to get the subject back on track: suggesting activities to him, not to entertain him or mindlessly occupy him, but to give him back the keys to understanding what it means to be occupied. When the subject begins to follow these instructions, a sort of dynamo is rekindled inside of him; soon, he will regain the ability to orient his space-time in a more personal way.

This is what it means to care for someone. It can be very simple, and can seem very humble, which is undoubtedly the reason for which the work of carers is so undervalued: it requires a great deal of technique, but the technique in question is almost invisible—that of a know-how and of a knowing-how-to-be. It means knowing how to guide the other when he is in pain, not disturbing him, not making him ashamed, annoying him, irritating him; it means being there, but also not being there, being invisible without making the subject think that he has been abandoned to himself; helping him to repair his damaged autonomy and letting him know that no one is judging him for doing so.

Providing this care has become more difficult in a world that only values and admires performance. Fanon learned this form of humble,

THE SEA: A WORLD OPENED TO MAN

simple, and effective care from Tosquelles. We see evidence of this in
the guidelines Fanon set out for the hospital's internal journal: speak
"in a simple manner," "call patients by their name," "organize a time
schedule in order to break with indifference and inertia," "prevent
orderlies from becoming a disruptive element," "apply the rule of
three times eight—work, recreation, rest," "maintain the patients'
relations with the outside and the necessity of writing," "live fully
by celebrating religious feast days," "allow recreation,"[358] etc. These
common-sense rules are useful for all those who are going through
a phase of self-weakening; every carer should be familiar with them.
For Fanon, caring is anything but self-evident: those who define
themselves as "carers" can easily be disruptive elements, and it is
thus important to ensure that they do not abuse their role, that they
respect distance, and that there are no mechanisms of power at work
behind their care—such mechanisms are all too easy to set in place.
Care, here, is enabling, and allows the patient to keep his "links"
with the environment that is most vital for him—not necessarily the
family, but the environment that allows him to live; it allows him,
in other words, to remain in contact with the world as an aesthetic,
perceptual, sensual, and intellectual resource. Fanon also speaks
of the "necessity of writing": making stories, setting down words,
verbalizing—simply establishing the thread of writing at the very
moment the subject feels fragmented. The rules also invite a form of
discipline so as to give organization to days that can feel endless: the
ineffectiveness of such days can give rise to feelings of guilt, or more
generally of weariness. Celebrating important days in the collective
consciousness is also a way of connecting with others—to the world
that keeps turning, and also to the ancestral world that preceded us.
As will be clear to everyone, it is not a matter of religious proselyt-
izing. It is a matter of accepting the presence of a ritual in its most
elementary form: the festive, communion with others, the sacred in
its convivial aspect rather than its sectarian one. This also allows
patients to recreate links with the notion of "work" even when they
are ill.

Fanon is concerned that patients will be infantilized, rendered even
more fragile by being overmedicated. Caring for them means making
them responsible, not punishing or overprotecting them. This is how
he describes the ideal of his profession: "Each time we disregard our
profession, each time that we give up our attitude of understanding
and adopt an attitude of punishment, we are mistaken."[359] What use
is the publication of a hospital journal? To ensure that the patients do
not withdraw into themselves, that they do not fall prey to apathy,

PART III

victimization, or a sense of exclusion. "On a ship," writes Fanon, with an almost naïve sensibility, "it is commonplace to say that one is between sky and water; that one is cut off from the world; that one is alone. This journal, precisely, is to fight against the possibility of letting oneself go, against that solitude. Every day a news-sheet comes out, often poorly printed, without photos and bland. But every day, that news-sheet works to liven up the boat."[360] Seeing the hospital as a ship, and the cure as a crossing, shows the humanity of Fanon's gesture of care. There is no irreversibility underlying his remarks. These are the crossings of life, of suffering, and he, as the head doctor, has the same responsibilities as the captain who is one with his crew, which is made up as much by the patients as by the carers. Patients and carers alike are invited to keep a journal, and to participate in the writing of the shared hospital journal.

Fanon is often disturbed by the lack of enthusiasm put into this task, for he knows that it is virtuous, therapeutic, and enabling, and that it brings all of the individuals in question back to the path of "doing," of a more dignified lived experience. "The discovery of writing is certainly the most beautiful one, since it allows you to recall yourself, to present things that have happened in order and above all to communicate with others, even when they are absent."[361] We could add that writing allows one to project oneself into the future and onto the world, and that writing remains the ultimate form—or the initial form, depending on your perspective—of temporal and spatial mobility. Writing means regaining movement. The words Fanon devotes to this in *Black Skin* resonate here with a new meaning, one that is less metaphysical and more clinical: "Man is propelled toward the world and his kind."[362] But when this man's physical capacity for movement is harmed, he must search the depths of his soul and his heart to retrieve those remnants of psychological energy that will once more propel him or set him in motion, and this can occur by way of writing: not writing that is spontaneous, solely for pleasure or inspiration, but the one that can lead him toward the passage he must undertake. This writing is less obvious and more laborious, and many do not initially know how to employ it. It can eventually lead back to the pleasure of writing as inspiration. But now is not the time for this: what is important now is helping a wounded being—one weakened by life and by himself—to recover in whatever way possible; what is important is getting him out of his discouragement and indeed his bitterness; as such, he must be invited, almost forced, to take the path of writing, just as others would go for a walk or force themselves to bathe. It is a question of more than bodily hygiene—unless it is a

THE SEA: A WORLD OPENED TO MAN

question of precisely this, in the most noble sense of the term, and not solely in the sense given to it by public order. This writing is a form of "taking care," a therapeutic gesture that one can undertake for others. Patients thus become able to listen to the other and show him the path of writing. Putting his words—his doubts, his sufferings, his sorrows—on paper allows him to reinscribe himself within an ethical circle within which he is welcomed with empathy. It is a matter of always seeking to involve the patient and make him an actor without giving him orders. Which is anything but simple, for the patient does not necessarily want to be an actor: he doesn't want anything, indeed he no longer wants; his illness is one of the will, in the sense that the latter is buried beneath a heap of anxiety and severe neuroses, which is too heavy—and above all too painful—to displace. The patient no longer wants. And yet, if he is not involved and he realizes this, he may rebel:

> Some days ago, I drew a very abrupt reply. I asked a patient from Reynaud what the date was. "How do you expect me to know the date? Every morning, I am told to get up. To eat. To go to the courtyard. At noon, I am told to eat. To go to the courtyard and afterward to go to sleep. Nobody tells me the date. How do you expect that I should know what day it is?"[363]

Principles and practices must constantly be reexamined, for it is easy to forget that establishments that are purportedly devoted to care are far more ambivalent than they seem. If Fanon seeks to enable, to involve, this does not mean that the employees consign themselves to following while the patients become agents. If I am lingering so long on this way of understanding care, and above all on the example of Fanon and the Blida-Joinville hospital in 1953—though I could have chosen Saint-Alban, La Borde, or Kingsley Hall, or so many other establishments that attempt to care in novel ways and as a result to help societies advance—it is precisely to illustrate a way of fighting psychological illness, especially depression, and all the different kinds of self-depreciation that tend toward resentment. To show, in other words, that combating this sometimes requires very little: a little can go a long way. But this "little" must be done in a regular and disciplined manner: every day, the patient must defy his own will to wander, a will that is common to us all. This is a very concrete example that shows how a resolutely singular psychiatrist operates within an extremely modest collective structure: how, in his uniqueness, he cultivates a public politics of care and solidarity; how

PART III

he works to reconnect public health with the psychological health of individuals.

I work within the context of the Chair in Philosophy at GHU[364] Paris–Psychiatry and Neurosciences, where we are attempting to create the kind of establishment in which care can be reinvented. We are still far from achieving our objective: we're in the very first stages. Our challenges are multiple: we are creating a unit that is dedicated to care, dedicated to other hospital units, dedicated to carers and to patients, dedicated to inventing new clinical methods, all by foregrounding humanistic study that is theoretical and academic, but above all experimental. Our unit, in other words, seeks to support all the other units, whose members are both necessary and exhausted. At stake is nothing more and nothing less than the invention of new ways of thinking about medicine—but also new ways of thinking connections—within collective institutions. We must nonetheless be vigilant, as Fanon has taught us, for while the need for this may be clear for some, this is in no way the case for everyone; and given how great the ambition is, time and resources, both human and material, are bound to be lacking. But giving up on this ambition makes no sense: it would be like abandoning medicine to the charlatans; it would be like abandoning all the decisive new technologies that are bringing us toward a new age of health.

— 9 —

THE RECOGNITION OF SINGULARITY

In an editorial from April 1954, Fanon notes that a ministerial circular has asked hospitals, and rightly so, to name patients correctly (for example, to not call a married woman by her maiden name), and to allow them to keep their personal effects, clothing, and wedding rings. This seems obvious today, even if the policy regarding personal effects is often challenged, notably regarding that interactive and complex personal object that is the cell phone. We recall here Goffman's devastating sociological inquiry that unveils the internal functioning of psychiatric asylums and their procedures of "profanations of self,"[365] procedures that are totally archaic and dangerous for patients, leading them to undervalue themselves in a way that is harmful and counterproductive from the standpoint of care. Reification was predominant at this time in so-called establishments of care, which were shown to be antihumanist. Fanon writes: "At each major shake-up of one's life, one needs to rediscover one's dimensions, one needs to stabilize one's positions. We ought not to collaborate in the destruction of these positions."[366] Let us not believe that these strong words are valid solely where hospitals are concerned. The same reification is at work in businesses, in schools, indeed in every public institution, as though this reification took pleasure in "destroying the positions" of the individual so as to infantilize him and take away his appetite for individuation. When we participate in this general system of reification, we "collaborate"—and we should hear in this term the historical reference of Vichy. We give rise to a colonization of beings at the very moment that we should be helping them to feel reassured.

This attachment to small details does not have any totalitarian ambition, contrary to what one might rightly suppose while reading

183

PART III

Goffman's *Asylums*. For Goffman, the functioning of asylums in the 1960s is that of a total reification whereby one seeks to control every detail of the patient's life, leaving him no initiative to propose something specific to his personality. This is an undertaking of normalization and indeed of stigmatization. Nothing must escape the total institution, as Goffman calls it. The refusal of singularity turns this institution into a site of mutilation for the individual, rather than one of thoughtfulness and care. When Fanon insists on paying attention to small details, he certainly does not have totalitarian aims. For him, paying attention to the private and the seemingly negligible is a question of respecting what the patient considers to be his own: his name, his clothing, his personal effects, his wedding ring, etc. Fanon seeks to reassure, to consolidate, and to recognize the identity that the patient has always had, independently of his experiences of vulnerability.

It is interesting to think about how this analysis can be broadened today to the more general functioning of society. What is the role of paying attention to small and negligible details, to the singular? Is there a place for this in politics—for what some have rightly called the "infra-political" in the face of which the state withdraws, thus allowing it to blossom without veering toward identity-based forms of community, which would contradict the initial aim of respect for singularity?

> Reason cannot be introduced by force into history and society, and it is pointless to imagine that it is already at work in these domains in a hidden way. This point was highlighted by the Frankfurt School, which showed that all efforts that seek to rationalize social life turn out to be destructive, in that they establish the conditions of a generalized slavery that is not perceived as such by those who endure its effects—which is the basic principle of the functioning of a norm-based society. It has become dangerous to place our faith in projects that seek an all-encompassing transformation of society. We must forsake great revolutions, at least for the time being, and resign ourselves to thinking a small version of revolution at the level of the concrete details of existence, knowing that at any moment the "better" can turn into its opposite.[367]

What the theory of the Frankfurt School teaches us here, not about reification in an institution of care, but about those more general institutions that are society and history, is that the latter are entering into a new era: that of civilizational changes that do not occur at

THE SEA: A WORLD OPENED TO MAN

a mass level, that do not seek a standardization that tends toward totalitarianism. Henceforth, the collective project entails an experimental insularity, "third places" that are able to express the local and the endogenous, on the one hand, and the general national interest on the other—in short, a new way of creating the general interest by insisting on the singularities that belong to the law-based state.

I'm not saying that we should lower our ambitions, but that we must not destroy our good intentions with means that are unsuitable, and whose consequences are too dangerous. This requires us to walk a fine line, for the rise in generality remains a major challenge for civic equality. Clearly there are two worlds that confront one another:[368] on the one hand, there is the world of a real and creative individuation whose talent is harmed by approaches that are too vertical, and that are not respective enough of people's own expertise—not to mention the fact that only this approach to governance is truly effective in comprehending the complexity of the stakes involved and the finesse that must be employed in dealing with them. Sadly, individuals must arrive at a high level of individuation to make this approach effective. Confronting this world is another in which individuals are besotted with individualism rather than individuation; these individuals are often more frail, more focused on the short term, less aware of the specificity of our current situation, and oscillate between cries for help and fanciful visions of messiah-like figures; at the same time, they reject governments composed of the elite, who are judged to be too oligarchical, not sufficiently typical, and hence unworthy of being recognized as leaders.

The other great movement that structures society today is well and truly resentmentist, or at least has strong tendencies toward being so: individuals are trapped, going back and forth between aggression and disparagement; they are childlike and feel helpless, but do not put in any effort to pull themselves out of the position of victim. This phenomenon echoes the well-known clinical situation whereby patients create blockages to their own escape routes. These patients are extremely ingenious when it comes to not finding solutions: they say they have already tried whatever is proposed to them, and that it has turned out to be ineffective; they discredit anything they have not already tried. Their arrogance, which is undoubtedly their only defense against an irrevocable invasion of self-deprecation, is immense: having spent all their time not creating solutions, they understand escape routes better than anyone. It is not easy for the analyst to position himself when faced with this fierce will—which borders on psychosis—to prevent the creation of any exit. Proposing

185

PART III

a way out, or several possible ways out, is inevitably rejected (the only form of enjoyment for these patients lies in the failure of their analyst); not proposing anything, on the other hand, does not put a halt to the production of impasses. The analyst must find a different site on which to work, a space in which mimetic rivalry no longer has any hold, a space in which the patient sidesteps "comparison," as Fanon would say—ceases to compare himself to others. The analyst must pull patients out of the narcissism of being inconsolable or incurable.

For the person suffering from psychosis, this refusal of a way out is the only sign that he still possesses his subjectivity; denying him this "negative," therefore, makes him even more aggressive. When all you have left is your own disturbance, it is almost impossible to give it up. The analyst must try to convince the patient little by little, without giving the impression that there is another subject elsewhere (precisely his own subjectivity), a subject who is at work, as opposed to one who is idle. A marvelous tool here would be humor—the *vis comica*, of course. But these are subjects who don't have any sense of humor, and who take any ironic observations about their skill at creating impasses very poorly. More gentle forms of humor are also powerless, for they are taken as signs of the analyst's incompetence: after all, he has clearly not understood how high the stakes are—he has not understood just how unique the problem is. The patients suffering from these deeply narcissistic pathologies pride themselves on being unmanipulable; in fact, they are easy to manipulate, but the mechanism of manipulation does not lend itself to a cure whose process is based on an aptitude for freedom.

In his editorial from December 1956, Fanon illustrates the irreducible difference between classical social functioning and life inside of a psychiatric hospital with a light-hearted example. He chooses this example from the world of sport, which is often used as a therapeutic element. But he is dismayed to see that the orderlies are incapable of playing the role of referee such as it is demanded by the hospital—according to the specific rules of the latter—instead becoming referees in the more classical sense of the term, according to the rules and codes of the outside world, which inevitably brings about serious dysfunctions:

> At the psychiatric hospital, a general law cannot be established because we are not dealing with an anonymous population. We are dealing with very determinate persons and as therapists we have to take these persons, in all their nuances, into consideration; we must

THE SEA: A WORLD OPENED TO MAN

necessarily adapt to each patient. At the psychiatric hospital, we cannot be hearing phrases such as: "I do not want to know, just do as everyone else." Because, precisely, the patient has to relearn to be like everyone else; it is often because he or she was unable "to do as everyone else" that he or she was entrusted to us.[369]

The man of resentment shares with this type of patient the fact of being afflicted by a narcissistic pathology, which leads him to demand (even if the demand remains inaudible) an absolute recognition of his uniqueness—while at the same time he silences this uniqueness due to the violence of resentmentist affects, for the mere awareness of this uniqueness causes him suffering, since he realizes that he is light years away from how he would like to see himself. It is also impossible to treat the man of resentment (again like the patients) in a general way: he disappears into the crowd, but this crowd is not general—it is a sort of aura of his ego that is lacking being, an extension of his disfigured ego, a great compulsive puddle that is tasked with liberating the tiny, shrunken ego that he has become. The only adequate response to this would be to stay with him twenty-four hours a day, recognizing him in his uniqueness, not putting any pressure on him through this recognition, simply being there, not to judge but merely to give sympathy (in the simple sense of "being with," thus avoiding a more onerous empathy)—all of this in spite of the patient's hostility. Once again, the best thing would have been to work on the prevention of resentment, because once the resentmentist border has been crossed, it is difficult to come back from it. I am often in lockstep with Jankélévitch's thought, but this is a point on which we completely diverge: it seems to me that resentment is very difficult to overturn—hence the work that must be done before it arises, so as to prevent it. Because once its threshold has been crossed, some aspect of our biological and intersubjective confidence is afflicted and indeed eroded. Jankélévitch denounced the "philosophy of good-riddance," which prefers to "forget it"[370]—which forgives so as to dispose with the need for justice and truth. This philosophy, he argues, produces only a simulacrum of forgiving. He thus expresses a preference for resentment, insofar as the latter implies "seriousness and profundity."[371] Because Jankélévitch always inclines toward hope, he believes that resentment can be "a prelude to cordial forgiveness."[372] I disagree. Just as forgetting can sidestep the mere simulacrum of forgiving—a subject can certainly decide to forget without forgiving—not forgiving does not necessarily give rise to

187

PART III

resentment; the latter is neither "serious" nor "profound" in the sense of being worthy of qualitative knowledge. Resentment cannot be equated to suffering. It is a purely subjective construction that develops as a toxic outgrowth of serious and deep suffering.

— 10 —

INDIVIDUAL HEALTH AND DEMOCRACY

In this chapter, I seek to link the psychological health of individuals with democratic health, not so as to calmly engage in a virtuous exercise, but rather so as to interrogate the proper functioning of society and its ability to resist its own entropy. Being in good health means getting sick and recovering from sickness, as Canguilhem and so many others have taught us. Democratic health shares the same ability: a healthy democracy is able to confront its internal malfunctions without being paralyzed by them, and to find a way of moving forward despite the interminable headwinds that it faces. These headwinds are not necessarily evidence of a proper pluralism: this would reflect an overly placid version of conflict, one that reduces the latter to a controversy that is completely respectful of a prior consensus on norms. The headwinds in question can be much more than this: they can be antidemocratic and antihumanist, making all attempts to integrate or digest them without being contaminated by them much more difficult.

Many rightly consider the analogy between the individual body and the collective body to be senseless. They are correct, insofar as great numbers often nullify qualitative reasoning. But not linking them is just as ridiculous, given that, today, societies are constituted by "individuals" who, with greater or lesser degrees of psychological health, claim the right to their individuality. This is not without consequences for the collective "body" that is society as a whole, even if its organic and unitary character is less and less graspable, given how many different "bodies" there now are within said societal body. Studying the political and social functioning of a society without raising the question of psychoanalysis thus seems insufficient. Even though he was not a psychoanalyst, Axel Honneth was

189

PART III

able to incorporate psychoanalytic concepts into his work, notably when he forged his very pertinent concept of "recognition." Why is psychoanalysis so essential in the study of democracy, and not only for the study of the person? Because it is "capable of clarifying the psychic, unconscious attachments that prevented oppressed subjects from perceiving what was in their rational interest."[373] Honneth, unlike Habermas, takes this extra step in the history of human singularity, and in thinking about what psychoanalysis can bring to critical theory:

A critical theory of society needs, on the normative level, a concept of the human being that is as realistic and close to the phenomena as possible; it should be able to accord an appropriate place to individuals' unconscious, non-rational attachments. Without taking into account such unconscious motives and affects, the theory runs the danger of succumbing to moral idealism, demanding too much rationality of individuals.[374]

We constantly return to this illusory conception of a rationality removed from drives and emotions, or, more simply, disconnected from that which structurally constitutes an individual: finitude, fear of death, "the existential foundations of one's life."[375] If we do not integrate these foundations into our way of thinking about and conceiving of democracy in its broadest political functioning, we consign democracy to entropy.

In doing this, we must avoid falling into a caricature of the study of the singularities who compose a law-based state—though in fact we are moving in this direction today, with the incessant collection of personal data that can in no way be equated to actual people. On the contrary, we must understand that the impact of the psychological health of individuals on the functioning of society is undeniable— and the impact only increases when this functioning becomes more quantitative. In my book *Les Irremplaçables*,[376] I sought to demonstrate this by imagining a reified individual who feels replaceable, interchangeable, disrespected by his environment from both institutional and professional standpoints—in other words, from a broadly public standpoint. I discussed how this individual, little by little, divides himself in order to resist this psychological mistreatment, which leads him to fall ill—on the assumption that he was healthy at the beginning of the process. If not, things would proceed differently: this collective dysfunction would lead him to reinforce his own internal dysfunctions, which are linked to his personal history—the latter already being linked, of course, to collective history. This individual would thus no longer be up to the task of protecting democracy, in other words of desiring and engaging in democracy. On the contrary, he would fall back into a frenzy of victimhood and persecution; this would lead him to search for a scapegoat and for a paternal figure who could provide him with a two-sided false belief: that of being protected, and that of being able to liberate his hostile impulses without paying the price.

Just as financial theory has now officially taken behavioral science into account (and has been rewarded for doing so with the Nobel Prize),[377] political philosophy must also do more to establish connections with the behavioral sciences, and notably the one that works with the notion of the unconscious: psychoanalysis. Understanding resentment as an evil that is dangerous for both the psychological health of the subject and the proper functioning of democracy must lead us to an awareness of how to protect ourselves from it, both institutionally and clinically, which brings us back to the study of the drive-related aspects of this resentment.

> Whether in the form of repressed instinctual fantasies, largely unconscious attachments or uncontrollable constellations of affects, the theory always takes into account human beings' unconscious drives, which impose certain, nearly inevitable restrictions on rational deliberation.[378]

Honneth continues by citing a second important argument for the proper development of a critical theory of society, one that is "explanatory" and not solely "normative."[379] Understanding the "motives of human action"[380] requires psychoanalytical theory: "In order to be able to take account of the opaque, unconscious motives expressed in anxiety, longings for attachment, desires for togetherness and fantasies of submission, we need a psychological theory of the subject, a theory of socialization that takes sufficient account of the genesis of unconscious affects in our individual biographies."[381]

Obviously, we cannot achieve this for all the individuals who constitute a society, since it is not desirable to allow politics onto this intimate terrain. We should thus not be aiming to look at human beings with absolute transparency—to do so would give rise to a veritable psychosis, a chaos of false selves. We should rather understand that our institutions—in a broad sense: schools, companies, administrations, hospitals, universities, etc.—must produce enough care that they will not end up reinforcing the vulnerabilities inherent

PART III

to the human condition: namely, the conflicts that arise from our impulses and the melancholy sense of finitude. These institutions must also be careful not to create reification, which, once it has turned against individuals and made them ill, will turn against democracy itself, translating into politics its disturbances at the level of the psyche—notably, resentment. Incorporating psychoanalysis, and more generally the humanities, into the way we speak about politics will be all the more necessary in the future, given that all considerations on the importance of emotional rationality, which is inseparable from all rational decision-making, is now inscribed within a digital and algorithmic framework the importance of which will only grow. Technology now puts forth its own understanding of human beings, and this understanding competes with that of the humanities, often stifling the latter and threatening their freedom. Technology already proposes to "track" personal emotions by collecting data in ever more expansionist ways; these data are called "personal," but the adjective is unfair, for they say nothing about the holistic truth of the person. All data are henceforth personal in that they "say" something about our personal freedoms. This reification of humans through digital data is the opposite of an analytic process that is respectful of the dignity and the freedom of human beings.

— 11 —

THE VIOLATION OF LANGUAGE

One of the most explicit and audible manifestations of resentment remains the vulgar use of language. The man of resentment, after a guilty silence that often seeks to conceal his submissiveness, finally "lets loose" and vomits up his rancor by way of his language. Language becomes vomiting—a way of soiling others. Indeed, this is the aim: using language not simply as a vehicle to verbalize feelings or as a tool that allows for communication with others, but as a way of striking the other. There is a need to strike the other, to commit violence against him, and since this violence cannot take a physical form, language is used as violence. Insulting, denigrating, delegitimizing, shaming, slandering, disparaging, cursing. Language becomes the most important terrain on which to expel this bile, and above all to cause harm to those whom one believes to be the cause of the evil of which he is the victim. Language can easily verbalize anger and rejection; it can be used to designate the other as a dangerous evil; it is also the catalyst of that which constitutes, at a later stage, a new legitimacy and the establishment of justice. Violence in the service of this cause exists, and it is completely legitimate. But the misology that is at work today, under the cover of anonymity and of unceasing denunciation, is evidence of a resentmentist hatred that has the hearts of many in its grasp.

It is no longer just the violation of the other that is at stake, but a violation of language itself—its capacity for symbolization and sublimation. This constitutes a return to a falsified use of language, one that is sophistic, complacent, and vulgar, and that turns language into a simple instrument in the service of power rather than critique. This misology, as described by Karl Popper, should be understood as a hatred of logos, of culture. The resentmentist man who is prey

PART III

to misology deliberately chooses to use language only to degrade the other, the world, and the relations he maintains with both. Language is put in the service of a de-symbolization. It is no longer in the service of the critical mind but of the drives. It is judged inauthentic if it does not spew forth its impulses. But in fact this is harmful for language, which, if it no longer has the power to symbolize, disappears as language. It becomes indistinguishable from the drives: it cannot be controlled and it loses power of transfiguration. It is no longer that essential tool for the construction of public reason, itself a protector of the law-based state and more broadly of a humanistic society.

Today, this vomiting is a quasi-permanent feature of social networks, all the more so because anonymity is one of the rules that organizes these spaces. It is a unilateral anonymity, in that it is precisely the man of resentment who spews out his hatred of the other—targeting this other who, since he is identifiable, can come to be the victim of a physical violence that ends up confirming the linguistic violence. This is the aim: doing harm, dealing a blow that is as violent as possible, destroying the image of the other, because today, this image is virtually consubstantial with identity. No one can deny that one of the weaknesses of modern society lies in its having strengthened this narcissistic rift, in its having made images even more powerful than facts. Today, we live in a world that is defenseless against new forms of idolatry, which are not exclusively religious or divine, but which deteriorate the mind and the faculty of judgment in the same way as religion—indeed, they are perhaps even more damaging for the fact that transcendence no longer exists. Idols are not icons, and nobody is fooled by them. The idol is inscribed in a register of alienation, of addiction, of behavioral disturbances, and of a generalized panoptics. It is thus unsurprising that these social networks are often caught in a ridiculous and well-known binarism that is in no way binary: spewing out hatred and spewing out flattery are indissociable and essentially equivalent.

Those who are called "haters" sometimes strike in organized groups and engage in targeted harassment. Linguistic hatred gets excited at the idea of a target, but does not need one to endure. It is the first manifestation of a resentmentist impulse that has been liberated— that still hides beneath anonymity, but bides its time, waiting for the explosive moment at which it will let loose in the light of day. Of course, in the face of this "destroyed" speech that has lost all value, there are always individuals who persist in engaging in qualitative dialogue, for they know that only such dialogue will protect the law-based state, or at least what is left of it. We should thank them, for their work is reminiscent of the vessel of the Danaïdes, always incomplete, never given a moment's rest.

Andy Warhol's prophecy that in the future everyone would have their fifteen minutes of fame has come to pass in an inverted form: today, everyone is assured of fifteen minutes of defamation in a world in which physical and virtual realities can no longer be distinguished. In a way, Orwell's "Two Minutes Hate" already heralded the emergence of a ritual of collective hatred at every appearance of an image and a face identified as the "Enemy of the People" by the "Thought Police." This is the contrary of public opinion, at least in its nineteenth-century form: hatred, belittlement, and defamation—in other words, a sort of di-*fama publica*—have always been instruments of moral and public order, as mediocre as they are effective.

In appearance, defaming others is less a matter of lying than of sullying someone's reputation.[382] But only in appearance, for to defame is to lie about one's motivations. It does not mean trying to tell the truth, but tarnishing what is judged to be too luminous. It is to incite people to no longer love a loved object. Defamation is an inciting to hatred that does not speak its name. It is not necessarily a lie about the other, but a lie about oneself. What are the links between hatred, defamation, and lies or falsehoods?

In the *Republic*, Plato distinguishes between the "true falsehood" and the "falsehood in words." We must "hate" the first, but not necessarily the second. The first is a deliberate act of trickery. The "true falsehood" is "hated not only by the gods but by human beings as well."[383] Since gods do not lie or engage in trickery, any poetic fantasy that claims the opposite can be equated to a falsehood, against which the city and education must defend themselves. This is one of Plato's arguments justifying the censorship of the poets: "Whenever [a poet] says such things about a god, we'll be angry with him, refuse him a chorus, and not allow his poetry to be used in the education of the young."[384] Regarding a "falsehood in words," this can be justified if it is shown to be useful: "Is it useful and so not deserving of hatred? Isn't it useful against one's enemies? And when any of our so-called friends are attempting, through madness or ignorance, to do something bad, isn't it a useful drug for preventing them?"[385]

In other words, the falsehood is justified if it is useful for the general interest, to the extent that it is used to divert others from a bad act.[386] As such, this drug cannot be used by everyone. It is reserved for "doctors"[387] and kept away from private citizens. "Then if it is

PART III

appropriate for anyone to use falsehoods for the good of the city, because of the actions of either enemies or citizens, it is the rulers. But everyone else must be kept away from them."[388] Finally, Plato speaks of a "noble falsehood,"[389] which would be told to citizens to protect them from discord by making them believe that they are born from the same earth, that they are all "brothers"[390] in the city, but nonetheless dissimilar in that some are made of gold and thus more precious, while some are made of silver or bronze and hence less so. This myth, championed by the political leader, is a falsehood the main use of which is to make instrumental use of citizens such that they will not call the existing order into question. The republic convinces them that their natural inequalities are not arbitrary, but meritocratic. The paradox of this, whether conscious or unconscious, is as follows: to combat the absence of fraternity among citizens, and indeed discord or hatred among those who are most similar to one another, the politician lies by spreading a myth that, over time, tends to arouse the very hatred and resentment that it seeks to avoid. It may be that the reason for the success of defamation begins to show itself here. Why, after all, do people have such a penchant for slander when they express opinions? Upon what original resentment does such an impulse establish itself? Is this impulse a reaction against the lies of power—against this power's usurpation and mythification? I'm not trying to justify defamation by ascribing to it some sort of regulative role, but rather to put forth the following hypothesis: hatred is born from the lies of power. It is a reaction to a usurpation that has been turned into a myth of fraternity and its creation of a hierarchy. What is presented as social order is already hatred, in that this order is nothing but the result of the force and the violence of one group that allowed it to prevail over all others. As Jacques Rancière comments:

> Between artisan and warrior, or between warrior and ruler, there can be no exchange of place and function; neither can two things be done at the same time without bringing doom to the city. The barrier of orders is the barrier of the lie. Nothing remains of the fine functionality of the division of labor. Each was obliged to do the one task for which nature destined him. But the function is an illusion just as nature is. All that remains is the prohibition. The artisan in his place is someone who, in general, does nothing but accredit, even at the cost of lying, the declared lie that puts him in his place.[391]

— 12 —

RECOURSE TO HATRED

Hatred comes about suddenly, as a return of the real in the face of a simulacrum that has come about only to be repressed and denied. The psychoanalyst does not consider hatred to be a simple reaction, but rather connects it with a more fundamental and self-conserving drive. Not the hatred of lies, but lying about hatred. "In the beginning was hatred, Freud said basically (contrary to the well-known biblical and evangelical statement),"[392] as Julia Kristeva writes. But is the scene of the horde[393] enough to contain the sons' hatred? The terrain of mimetic rivalry between ultraliberal democracies is a perpetual scene of the horde. Per Freud: "Hate . . . is older than love. It derives from the narcissistic ego's primordial repudiation of the external world with its outpouring of stimuli."[394] There is another myth, this one biblical, that expresses this fraternal impossibility. The first murder is that of brotherly hatred—of Cain's ontological impossibility to be his "brother's keeper."[395] The consequence of this is our culture's current inability to sublimate original hatred. Culture consists not so much in the prohibition of one killing one's brother as in the existential resources that are offered to man to resist the abyssal nature of his desire. "Am I my brother's keeper?" is not a question but a lie told to both God and himself, for Cain knows that being a man means both being created and being a brother—it means nothing but being created and being a brother. Hatred is inherent to the weakness of the creature.

Another name for culture, and for a resistance to hatred, remains *philia*:

> The successive processes of the unification and the expansion of human groups that punctuate our anthropological development are

PART III

historical concretizations of a process of psychological and collective individuation that characterizes the development of human societies. A libidinal economy presides over this, in that this economy serves to transform the psychological energy of the drives into the social energy of desire, which is the condition of the constitution of a *philia*—the constitution, in other words, of a durability of the social bond.[396]

It is sadly revealing that the enormous social network Facebook chose friendship as a new territory of Newspeak. But friendship, like culture, demands a little more "mystery." Recall the dialogue between Oronte and Alceste in *The Misanthrope*:

> ORONTE: I mean it. Cross my heart, and hope to die!
> Look here, to show you that I'm really serious, I
> Would like to put my arms around you, if I may.
> Well, do you think we can be friends, starting today?
> Your hand, Sir, if you please. Now, do you promise me
> Your friendship?
> ALCESTE: Monsieur . . .
> ORONTE: Oh, what's this? You don't agree?
> ALCESTE: Monsieur, you honour me far more than I deserve;
> But friendship really needs a little more reserve [*mystère*].[397]

Undoubtedly, we will at some future stage see a switch from "friends" to "brothers" in the network in question, which furthermore does so much for forms of hatred linked to parricide and fratricide. The strength of virtual space is its ability to bring together different veins of hatred, and to do so, amazingly, without—for the time being— damaging their proliferation. They coexist despite their antinomy. The fact that the borders between them have become virtual makes it possible for different primal scenes to exist side by side, without their hordes devouring one another. Far from causing the horde to disappear, modernity has multiplied it, thereby creating a new challenge for culture: that of developing resiliency in the face of the expansion of forms of hatred. The *Nom-du-Père* has given way to the *Nom-des-Pairs*—the Name-of-the-Peers—which is even more ferocious. For in the same way as Machiavelli's prince, who takes the side of the people against the great figures, the Name-of-the-Father is, for the subject and his emancipation, a less formidable foe than the Name-of-the-Peers.

There is nothing new in any of this. In the wake of the First World War, and in anticipation of the Second, *Civilization and Its*

198

THE SEA: A WORLD OPENED TO MAN

Discontents already discussed culture's complete failure to contain the death drive.

> The fateful question for the human species seems to me to be whether and to what extent their cultural development will succeed in mastering the disturbance of their communal life by the human instinct of aggression and self-destruction. It may be that in this respect precisely the present time deserves a special interest. Men have gained control over the forces of nature to such an extent that with their help they would have no difficulty in exterminating one another to the last man.[398]

Even before these remarks, the dialogue between Charles Péguy and Jules Isaac had already set things out in a similarly impressive manner, in a scene whose durability lies in its ambivalence: in the context of a great friendship between these two men, the first—reflecting that "tolerance leads to degradation"—says to the second: "it is necessary to hate."[399]

I know that some will defend this primitivist idea of hatred as a great rampart against the aggression of others. And nothing would be truer—if the hatred in question really were self-defense, rather than a phantasy of the latter. For my part, simply reading Péguy is enough to prove to me that man is not resentmentist for the mere fact of being wounded and antimodern—antimodernity being perhaps the only way to live this modernity, all the while remaining critical of it. Péguy's style, immense and sublime, speaks for him, and serves as an eternal sublimation. I want to believe that his appeal to hatred expresses his fear of seeing the French republic destroyed by its own degradation—the degradation of its values and its relativist tendencies—which is no more than a parody of the notion of tolerance, which for its part is normative, and not permissive, as we too often believe.

— 13 —

THE *MUNDUS INVERSUS*

Conspiracy and Resentment

A hatred of others such as this is also aimed at institutions, and also the press, which is seen to "direct" public opinion and, as such, is suspected of being dishonest. This hatred, which today has become resentment, undermines living conditions and frameworks of thought, for there is only a very small step from resentment to conspiratorial frenzy: this is the collective version of persecution frenzy. Post-truth, alternative facts, fake news: this is a universe of permanent bad faith—and even worse, for truth, in this universe, turns into the outcome of a false and indeed sullied procedure in which it is fabricated by a closure, by a refusal to think differently, and by the psychological certainty of being a victim of injustice and of an order that disavows me. To think about these points properly, I would have to devote an entire book to them, and I don't want to engage in this sort of reflection in the present book. At present, this phenomenon is already widespread, and so great is its assault on rationality that it will only continue to grow. We're entering into an era marked by ever-stronger drives and impulses which will not simply be soothed by appeals to reason—the impulses in question have long since disavowed reason, classifying it as a kind of conspiracy.

Marc Angenot has already observed this indisputable kinship between resentment and conspiracy-based ideology: each incessantly feeds the other.

> At the heart of resentment, we find an inverted or reversed axiology, an axiology that has been turned on its head, whereby baseness and failure are signs of merit, and all superiority—including the instruments and creations of this superiority, are reprehensible in their very

THE SEA: A WORLD OPENED TO MAN

nature (for they have been usurped), and are hence devalued from the standpoint of whatever moral transcendence that resentment has constructed for itself. The axiology of resentment at once moralizes and radicalizes hatred for the dominant. Success is evil, failure is virtue: the entire "genealogy of morality" might be reduced to this little formulation. "No one reigns innocently," as Saint-Just said.[400]

We see here the strength and the unstoppable character of Saint-Just's reasoning, but also the proof of its ideological nature, for nothing can disprove it: it is just as infallible as the words of religious dogmatism. Why was it necessary to knight the regicide? Because it was a matter of killing the function of the king, but above all of understanding that Louis Capet, as king, was implacably and from time immemorial a usurper—which is true. From time immemorial, he was the one who stripped the people of their rights; the question of whether he was a good or a bad king has no significance for such reasoning. Resentment creates the same logic by implementing an inversion of values: if you are rich and in good health in this iniquitous universe, it is because you are complicit with this iniquitous universe, which is systemic and does not take into account the individual value of people. This sort of reversal of values can only lead to the advent of a totalitarianism that is egalitarian in a reifying way: in the place of dominant reification, it gives rise to a reification of the dominated, who thereby become dominant. The vicious circle is not broken—it simply benefits a new group. Resentment is therefore not a form of thought that brings about social justice but an ideology, a relationship of force that seeks to establish itself and to promote the interests of a new group that judges itself to have been dispossessed.

In discourses of resentment, we see the functioning of a summarily eristic dialectic, in other words something like the art of always being right . . ., of being impervious to objections, refutations, and the revelation of any contradictions someone might reveal in your arguments. All of this forms an unassailable system and an inexhaustible reserve: we have never won anything; there always remain past wrongs that have not been corrected, scars that recall this past and its misery; the dominant group is still there, hostile and contemptuous, and—so long as we have not been able to completely get rid of them, to annihilate them through some "final solution"—they still retain certain advantages that turn them into an endless obstacle to the positive image we would like to have of ourselves.[401]

201

PART III

The former dominant group must be annihilated to have any hope of restoring a "self-image" that is more in keeping with the ego ideal of resentful subjects. So long as the others have not been annihilated, there remains a sort of sting in the soul, the breach of an acridity that becomes so strong as to be unbearable. Precisely this mechanism is at work in the genocidal madness of an "ultra" solution, namely a solution that makes the "problem" disappear instead of fixing it: the belief, in other words, that total eradication will finally reassure, calm the resentmentist impulse, reestablish a just order, when in fact what is being organized is simply a new inegalitarian order in which the former victim is now the perpetrator of injustice. We can easily see that this mechanism is endless, unless the eradication is believed to have been total—and only from a romantic standpoint, one that sprouts from a hateful Mafioso logic, can one believe that the eradication of the other is possible, and that the resulting "purity" will remain unscathed. In fact, new forms of resentment will arise, for only the deconstruction of the impulse (and not the liberation of this impulse) will constrain and indeed assuage it. No one can evade this work of deconstruction, neither individually nor collectively. And it is never complete, for both individual and collective histories always bring forth new challenges to overcome. Those who do not undertake this analytic work feel the need to disavow it in a certain way, countering it with an entire order of "unfalsifiable" and infallible facts—facts that are thereby "mythological" in that they put forth a reading of the world that is "grandiose" in an illusory way. Angenot calls these facts "extra-dialectical elements," in that they cannot be contradicted by scientific reasoning, which is always held in suspicion:

> Besides its tortuous reasoning, resentful thinking can also be recognized by its extra-dialectical elements—namely, its "myths" of predilection. This thinking, marked by denial and suspicion, is also a great consumer and producer of certain well-known forms of "myth": the myth of evil plots, of heinous conspiracies, the myth of origins and of rootedness, the myth of the righter of wrongs who will come forth from his people. We can understand the persuasive effects of such myths: they are invented to contribute to a Great Explanation of this mundus inversus, of this upside-down world in which we—I, my loved ones, my people—have not been accorded our rightful place.[402]

The notion of the *mundus inversus* is very important for understanding the indestructible link between resentment and conspiracy

THE SEA: A WORLD OPENED TO MAN

theories, because its all-encompassing nature allows it to have an answer for every question, for everything that is lacking in the contemporary world. It is a kind of magical solution with a response for everything, able to explain all the narcissistic irritation of the resentmentist individual, and allowing him, furthermore, to dilute his responsibility. Conspiratorial reasoning is well known in psychiatry, for it is the preserve of paranoid structures that interpret every exterior sign in a single way—the one that validates their initial thesis. There is no escape. "Many political scientists . . . have identified, within contemporary public culture, a strong resurgence of 'paranoid logic,' the symptoms of which are right-wing and left-wing conspiracy theories."[403] It is one of the characteristics of psychosis to block all ways out, to prevent care and repair, and it is for this reason that it is so difficult, indeed almost impossible, to heal from this illness.

The paranoiac thesis is all the more difficult to deconstruct in that it purports to embody supreme clarity. Let us not forget that paranoia plays an important role: that of restoring the subject's narcissistic drive, of making him feel intelligent again, where before he was scorned and unrecognized. What society had refused to him, paranoia offers up on a silver plate, and it is thus logical that he should cling to it, for it is the only form of reparation that is easily accessible. We must recall that, in the context of this broad movement of the destruction of the other, psychosis is always a form of conscious or unconscious self-conservation. It is this dynamism, this self-conservational energy, that raises the question of whether we can qualify psychosis as a real "illness": it is, after all, the very life force of something harmful. However, if we refer to the more dynamic and subjective definitions of illness in the work of Canguilhem (others could be cited as well), we see that illness remains "a positive, innovative experience in the living being,"[404] allowing the latter to persist as a healthy body. It is an innovation by the living being which is "designed to bring about healing,"[405] writes Canguilhem. Psychosis, however, has no healing intention: it generally denies that there is any illness at all. We must differentiate the perverse denial of illness from the anosognosia that arises from neurocognitive disturbances.

The metaphoric use of the term "health" helps us to grasp the internal dynamics of the subject and of democracy: the latter turns out to be pertinent for discussing the kind of *vis medicatrix naturae* that we must put into place, invent, strengthen, and conceptualize to protect the health of the individual and the structure within which he lives. The long-term goal of education and care is the construction

203

PART III

of a *vis medicatrix naturae* that is capable of creating innovations that can bring about healing—in other words, reforms dedicated to maintaining democratic durability.

> Resentment, for the one who denies it, has always operated as a reaction to disenchantment—*Entzauberung*, per Max Weber's central concept. Ideologies of resentment are intimately linked to waves of anxiety in the face of modernity, rationalization, and deterritorialization. This is the mentality of the *Gemeinschaft*, which is homogeneous, warm, and stagnant, and has a tendency to turn sour in open, cold, rational-technical societies. Resentment, which recreates solidarity between those who are bitter and feel victimized, and favors the withdrawal into identity-based communities, appears as a low-cost way of reviving warmth—communion within a warm irrationality—in the face of social and international development mechanisms that are anonymous and cold, uncontrollable "cold monsters" that do not allow us to imagine strategies for collective success.[406]

Angenot's association of resentment and disenchantment is perspicacious, in that the absence of sublimation that disenchantment entails makes resentment inevitable. In order to protect ourselves from the spread of anxiety—and sidestepping, for the moment, the need to sublimate anxiety (which is really what is at stake)—we must avoid reinforcing extreme processes of rationalization and deterritorialization, which inevitably give rise to a feeling of reification, and hence, as a reaction to this, to a resistance that seeks to submit to passions of victimhood, rather than a more active resistance of a civic and democratic nature.

— 14 —

TOWARD AN ENLARGEMENT OF THE EGO, 1

It is intellectually ridiculous and ethically dangerous to deny the existential conditions of the individual, which are both psychological and social—in other words, to overlook their intense interaction and hence to believe that a ready-made rationality will be able to control the unmastered freedom of the individual's lethal drives. Hermann Broch, in his great work *The Theory of Mass Hysteria*, championed the teaching of political psychology and the study of phenomena of collective hysteria,[407] which he called "down-to-earth blindness and down-to-earth intoxication."[408] If nothing is set up to counter this, two risks ensue, both extremely harmful in that they can give rise to the "psychological contamination of the masses":[409] namely, a "rise in irrationality" and a "loss in rationality."[410] The first arises mainly from an excess of religious aspirations, and the second, from an excess of populist aspirations—though the phenomena are undoubtedly connected.

Why "political psychology"? Because Broch is well aware that there does not exist any mystical entity called "the mass," as though the latter were an entity unto itself with a single will. Collective psychology is the study of the "exterior conditions in which the Ego finds itself to be located due to the presence of a sociological group such as the mass."[411] When the ego can no longer connect itself to the world—in other words, when it considers itself to be excluded from the world, or finds that it is no longer able to transform the world, even in a minimal or gradual way, in the face of an impossibility of self-expansion within the world—it creates the exact contrary of this: namely, a "retraction of the ego" that leads the individual to "fall into a feeling that is opposed to ecstasy, the feeling of fear, which, as we know, is always fundamentally a fear of dying."[412] The ego can only resist its own lethal drives, its anxiety in the face of nothingness and death, if it is able to engage in a kind of suspension of these assaults, by opposing them with a vital creative energy, a force of sublimation.

Many paths exist for doing this, for the expansion of the ego can take place in various ways: love and friendship, in the Aristotelian sense of these terms (in other words, broader than that of simple elective affinities), are one cause of—let us say, one occasion for—the enlargement or the expansion of the ego. This is just as true of aesthetic experience, art, and the humanities. We have also seen that the *vis comica* is a way of expanding the ego, or, more precisely, a very effective dynamics for deconstructing the contraction of the ego, in that it constantly overturns represen- tations of the world that are judged to be too stereotypical and restrictive. Laughter is a form of discernment. I was raised on this laughter that often left me doubled up—which thus allowed me to see things at an angle, in oblique ways, from beneath. Laughter is a way of deconstructing the illusion of possession: "The knowledge of the world, the knowledge of the non-ego, becomes a sublimated way of possessing the world—a sublimation of the drives. Truly possessing the entire world has been shown to be impossible, but it is possible to possess it symbolically; as such, we beckon this symbolic relationship to do what the primitive, possessive approach could not have done: to abolish time."[413] We can all see how the contemporary, modern illusion aims to go beyond symbolization in order to "expand" the ego, thus turning this properly ethical, intellectual, metaphysical, and symbolic concern into one that is material and technological. And of course, this does not work: it creates addiction and an ability to create false compensations, but mental panic ensues as soon as the Wi-Fi doesn't work. The expansion of the ego does not mean the omnipotence of the ego, but precisely the reverse. It is a testament to the knowledge of the ego and its limits, and the need to sublimate these limits to avoid potentially lethal ramifications. Symbolization is the antithesis to omnipotence, in that the subject accepts absence, but produces alongside it a qualitative relationship that enables him to go beyond the pain associated with the absence of possession. This is one of the fundamental teachings of psychoanalysis, which responds to the question of how to resist separation, the absence of the object and the other—how to resist this invasive "non-ego" that surrounds me. The child believes at first that he is insepa- rable from his mother, that she and he are the same being, but the

THE SEA: A WORLD OPENED TO MAN

illusion falls away quickly; from the moment of birth, the intuition of separation is unavoidable, and little by little, education will help the child to open himself to the emergence of the power of symbolization: here lies the mother [*ci-gît la mère*].

— 15 —

WHAT SEPARATION MEANS

Separation is not abandonment—the refusal of debt to one's elders, the refusal of a certain form of affective dependence, the illusory belief that one is independent and free of obligations. This would be a caricature of understanding. In fact, accepting separation, considering it as a task, accepting a certain form of distance, does not commit the subject to a denial of filial attachment. Nonetheless, the fear of separation and the inability to sublimate it can confine the subject within a logic of victimization, for he no longer feels protected, counted on, loved as a unique being. It is never quite this clear: it is not necessarily our real and physical "parents" who are at stake in the impossibility of mourning this fantasized and almost magical protection.

There is an author whose work sheds light on the ambivalence of the parental relationship, which is immensely important and accompanies all of childhood development. While recognizing this, this author was able to withdraw, to stop expecting what she had expected in the past. Ambivalence, once again.

As she is departing for New York, waiting on the dock, Simone Weil addresses herself to her parents: "If I had many lives, I would devote one of them to you. But I only have one, and I must spend it elsewhere."[414] *I owe you everything*, says the child to her beloved parents; but I also owe this debt to the "elsewhere"—and this is how the Open takes shape. Weil's "here lies mother" never closed off her access to her childhood.[415] "It is as if the familial gaze unified—and reunified, if necessary—her being, as if no exterior gaze dissociated her from herself. The parental gaze—above all maternal—confirmed, well beyond adolescence, the identity of this brilliant and turbulent child, who believed that she had been born with mediocre intellectual

THE SEA: A WORLD OPENED TO MAN

faculties."[416] The separation wasn't easy, but it happened. Weil often complains to her mother, accusing her of not writing often enough, only to admit a few lines later that the accusation is unfounded, and indeed Simone's life is heartless where the time she is able to devote to others is concerned. Her parents are omnipresent in her heart and her mind, but the roads of the world are infinite, and there is no going backward: she must keep going, she must write, take up the challenge of learning mathematics and Greek philosophy, take up the challenge of reconciling the ancient and modern periods; staying within her mother's embrace was always going to be unlikely, for it would prevent her from doing what she wanted to do, and would also pervert the educational ambitions her parents had for her. A month before her death, while she is ill and exhausted by weariness, she thinks of them: "'I am finished, broken, beyond all possibility of mending. . . . In the most favourable hypothesis . . . it may be possible, not to mend the object, but to provisionally glue it back together. . . . I believe, I am almost convinced, that even this provisional regluing can only be accomplished by my parents, not by anyone else.'"[417] Her whole life, Weil equivocated between this awareness of distance and this need for a rediscovered unity, this desire for love as Aristophanes conceived of it in Plato's *Symposium*,[418] which recalls to each of us our original destiny of being one and only one, prior to the two of man and woman. Her divine quest is undoubtedly linked to this sensibility of fusion. Being glued back together, mended by the one: who has not hoped for a healing such as this? As for me, when the great split took place, I no longer had access to such understanding. It turned out that at every hour of the morning and the evening, and during the day as well if necessary, they were there: father and mother, grandmother as well, and not only as family, for at a moment like this one, something else is at work, some task beyond age and beyond life, a loving and silent fraternity that is responsible, agile, and effective. It is like a commandment.

At the age of fourteen, Simone Weil fell into "one of those bottomless forms of despair that happen during adolescence,"[419] aware that she was not her brother (whose genius was obvious—at least, she was persuaded of this); and what saved her was the sensation that only the force of persistent and authentic effort, the careful effort to arrive at the truth—one might say think of it as a sharp philosophical desire— could save a soul of such proven mediocrity. She would later thank André Weil, her brother and confidant, for having told her that "the future needs [her],"[420] and adding that her love of Greek antiquity was a way of binding herself all the more tightly to this "future" as

209

PART III

it presents itself. In her correspondence with her brother, Weil revisits the Nietzschean interpretation of Greek tragedy, and suggests that the philosopher is mistaken when he describes the Greeks as "desperately attached"[421] to proportion. Nietzsche's phrase, she thinks, is not an oxymoron, but it does bear witness to the incomprehension of the ancient mind on the part of the moderns. There is no despair. There is certainly the bitter taste of necessity, but the latter simultaneously maintains a form of happiness, perhaps of obligation. Was this the meaning of this quasi-innate or implicit sublimation? Was Nietzsche only capable of creating melancholy sublimation? Whatever the case may be, Weil chose her camp: that of measure and harmony against the Dionysian, that of mathematics and geometry in the face of the prevailing chaos, even if she did experience this chaos on numerous occasions in her own flesh during the years preceding the war—active years that shaped her thought. But she refuses to be attracted by disequilibrium, temptation, and madness. All those whose eyes are open have a painful conception of existence.[422] For all that, they do not subject themselves to annihilation and anxiety. Anxiety was unknown to the Greeks.

— 16 —

TOWARD AN ENLARGEMENT OF THE EGO, 2

Democracy as an Open System of Values

Anxiety is a truth of the moderns. If the withdrawal of the ego persists, anxiety deepens into what Broch describes as "an anxiety with no exit."[423] Broch thus introduces various "support"[424] structures. The most traditional of these refer back to material reality (in short, property), relations with power or with intellectual reality and knowledge, or to emotional reality: the aim is to create "systems of values" that are capable of "proscribing panic,"[425] especially the panic linked to finitude or to the danger that the other sometimes represents. All our systems of values thus seek to calm our existential anxiety and liberate the subject from its grasp, with the aim of creating something. Resentment, on the other hand, brings about an inversion of this system of values: it does produce a system of values, but one from which the subject cannot emancipate himself; on the contrary, he repeats his impulse-related tendencies, strengthening them and, in doing so, giving rise to a state of withdrawal into himself and his certainties. Broch thus reminds us of Karl Popper and his description of open societies, for he employs an equivalent term to define a healthy system of values versus one that is unhealthy.

Even if man tends naturally, as if by a sort of protective reflex, to want to subsume the world within his system of values, he must nonetheless realize that something is left over, something that resists this synthesis.

Every individual, every social group, every professional category, etc., seeks to understand the world according to its own specific framework of apperception, which is precisely that of its system of values, and to subsume it entirely within this system.[426]

PART III

The problem is thus not that the individual or the group seeks to do this, for it is quite natural, at least at first; the problem arises if they cling to their subsumption, thus becoming incapable of going beyond the borders of their system of values, such that everything that transgresses these borders is judged to be illegitimate for the very fact of this transgression. It is not a matter of affirming those relativist systems that do not hierarchize their values and their ways of reasoning. It is a matter, on the contrary, of creating systems of values that are compatible with a spirit of critique, and that welcome discussion with those who reason differently, possibly rejecting their arguments, but doing so in good faith, and not by practicing bad faith in the way Schopenhauer theorized it. "A system that finds itself dominated by dogmatic values can be described as a closed system."[427] This has generally been the case for religions, or for fundamentalist and totalitarian ideologies. "Open systems, on the contrary, are distinguished by the fact that they do not seek to subsume all of the world's phenomena within a dogmatic framework of material values, but rather strive to reach the absolute value that they seek through an ever further development of the system."[428] Science is a paradigmatically open system, one that proceeds via a successive stabilization of truths, even if these truths sometimes fade away in the face of new forms of reasoning that call them into question according to scientific rules.

Broch thus goes a step further in linking individual and system of values—whether the latter is open or closed—and hence to describe the resources at the individual's disposal to resist his lethal drives, for the choice of a system of values is not without consequences for the psyche of the individual or the collective. A system of values that is present within the individual obviously does not arise simply from the choices of the individual: on the contrary, it arises through a continuous interaction between the personality of the individual and the societies (familial, cultural, institutional, economic) within which he develops. Broch thus recalls the necessity, for the individual—even if he is aware that he belongs to various communities, and even if he is aware that this belonging comforts him—of being able to think critically with respect to these communities, even at the risk of being alienated from them. Broch describes the "ideal type of community" which must offer to the individual at once "a maximum of rational values and a maximum of irrational values, the latter at once in the form of a free development of his personality and in the form of community-related feelings."[429] Broch's thesis is all the more

212

THE SEA: A WORLD OPENED TO MAN

interesting in not opposing the rational and the irrational: it concedes that both are essential for man.

We could add, furthermore, that reason, as a whole, does not necessarily express itself through scientific paths, or by following a methodology that has been certified beforehand; little by little, reason invents new tools of evaluation and measurement, tools that were previously judged to be lacking in terms of scientific rationality. The fact is that the human mind and the related cognitive emotions are driven just as much by the irrational as the rational—in other words, by that which is not yet, and may never be, scientifically proved. Both are essential to "care" for the soul of the individual and to give forth resources that permit him to overcome his existential anxiety, and the latter's potential metamorphoses into resentment. If Broch is particularly sensitive to irrational reality, it is because he experienced, in his soul and in his flesh, the inanity of the world in which he lived—Nazi Germany—and because, as an inverted mirror of this world, he conceived of a form of mystical resistance, capable of extirpating itself from its murderous degradation of values while retaining an opening. Broch's mysticism is an open system, one that is in no way dogmatic, but it is a system that also does not allow itself to be confined solely within mathematical logic. Scientism is just as capable of carnage as fanaticism.

> We can say without risk of error that every central system of values, whatever its contribution to the construction of civilization, collapses and degenerates into a veritable collective hysteria from the moment its theology comes to constitute itself as an autonomous, closed system, thereby hyptertrophying.[430]

It is thus important for the central system of values to be able to create a sort of regular homeostasis, in the face of new values and "facts" that have not yet been tried out or thought through. Once again, adaptation to this new reality is not immediate, and can bring about a feeling of deep destabilization. If the subject maintains himself within his closed system, and is thus incapable of new symbolizations and sublimations, the consequence is inevitable: he falls into a psychosis that is dangerous for himself and for the collective. If he maintains an open system, this in no way means that he will be immediately protected from the assaults of insecurity (material, intellectual, or emotional insecurity) brought about by this new reality, but it does mean that he will be able to confront them. Broch speaks of a possible "psychological tearing,"[431] which he classifies

PART III

as a neurosis rather than as a psychosis, but a neurosis that can be very severe. If it is possible to put Popper and Broch into dialogue, it is precisely because both sought to think democratic society as an open system: Broch went so far as to judge democracy's very object to be that of "fighting against mass hysteria" and of "bringing man back within an open system of feelings of humanity."[432] Certainly, Broch's theory is infused with Christian mysticism, in that it seeks to think a "democratic conversion"[433] that is analogous to religious conversion. In this, he is not far removed from the French revolutionary pioneers—at least some of them, including Robespierre and Rousseau—who criticized religion for its sectarian aspect, but who sought to understand its mechanism of unification and creation of social sentiment. Rousseau spoke of civic religion, while Robespierre sought to sanctify the principles of the republic. In *Pathologies de la démocratie*, I attempted to explain this very French phenomenon, and formed the following hypothesis: if the notion of *laïcité* is the norm in France, it is perhaps to allow everyone to develop a relationship to transcendence without dogma, or at least to allow the potential for a common, non-conflictual territory within this personal and civic link to transcendence. "The framework of all religious conversions can thus easily be applied to their secular prolongation."[434] Broch's reasoning is interesting—and we can appreciate it without having to share its penchant for mysticism—insofar as it allows us to understand how democracy should "tend," for the individual, "toward a constant gain in rationality";[435] this type of gain in rationality brings us toward a very personal space, one that is intimate and in no way political.

— 17 —

THE MAN FROM UNDERGROUND

Resisting the Abyss

Resentment always exists in very close proximity to the heart of a man, which means that falling into resentment is sometimes inevitable. But sometimes atonement is possible in literature: on the one hand, by way of style, in its power to symbolize; on the other hand, by way of the plot, which can tell the story of a reversal: the impossibility of surviving one's own resentment intact. Dostoyevsky deals with this major problem, notably in *Crime and Punishment*, at the very time that he is undergoing a difficult personal situation marked by debts and bitterness.

In his letters from 1865,[436] the writer speaks of how he lost his appetite for food after being obligated to fast—that is, out of a lack of means to feed himself properly. He explains that one of his projects was to write a story that was a "psychological account of a crime."[437] The crime that he describes is decidedly odious, even if one might think that the fate of the young man who is an aspiring criminal is unjustified, in that this man is just as miserable as the world that he loathes. The hero is poor and completely desperate. He thus comes to be won over by "certain strange, 'incomplete' ideas,"[438] writes Dostoyevsky, ideas that will lead to his downfall by way of the murder of an old woman, a foolish, deaf, and ill usurer. Should this be called a crime, he asks himself, given that the woman is very old, that she will die sooner or later without anyone's help, and that she is the mediocre and selfish reflection of the world that surrounds her? The response is positive. And it is here that the book saves the author of the crime by condemning him: not to resentment and to imprisonment within his murderous certainty, but to repentance, by showing him the way to a path that, while much more difficult, is also salvational.

PART III

Insoluble problems arise before the murderer; unsuspected and unforeseen feelings torment his mind. Divine truth and human law take their toll, and he ends up by being *driven* to give himself up. . . . The feeling of being cut off and isolated from humanity that he had experienced from the moment he committed the crime had been torturing him. . . . The criminal himself decides to accept suffering to expiate his deed."[439]

This study of the psychological reversal of the criminal will allow Dostoyevsky to develop a new figure of man, one who simultaneously overcomes disenchantment and resentment, even if he tirelessly flirts with them and risks succumbing to them—becoming, in other words, the "man from the underground." What better name to give to this man who, confronted by modern, technological, urban, and industrial revolutions—which have not yet arrived at any form of social moderation or just repartition, especially in Russia, which at this time is not moving toward any form of law-based state—is only able to overcome such a level of material and immaterial insecurity with great difficulty, at the price of his consciousness and his life. He succumbs, but as a latter-day Orpheus (the Orpheus of a new genre), he will be able to get beyond this underground wandering.

This late nineteenth-century literature is the one in which the antihero is born, the "men without qualities": the ordinary, the mediocre, the sad; orphans of privileged birth who also see themselves as orphans of the future, for nothing seems to appoint them as chosen ones. They feel terribly offended from a narcissistic standpoint, so they give themselves the "right to crime,"[440] which foresees Aragon's later formulation of the "right to be ferocious."[441] There is another great writer who will make of weary wandering the leitmotiv of his oeuvre. Each of Joris-Karl Huysmans's books paints the portrait of this individual grasped tightly by modernity, surrounded by atrocious mediocrity, struggling to find transcendence, seeking meaning but only coming across the absurd, struggling with his freedom and his talent, too aware to be happy: "the atrociousness of modern life," "moral Americanization," "the eulogy of brute force," "the beautification of the safety-deposit box";[442] we could be reading a description of the contemporary world's fascination with mercantilism and the spectacle of histrionic relations of force. And of course, this denunciation of "the ghastly taste of the masses," of the rejection of "every ideal," the refusal of "every aspiration toward the supernatural," and this final judgment that could sound the death knell of literature and its all-encompassing ability to sublimate: the fact of "the repudiation of style."[443] Huysmans recounts these torments of modernity and of unhappy consciousness while flirting with bitterness, but without ever tottering into a crystalized resentment, instead remaining on the side of melancholy and weariness, of a discouragement that capitulates even if it remains ponderous in its address to style. For no one can deny the quality of Huysmans's style: his ability to sting in the manner of irony, to accurately convey the baseness of the soul, to at times grasp the grace of beauty, to recount how the individual does not escape from modernity—as though the latter were a sort of dark pool. A simple glance at the titles of Huysmans's books allows us to understand the nature of his quest as an author and as an individual: that of finding a place to retreat without falling prey to resentment; that of finding a refuge, in short. *Pack on Back* narrates this wandering through the beyond of war and illness; *Against Nature* renders this wandering impossible once and for all; *The Damned* attempts it once again; *Married Life* ridicules it. "Living alone, far from his own century":[444] this is what he aims for, but this is impossible as well. It is a commonplace in the contemporary world: the refuge seems unattainable; connectivity, with its ideal of the "without remainder," makes the physical reality of any refuge technologically impossible. Certainly, we still have symbolization and sublimation, and hence the possibility of creating refuges everywhere; indeed, we have a moral obligation to do this, since from a technological standpoint it is forbidden. Huysmans was not yet living in the giant panopticon that we all know today, but he foresaw the spirit of modernity in the idea of imposing a new form of imperialism: subjection to a single and solitary space-time.

Let us recall those brilliant lines that seem to denounce a sort of lack, when in fact they undoubtedly describe the only way of living in the world: namely, allowing oneself to be inhabited by several temporalities. We do not all live in the same now, as Bloch wrote. And is there really anything wrong with this, when all is said and done? Certainly those who have nostalgic feelings are in a sort of exile, and might fall into resentment. But nostalgia often remains a territory of refuge, one that gives forth a "now," a space-time in which the illusion of being able to live calmly is maintained. It is true that this nostalgia is rather untenable for oneself and for others. It is exhausting and also isolating, for those around us grow tired of trying to prevent it or counter it with rational arguments. But we're dealing here with an existential and emotional truth that is not really affected by those who seek to contradict it. Let's be realistic: those who practice the contemporary form of melancholy

PART III

that is nostalgia are in no way wrong; they simply choose, from among innumerable disappointing facts, those that reinforce their ideas. What protects those who are nostalgic and melancholic from resentment is the fact that they no longer live in a state of envy: they live within regret, disappointment, the impossibility of forgetting an imaginary past, but in the end, all this protects them, for they no longer "desire" anything from this world. "Like a hermit, he was ripe for seclusion, worn out by life and expecting nothing more of it; and also like a monk, he was overcome by a tremendous lassitude, by a need for contemplation, by a desire no longer to have anything in common with the heathen—which was what he called Utilitarians and fools."[445] Huysmans perfectly describes this "desire no longer to have anything in common" with others, which is not the desire of the resentmentist man to make others pay for his feeling of being excluded from this common. The relations between the nostalgic subject and modernity resemble those between Durtal and Madame Chantelouve in Huysmans's *The Damned*: Madame Chantelouve pounces upon Durtal with all her desire, and Durtal repels her as best he can, virtually horrified by her lustful assault; when she asks "Shall I see you again soon," he responds: "There is no reason why we should. You want too much; and I want nothing. Better to put a stop to it now; otherwise things might drag on like this until they end in bitterness and recrimination."[446] At the very moment that the nostalgic subject wants nothing, modernity wants everything, and refuses to renounce its desires: everything that technology allows will be done; the will to power must not have any limits, for limits entail irreparable frustrations; they afflict progress at the very moment that it is helping us to strive toward perfection—to sublimate limitations, in other words, not to deny them. Everyone understands that it is possible to push back the limit, to ensure that it is elsewhere, but everyone also understands that this is not enough to satisfy modernity, and that the latter ensures that there are no structural limits for man.

If literature saves history, it is because it is better able to envision a potential road to redemption for this man from the underground who resists resentmentist assaults so as to finally choose the road to repentance, and to the possibility of a new life. History, on the contrary—or what will one day be called history—is often the theater of a resentment that has been freed from its chains, believing that it is the historical force for change, when in fact it is nothing but inertia, the workings of cowardice. History at once bears resentmentist impulses and the long durations that are necessary to "mend"

THE SEA: A WORLD OPENED TO MAN

resentment; this mending will not last forever, but history allows for the advent of something different, for escaping from resentment often requires several generations, as psychoanalysis, in clinical work with families, knows all too well. Many generations are required to stop the logic of reproduction—to escape the trap of confronting and reacting to everything associated with the family and the cultural milieu from which one stems. Sometimes, many "psyches" are necessary to confront an immense wound.

Hegel would undoubtedly see in this an example of the cunning of reason, whereby one employs the lowest human passions to transform history. But this is an "optimistic" vision, for Hegel believes that history has a direction, and that its development is irreversible. As such, all passions, great or small, serve the interests of historical reason. But the postmodern mind does not share the idealist vision of Hegelian thought, which finds a place for every event in the great totality of history. Different phases of history have different roles and different weights in the advent of humanist civilization. Great collective moments of resentment bring about reactions that create a movement of regression from which it is difficult to recover. This is where conceptions of history that are based on progress get bogged down. We must try to bring about the redemption of literature in the "real" world, like a sort of sign of "great health," in other words of the capacity, for society and for the individuals who comprise it, to experience the breadth of the "underground" sentiment, while at the same time being able to find resources for resisting its abyss. Getting sick and recovering, as Canguilhem said. This is our task: going through the agony of resentment without succumbing to the temptation to make of it a concrete historical moment, one that might lead to war or to the hatred of others, with all of the well-known consequences of this.

I would have liked to divide these three "here lies"—bitterness, mother, the sea—with greater precision. But this seems unlikely, given the extent to which the dynamics of all three are intertwined—how these dynamics respond to one another, support one another, serve to correct one another. The antidotes to individual and collective resentment resemble one another: it is a matter of material security, or rather of controlling material insecurity such that it does not cause emotional insecurity to overflow. This is the aim of a political and socioeconomic combat: to create the least anxiogenic milieu possible, one that serves as a structure for potential support, in the sense that, even if support is not its foremost objective, it nonetheless does not make all emotional support impossible. It cannot be solely

PART III

a question of material reality: even when material issues dominate, they must not call into question all psychological and physical safety. For all that, "material" support alone is not sufficient for avoiding resentment, for disturbed emotions can always overwhelm the subject in more profound ways. Pierre Bourdieu identified this when he differentiated misery of position from misery of situation. While the latter refers to a subjective fact, the former arises from the sense one has of a gap between oneself and another: from the comparison one makes between himself and another who mocks him, from his feelings of nonrecognition and humiliation, from his feeling that he is not getting his "due." Miseries of position, if nothing is done to assuage them, create the perfect terrain for the spread of individual and collective resentment. Independently of material and economic support, there is symbolic "support," the subject's capacity for symbolization and sublimation so as to overcome his own tendencies toward resentment. Many possibilities exist for this, such as the *vis comica*, which allows one to overturn anxiety and to avoid being sensitive to the sting of sad and potentially lethal emotions. At some point I will dedicate a book to this *vis comica*: it has been sleeping in a drawer, as it were, for twenty years; I'll have to wake it up sometime soon. Other possibilities are those of style and of the work: one could speak of *poiesis*, the act of doing and thinking, an act that sometimes borders on art and sometimes on know-how; and then there is of course the path of *philia*, in the broad sense of the term: the virtues of love and of friendship. These different territories offer possibilities for sublimation and symbolization that are absolutely decisive for escaping rancor. They allow two things: the creation of a common world and the expansion of the ego.

* * *

Some may think that I have dealt with "here lies mother" less than the other forms of "here lies," but this is not true. I have already devoted a book to this subject, to the *pretium doloris*, the risk of truth, the separation from the faculty of proper judgment, the mourning of the puerile demand for protection. The state of leaving childhood behind, as Kant wrote. The mother is also what Winnicott called the mother's primordial worry, or how a parent becomes a resource of support in the world: how, by way of the care he gives, which comes to feed the development of the imagination, he accompanies the emergence of individuation in the child. Winnicott often told the story of how he became a psychiatrist. We know that history is always written after the fact, but it is no small matter that

THE SEA: A WORLD OPENED TO MAN

Winnicott chose this story to describe his own conversion to care—in other words, the birth of his vocation. As Winnicott writes in his 1963 poem "The Tree":

Mother below is weeping
         weeping
         weeping

Thus I knew her

Once, stretched out on her lap
    as now on dead tree
I learned to make her smile
    to stem her tears
    to undo her guilt
    to cure her inward death

To enliven her was my living[447]

Separating oneself cannot be reduced to mere physical separation, but rather bears witness to an aptitude for symbolization: making something of this, the infinite sorrow of his mother, her depression, even though this weighs too heavily for a child. Not denying this difficulty, but learning to grow with it, to distance oneself from it, to find the right distance to provide care for her and above all for himself and others, for repetition must be stopped in its tracks. Here lies mother: these are the first renunciations, the first forms of mourning, that one undertakes in order to grow: it is a question of maintaining the demand of Rilke's Open at the very moment that certain roads that are proper to childhood are closed off. One must leave this safe universe in which everything is possible, nothing needs to be achieved, everything can simply be imagined or hoped for, and in which everyone smiles beatifically, satisfied by this pure potentiality. This is the world of childhood and the world of the adults who gaze upon this marvelous child: it is a world that mends all narcissistic cracks by its simple existence. But this cannot last, neither for the child nor for the adults: the child risks being devoured by the "benevolent" scope of the parental omnipotence; it is even worse if he comes to bask in it. One must separate oneself from this as well, and create another form of the Open, one that has a connection with the *pretium doloris*; he must step outside of this, into risk and even death; he must leave behind this great mirage of pure potentiality

PART III

without being too disenchanted. Here lies, in short, the ego ideal, the one that is transmitted (even if lovingly) by others. Only now can he begin to sculpt a self.

"Here lies"—in other words: "you have left it behind," it is at rest, in peace, even if not exclusively: it has a share of peace. Is it buried, outdated, repressed, or sublimated? I don't know; all I know is that it has been left behind by the demand to not repeat, to not allow yourself to sink into involuntary repetition. It is not a matter of resisting the unconscious, but more simply of playing with the unconscious, of understanding its meandering, and of not allowing yourself to be seduced by its dark call, should it arise. We are all convalescents, as Nietzsche says of Zarathustra, this man who resists the resentment of weak spirits who are deeply "ill" but have no intention of healing. Are you "ill" if you refuse to define yourself as such, so that the very idea of healing seems incongruous and condescending? The convalescent, by contrast, is always halfway between the illness that must be defeated and the healing that must be won. He has gone through something: he has crossed over. He has undertaken the effort of this crossing, of crossing over that which has tormented him—namely, the "abysmal thought."[448] "Here there is thunder enough to make even graves learn to listen!"[449] exclaims Zarathustra, confronting the assault of the nothingness that threatens to carry him away. The attack is real: "Nausea, nausea, nausea, oh no!"[450] cries Zarathustra, collapsing like a dead man. And then—here lies bitterness—Zarathustra gets back to his feet, takes an apple in his hand, smells it, tastes it, and the time of speaking with the world emerges once more. Nietzsche has a magnificent way of expressing the sublimation that has been our theme since the beginning, the one that makes us capable of leaving the cave, that is capable of nourishing itself with aesthetic experiences, and of making us feel that our existence is worthy of the name. How? What is the path proposed by Zarathustra? "All things want to be your physician!": in other words, if Zarathustra is able to lend his ear so as to welcome all of the phenomena that surround him, to mingle with nature, the world will lie before him "like a garden."[451] If he is able, like Orpheus, to nourish himself with nature's veils (the veils of Isis, as Pierre Hadot said), to experience the mystery of the living without being wounded by its breadth, to simply be conscious of its *tremendum*[452]—if he learns to do this, his soul will expand; it will be like the universe, transcending finitude, not by negating it, but by becoming capable of sublimating it, and of creating the theory of the eternal renewal.

222

THE SEA: A WORLD OPENED TO MAN

It is clear that the *amor fati*[453] is a theory of anti-resentment in that it is a matter of desiring something, whatever it is, in such a way that can eternally return—but with this very Nietzschean caveat of the need to invent creative repetition. "Everything breaks, everything is joined anew; the same house of being builds itself eternally. Everything parts, everything greets itself again; the ring of being remains loyal to itself eternally."[454] Conversely, there are those whom becoming wounds by giving them the sense that they are its victims. These are the "tarantulas," a term used by Nietzsche to describe the execrable nature of the man who is subjected to the need for vengeance, and who is incapable of leaving the "lie-hole lair" that his "rage"[455] and his vindictiveness create. There is of course something of the Odyssey in man's ability to defeat his resentment, even if doing so does not require reproducing Ulysses' journey. But it is indeed an epic—that of bitterness transforming itself into a sea [*celle de l'amer se transfigurant en mer*]. To understand this, Pound's *Cantos* are required reading—at the risk of a dizziness that can ensue from their twirling language and incredible polyphony. This is a great book about sublimation and the crossing of individual and collective history. "And then went down to the ship, / Set keel to breakers, / forth on the godly sea, and / We set up mast and sail on that swart ship."[456] It is thus that the voyage begins: the same call to the open sea as in Melville's work; the same darkness, that of a consciousness that does not know that it can die, that it is undoubtedly taking this risk to escape a death that is even more certain if it remains at the dock. The swart ship thus sets forth.

The *Cantos* is also required reading for its attraction to fascism. Within the book, we thus see—like always—the outlines of a need for dissociation from the author. Pound's style is a permanent battle, that of a pen caught up in its torments as well as its enthusiasm, in its will for renewal and indeed for a quasi-resurrection of the soul and the people. But we also see the signs of bitterness, one that threatens to spill into resentment, its style saving it from an irrevocable fall. The *Pisan Cantos* undoubtedly describe this state of mind that is hard on itself and on others—hard and poetic; hard, and at times giving free rein to its own hardness: "'Master thyself, then others shall thee beare' / Pull down thy vanity / Thou art a beaten dog beneath the hail / . . . Pull down thy vanity / How mean thy hates / Fostered in falsity, / Pull down thy vanity."[457] And above all the conclusion, which suddenly illuminates that which had for a long time remained in the dark within Pound's discourse: an ode to humanity and above all to the work, in which doing and thinking are united. For we find

PART III

in Pound's work this conjunction between saying and doing, between words or names and acts, between *praxis* and *poiesis*. Regarding this, Pound never tires of citing the Chinese term *zhengming*, which can be translated as "the rectification of names." "The expression comes from the *Analects of Confucius*, and refers to the idea of a harmony between the name (*ming*) and reality (*shi*). According to Confucius, 'only a sovereign who comports himself according to the principle of the sovereign deserves to be called a sovereign.'"[458] This duty to rectify names shows the way to the morality that it attempts to put into place: a coherence between being and saying; the ultimate and impossible challenge of a total reconciliation between the sensible order and the symbolic order, such that the name is completely embodied in a body, allowing them to work together without separating. This dream of an entity without remainder is very typical of absolutist thought, and indeed, where this case is concerned, thought that tends toward fascism: it is as though there existed a dream of purity for oneself in opposition to the impurity of the other. Thankfully, the *Cantos* keep coming, weaving a more complex web than they appear to at first glance, and ending up being positioned on the side of impurity—of that which is doable, of that which can be attempted even if it is not perfect, even if it lacks an end. The sea is also linked to shipwrecks. Indeed, this is the figure employed by Pound to speak the truth of his being.

> But to have done instead of not doing
>   this is not vanity
> To have, with decency, knocked
> That a Blunt should open
>   To have gathered from the air a live tradition
> or from a fine old eye the unconquered flame
> This is not vanity.
>   Here error is all in the not done,
> all in the diffidence that faltered.[459]

This is in no way an attack against the fear of those who are vulnerable, but a denunciation of those who tremble and who resign themselves to cowardice, and who no longer even notice; a denunciation of those who decide (but the word is inadequate: it would be better to write "decide") to do nothing. To understand Pound's attraction to Mussolini, a sign of his lack of discernment, we must analyze his thought: naïve, all in all, on the subject of pseudo great men, but very alert on the potential for the confiscation of power by

THE SEA: A WORLD OPENED TO MAN

oligarchs: "'You fear the one, I the few.'"[460] Pound is one of those poets who believe in an alliance between the "great man" and the people, as though each could save themselves by way of the other. A very idealistic vision, in short, that will be tripped up by the reality of human psyches, and that will end up fading away the more he opens his eyes, with the flow of the years and the *Cantos*, with the flow of his pen and his life, of exile and asylum—for Pound will be detained for thirteen years and accused of high treason for having been a fervent admirer of fascism. In the great movement of the *Cantos*, he recognizes his error and asks forgiveness: "That I lost my center / fighting the world / The dreams clash / and are shattered— / and that I tried to make a paradiso / terrestre. . . . Let the Gods forgive what I / have made / Let those I love try to forgive / what I have made."[461] The shipwreck, as figuration of bitterness that has become the sea [*l'amer devenu mer*]; the shipwreck, to express his mistake and that of the world, not in order to deny it, but to announce the birth of Europe after two world wars and the disaster of the crime against humanity. We have already seen this with Jankélévitch: what is born with Europe is something imperishable. "As a lone ant from a broken ant-hill / from the wreckage of Europe, ego scriptor."[462] If Pound is an interesting figure, it is also because there is a psychotic dimension within him. The extent to which his internment in a psychiatric ward protected him from charges of high treason is far from easy to determine. Nonetheless, a reading of the *Cantos* allows us to understand that its words undertake work to bring about health, following the wanderings of an ill and wounded soul who ruminates his enthusiasm like others ruminate their hatred. These words are also febrile, agitated, incomprehensible. They cause us to lose our bearings as readers, just as they did for Pound.

Everyone would of course be happy if the art of sublimation offered more than a craving for bitterness. This does happen, for there are always new things that emerge, things that were totally unexpected. The clinical function of sublimation allows us to envision what Reich called sexual economy, or more simply sexual life, in different ways. This resonates clearly with what Freud called libidinal cathexis or investment. The question is how, by symbolizing and sublimating, the individual can expand his domain of libidinal investment, hence strengthening his desire to encounter the world and to employ his vital power in the service of a superior ideal. Some will call the extension in question an extension of the zone of struggle: after all, sublimation is a theory of action and desire in which an ethics of recognition for oneself and for others plays out. Within this taste for

PART III

bitterness, there is an awareness of the harmful unrest of the world, and an ability to resist: sometimes by way of the *vis comica*, and sometimes through escape, fleeing, a flight to the outside—an ability to furtively move elsewhere, a talent for stealth.[463] The territory of literature allows us to sublimate all forms of resentment, and to taste the bitterness of things, beings, ideas. But there are also symbolic territories that do not belong to literature, and that can bring us those "magisterial" elements that we need in order not to go under. Developing the faculty of the taste of bitterness helps us to become surveyors of the world. When we do not fear this taste, when we know how to appreciate it, it expands the density of the world, or rather our representation of the world.

This taste for bitterness is also a way to heal from resentment.

NOTES

1 [Trans. note: With few exceptions, I translate *l'homme* as "man" throughout the book, for two reasons. First, Fleury insists on this term, both in her use of *l'homme*, and in the distance she takes from "inclusive writing" (see her comments on this in Part III, Chapter 2). Second, one of Fleury's arguments is that resentment has traditionally been too closely associated with women; from this standpoint, her constant use of "man" may serve to emphasize that resentment is far more universal than it is often assumed to be, and indeed that certain forms of it are much more masculine than feminine.]

2 [Trans. note: "Resentment" in this sentence and throughout the book translates the French *ressentiment*. There is a long history of using this French term in English, especially within philosophy; this follows in part from the fact that Nietzsche (an important reference for Fleury) employs the French term throughout his work, which has led English translators of Nietzsche simply to leave the term as is. I have chosen to translate it as "resentment" (except when citing works that specifically opt for the French term) in part because Fleury's aims are not solely philosophical: they are also (to name just a few) literary, clinical, and political. Using the French term *ressentiment* would make little sense within Anglophone clinical contexts. In contemporary politics, meanwhile, it has become more and more common to speak about the "politics of resentment," and Fleury herself comments on this.]

3 [Trans. note: The French title of this book is *Ci-gît l'amer*, and my decision regarding the translation of the title's final term requires a word of explanation. The direct translation of *l'amer* is "the bitter"; for stylistic reasons, I have translated it throughout as "bitterness." What is important here is that *l'amer* in spoken French is indistinguishable from *la mère*, which means "the mother," and *la mer*, which means "the sea." Fleury plays on this homophony here and throughout the text. This is impossible to reproduce in English, but the reader

227

NOTES TO PAGES 3–8

should remain aware of it, given its importance for several of Fleury's arguments.]

4 The *Littré* dictionary gives the following etymology for stance: "Ital. *stanza*, stance, (properly speaking) stay, sojourn, stop, from the Latin *stare*, to stay, to stop; one speaks thus of a stance because it is a kind of stop."

5 Herman Melville, *Moby-Dick; or, The Whale* (1851; New York: Penguin, 2009), p. 3.

6 Ibid.

7 Ibid.

8 The oceanic feeling was defined in 1927 by Romain Rolland in his correspondence with Freud to describe this *universal* desire to be one with the universe. In his work, Rolland turns this into a foreshadowing of religious feeling: the oceanic bears witness to a spontaneous spirituality of man that is independent of this feeling. The oceanic enters into a dialectical relationship with an originary sense of abandonment, permitting the subject not to feel a sense of "lack," to confront separation and finitude (here lies mother) without giving in to melancholy. It arises from a feeling of eternity, of a quick flash and then of rest. Freud, without naming him, addresses Rolland at the beginning of *Civilization and Its Discontents* (1929), in which he deals at length with the oceanic feeling of the Ego.

9 Melville, *Moby-Dick*, p. 4.

10 Cornelius Castoriadis, "The Revolutionary Exigency," in *Political and Social Writings, Volume 3, 1961–1979: Recommencing the Revolution: From Socialism to the Autonomous Society*, trans. David Ames Curtis (Minneapolis: University of Minnesota Press, 1993), p. 243 [translation modified].

11 [Trans. note: On Reich's "capacity for freedom," see Part II, Chapter 7.]

12 Castoriadis, "The Revolutionary Exigency," p. 243.

13 Cornelius Castoriadis, "The Subjective Roots of the Revolutionary Project," in *The Imaginary Institution of Society*, trans. Kathleen Blamey (Cambridge: Polity, 1975), pp. 90–5, here p. 94.

14 [Trans. note: "Resentmentist" in this sentence and in what follows translates *ressentimiste*, a neologism employed by Fleury; per the *OED*'s definition of the suffix "-ist," one might think of a "resentmentist" person as someone who actively practices resentment, or who adheres to it as though it were a creed.]

15 Max Scheler, *Ressentiment*, trans. William W. Holdheim (New York: The Free Press of Glencoe, 1961), p. 39 [translation modified].

16 In his book *The Great Transformation*, first published in 1944.

17 [Trans. note: I use "enjoyment" here to translate *jouissance*, which has a much stronger sexual connotation.]

18 Scheler, *Ressentiment*, p. 9 [translation modified].

228

NOTES TO PAGES 8–15

19 According to the Freudian definition of breach:

> We describe as "traumatic" any excitations from outside which are powerful enough to breach the protective shield. . . . Such an event as an external trauma is bound to provoke a disturbance on a large scale in the functioning of the organism's energy and to set in motion every possible defensive measure. At the same time, the pleasure principle is for the moment put out of action. There is no longer any possibility of preventing the mental apparatus from being flooded with large amounts of stimulus, and another problem arises instead—the problem of mastering the amounts of stimulus which have breached the surface and of binding them, in the psychical sense, so that they can then be disposed of.

Sigmund Freud, *Beyond the Pleasure Principle*, trans. James Strachey (New York: W. W. Norton and Company, 1961), pp. 23–4 [translation modified].
20 Scheler, *Ressentiment*, pp. 39–40 [translation modified].
21 Friedrich Nietzsche, *On the Genealogy of Morality*, trans. Carol Diethe, Cambridge: Cambridge University Press, 2006, pp. 19 and 94; see also *Ecce Homo*, in *The Anti-Christ, Ecce Homo, Twilight of the Idols, and Other Writings*, trans. Judith Norman, Cambridge: Cambridge University Press, 2005. The affect of resentment, born from an intoxication that cannot be separated from Judeo-Christianity, allows one to distinguish between the morality of slaves and that of masters.
22 Scheler, *Ressentiment*, pp. 45, 47.
23 Scheler, *Ressentiment*, pp. 45–6 [translation modified].
24 Ibid., p. 46.
25 See ibid., p. 49.
26 Ibid., p. 52.
27 Ibid., pp. 52–3 [translation modified].
28 As Freud conceives of it in his 1927 book *Fetishism*.
29 Scheler, *Ressentiment*, p. 58 [translation modified].
30 [Trans. note: The Palo Alto School refers to a group of researchers associated with the Mental Research Institute in Palo Alto, California. The term "ultra-solution" was developed by Paul Watzlawick in his book *Ultra-Solutions*, which appeared in English in 1988.]
31 There are many versions of the "ultra-solution." Certainly every version that is extremist, unsuited to the dynamics of negotiation (proposing a solution that no one can revisit doesn't count as negotiation), is a classic ultra-solution; everything that rejects discernment, nuance, and complexity, on the pretext that these are unacceptable compromises—there are thus unacceptable compromises that are not compromises, but simulacra of compromises. But not every

NOTES TO PAGES 15–18

compromise is inherently unacceptable. The problem with the ultra-solution is the illusion of knowing which solution it rests upon: no solution is inherently irreversible; certain principles can be, but no solution of itself ever possesses, in the space-time that belongs to it, the key to the resolution of a problem. Or rather, it might, if the problem is simple, but in this case it is not really a "problem" as it lacks its own dynamics. A problem refers to an awareness of the complexity of an entire ecosystem: a problem is always in a state of movement. Consequently, believing in an ultra-solution that will put a halt to the "motility" of the problem—which is always in a state of interaction with its environment—is quite insufficient in intellectual terms. This does not mean that there is never a solution, but that the resolution is always dynamic: it brings us toward a cycle that puts into play different and successive space-times.

32 Scheler, *Ressentiment*, p. 70 [translation modified].
33 See Catherine Fino, "Discernement moral et discernement spirituel à l'époque moderne. Une collaboration en vue de la liberté du sujet," *Revue d'*éthique et de théologie morale, Éditions du Cerf, 2018/2, no. 298, pp. 11–24. Fino cites Ignatius of Loyola: "We call Spiritual Exercises every way of preparing and disposing the soul to rid itself of all inordinate attachments, and, after their removal, of seeking and finding the will of God in the disposition of our life for the salvation of our soul." Ignatius of Loyola, *The Spiritual Exercises of St. Ignatius*, trans. Louis J. Puhl (New York: Vintage, 2000), p. 5. The *Exercises* were printed for the first time in Rome in 1548.
34 As Fino notes: "Good discernment thus demands that one clarify one's motivations, purify one's emotions, and bring judgment upon one's desire, in order to valorize what is good and reject what is bad" (Fino, "Discernement moral," p. 298).
35 [Trans. note: This is the title of one of Michel de Montaigne's most famous essays. See Montaigne, *The Complete Essays*, trans. M. A. Screech (London: Penguin, 1987), Book I, Chapter 20.]
36 Montaigne, *The Complete Essays*, Book I, Chapter 19.
37 Ibid., Book III, Chapter 12, p. 1177.
38 [Trans. note: Montaigne, *The Complete Essays*, Book III, Chapter 12, p. 1190.]
39 [Trans. note: See ibid., Book III, Chapter 12, p. 1191.]
40 Tocqueville writes: "When inequality is the common law of a society, the strongest inequalities do not strike the eye; when everything is nearly on a level, the least of them wound it. That is why the desire for equality always becomes more insatiable as equality is greater. In democratic peoples, men easily obtain a certain equality; they cannot attain the equality they desire. It retreats before them daily but without ever evading their regard, and, when it withdraws, it attracts them in pursuit. They constantly believe they are going to seize it, and it

NOTES TO PAGES 18–33

constantly escapes their grasp. They see it from near enough to know its charms, they do not approach it close enough to enjoy it, and they die before having fully savored its sweetness. It is to these causes that one must attribute the singular melancholy that the inhabitants of democratic lands often display amid their abundance, and the disgust with life that sometimes seizes them in the midst of an easy and tranquil existence." Alexis de Tocqueville, *Democracy in America*, trans. Harvey C. Mansfield and Delba Winthrop (Chicago: University of Chicago Press 2000), pp. 513–14.

41 I first examined it in *Les Pathologies de la démocratie* (Paris: Fayard, 2005).
42 Scheler, *Ressentiment*, p. 50.
43 See ibid., p. 61.
44 Ibid., p. 143 [translation modified].
45 Ibid., p. 146.
46 Ibid., p. 146 [translation modified].
47 [Trans. note: See ibid., p. 43.]
48 Ibid., p. 141 [translation modified].
49 Ibid., p. 142 [translation modified].
50 Quoted in ibid., p. 121.
51 Quoted in ibid., p. 122.
52 Ibid., p. 109.
53 Quoted in ibid., p. 109 [translation modified].
54 See ibid., p. 84.
55 [Trans. note: See ibid., p. 62.]
56 Marc Angenot, *Les Idéologies du ressentiment* (Montreal: XYZ Éditeur, 1996), p. 107.
57 Søren Kierkegaard, *The Sickness unto Death: A Christian Psychological Exposition for Upbuilding and Awakening*, trans. Howard V. Hong and Edna H. Hong (Princeton, N.J.: Princeton University Press, 1980), pp. 55–6. This passage is cited in Danièle Zucker, ed., "Pour introduire le faux self," *Penser la crise. L'Émergence du soi*, De Boeck Supérieur, 2012, pp. 19–21.
58 Friedrich Nietzsche, *La Volonté de puissance, II*, trans. Geneviève Blanquis (Paris: Gallimard, 1995), p. 56.
59 Ibid.
60 Ibid.
61 Friedrich Nietzsche, *The Will to Power*, trans. Walter Kaufmann and R. J. Hollingdale (London: Weidenfeld and Nicolson, 1968), p. 16.
62 Nietzsche, *La Volonté de puissance, II*, p. 58.
63 Ibid.
64 Montaigne, *The Complete Essays*, Book II, Chapter 11, p. 472.
65 Ibid., p. 478.
66 Ibid., p. 480.
67 Ibid., Book II, Chapter 20, p. 764.

NOTES TO PAGES 33–46

68 Quoted in ibid.
69 Quoted in ibid., p. 765.
70 Victor Hugo, *William Shakespeare*, trans. Melville B. Anderson (Chicago: A. C. McClurg and Company, 1911), p. 7.
71 Ibid.
72 Ibid., p. 8.
73 Ibid. [translation modified].
74 Nietzsche, *The Will to Power*, p. 327.
75 Nietzsche, *La Volonté de puissance, II*, p. 73.
76 G. W. F. Hegel, *Phenomenology of Spirit*, trans. A. V. Miller (Oxford: Oxford University Press, 1977), §187 (p. 114).
77 Nietzsche, *On the Genealogy of Morality*, trans. Carol Diethe (Cambridge: Cambridge University Press, 2006), p. 20.
78 Ibid., p. 21.
79 Ibid., p. 22.
80 "We shall suppose that a system in the very front of the apparatus receives the perceptual stimuli but retains no trace of them and thus has no memory, while behind it there lies a second system which transforms the momentary excitations of the first system into permanent traces." Sigmund Freud, *The Interpretation of Dreams*, trans. James Strachey (New York: Basic Books, 2010), p. 540. See also "The Unconscious" (1915) and *Beyond the Pleasure Principle* (1920). In addition, see Gilles Deleuze, *Nietzsche and Philosophy*, trans. Hugh Tomlinson (New York: Colombia University Press, 2006), p. 112.
81 Nietzsche, *On the Genealogy of Morality*, p. 22.
82 Nietzsche, *The Will to Power*, p. 449.
83 Ibid., p. 450.
84 Sigmund Freud, *Civilization and Its Discontents*, trans. James Strachey (New York: W. W. Norton and Company, 1962), p. 44.
85 Ibid., p. 50.
86 "What he employs for cultural aims he to a great extent withdraws from women and sexual life. His constant association with men, and his dependence on his relations with them, even estrange him from his duties as a husband and father. Thus the woman finds herself forced into the background by the claims of civilization and she adopts a hostile attitude towards it" (ibid., pp. 50–1).
87 "'Beyond this first stage of the child's development, the primary maternal preoccupation, for Winnicott, is a metaphor of therapeutic work. He views therapy as an attempt to imitate 'the techniques which come naturally to a mother who is preoccupied with the care of her own infant.' D. W. Winnicott, *Through Paediatrics to Psycho-Analysis* (New York: Basic Books, 1975), p. 219. '*There is no such thing as a baby*' (ibid., p. 99), writes Winnicott, to emphasize that a baby does not exist without a mother or someone who takes the place of the mother to care for the baby. In Winnicott's work, the individual

NOTE TO PAGE 46

ceases to be an isolated unit: 'The centre of gravity of the being does not start off in the individual. It is in the total set-up' (ibid., p. 99). To define maternal care, Winnicott employs the notion of devotion, as if to emphasize its unlimited, undiscriminating, infinite, and in some way providential character. 'Mental health is something which cannot be except as a fruition of previous development. The mental health of each child is laid down by the mother during her preoccupation with the care of her infant. The word "devotion" can be rid of its sentimentality and can be used to describe the essential feature without which the mother cannot make her contribution, a sensitive and active adaptation to her infant's needs—needs which at the beginning are absolute. This word, devotion, also reminds us that in order to succeed in the task the mother need not be clever. Mental health, then, is a product of the continuous care that enables a continuity of personal emotional growth' (ibid., p. 220). Devotion is not a theoretical act: it is the unrestricted giving of oneself, a way of being totally available and totally attentive. At stake here is not solely the most essential forms of care that the mother gives. It is also a matter of the feelings of safety that the child experiences thanks to the mother's attention: he feels 'supported,' protected, and this support—this concern—allows him to develop an initial contact with the world. 'The baby does not know that the space around is maintained by you. How careful you are that the world shall not impinge before the infant has found it! By a live and breathing quietness you follow the life in the infant with the life in yourself, and you wait for the gestures that come from the infant, gestures that lead to your being discovered.' D. W. Winnicott, 'Knowing and Learning,' in *Winnicott on the Child* (Cambridge, Mass.: Perseus Publishing, 2002), p. 22. The support of the mother is thus the support of the world, in that the infant can discover the world without being traumatized by it; the world doesn't become a world without this initial support of the mother. This makes separation possible, which will allow the child to build his own relationship with the world. 'So a great deal depends on the way the world is presented to the infant and to the growing child. The ordinary mother can start and carry through this amazing business of introducing the world in small doses, not because she is clever, as philosophers need to be, but simply because of the devotion she feels for her own baby.' D. W. Winnicott, *The Child, the Family, and the Outside World* (Reading, Mass.: Addison-Wesley, 1987), p. 74. At stake here is the psychological health of the individual to come: while this is wholly determined in infancy, it must be said that mistreatment during this time is profoundly harmful for the future subject, in that this initial rift will undoubtedly grow in the absence of tools that would allow this subject to surpass it. The mother gives the baby 'a belief that the world can contain what is wanted and needed, with the result that the baby has hope that there is a live relationship

NOTES TO PAGES 46–50

between inner reality and external reality, between innate primary creativity and the world at large which is shared by all' (ibid., p. 90)." Cynthia Fleury-Perkins, "Irremplaçabilité et parentalité," *Spirale* 79, no. 3 (2016), pp. 41–52.

88 Freud, *Civilization and Its Discontents*, p. 36.

89 See Cynthia Fleury, *Mallarmé et la parole de l'imâm* (Paris: Gallimard, 2020).

90 Deleuze, *Nietzsche and Philosophy*, p. 36.

91 The thiasus is the retinue that accompanies Dionysus on his journeys, comprising satyrs, sileni, and maenads.

92 I have often appealed to Rilke's notion of the Open, to endorse it and undoubtedly also to confer upon it a clinical function (even if this is not present in Rilke). For the poet, the Open has to do with the Real—the profound destabilization of that which cannot be synthesized—but also with calm, such as that of the animal gaze that he is so fond of describing in his elegies. The Open also echoes the notion of the "numinous" in the work of Rudolf Otto, taken up by Jung, in his letters, for its therapeutic function. Choosing the Open, choosing the Numinous, means choosing the principle of individuation against resentment, placing it outside as that which resists the death drive, as though the creative drive of life drew its vitality from this exteriority: existence as the state of being outside of resentment. As Jung wrote in a letter to P. W. Martin in 1945: "You are quite right, the main interest of my work is not concerned with the treatment of neuroses but rather with the approach to the numinous. But the fact is that the approach to the numinous is the real therapy and inasmuch as you attain to the numinous experiences you are released from the curse of pathology. Even the very disease takes on a numinous character." C. G. Jung, *C. G. Jung Letters*, Volume I, trans. R. F. C. Hull (Princeton, N.J.: Princeton University Press, 1992), p. 377. In the work of Otto, Freud, Jung, and even Rilke, there is undoubtedly a dialectic between the Numinous, the sacred, the spiritual, even more than with the idea of knowledge, undoubtedly judged to be too rational, or with an overly narrow understanding of reason. By contrast, it is certain that the Numinous and the Open dialogue with the notion of *imaginatio vera*, which is indissociable from the process of the growth of the I, which itself forms a matrix, or turns on the process of individuation. Once again, the *imaginatio vera* has more to do with the notion of discernment than with that of the imaginary. Choosing the Open, resisting resentment, means choosing the creative path of discernment. We will look below at the clinical and therapeutic function of discernment. Discerning is indispensable for health, for instance in the example of a correct diagnosis.

93 Nietzsche, *The Will to Power*, p. 543.

94 Maurice Blanchot, *The Infinite Conversation*, trans. Susan Hanson (Minneapolis: University of Minnesota Press, 1993), p. 203.

NOTES TO PAGES 50–61

95 Ibid., p. 216.
96 See the chapter entitled "Insurrection, the Madness of Writing" (ibid., p. 217).
97 Bruno Latour, "Pourquoi Péguy se répète-t-il ? Péguy est-il illisible?," in Camille Riquier, ed. *Péguy* (Paris: Les Éditions du Cerf, 2014), pp. 339–41.
98 Bruno Latour, "Nous sommes des vaincus," in Riquier, ed., *Péguy*, p. 28.
99 See Nietzsche, *The Will to Power*, pp. 460–62.
100 Deleuze, *Nietzsche and Philosophy*, p. 35.
101 Vladimir Jankélévitch, *Henri Bergson*, trans. Nils F. Schott (Durham, N.C.: Duke University Press, 2015), p. 223.
102 Vladimir Jankélévitch and Béatrice Berlowitz, *Quelque part dans l'inachevé* (Paris: Gallimard, 1987), p. 119.
103 René Descartes, *The Passions of the Soul*, trans. Robert Stoothoff, in *The Philosophical Writings of Descartes*, vol. 1 (Cambridge: Cambridge University Press, 1988), p. 385.
104 Deleuze, *Nietzsche and Philosophy*, p. 117.
105 Ibid.
106 See the notion of the "perverse whatever" in Eugène Enriquez, "L'Idéal type de l'individu hypermoderne: l'individu pervers?," in Nicole Aubert, ed., *L'Individu hypermoderne* (Toulouse: Érès, 2004), pp. 45–6; on "perverse mediocrity," see Fleury, *Les Pathologies de la démocracie*.
107 Deleuze, *Nietzsche and Philosophy*, p. 117 [translation modified].
108 Ibid., p. 118.
109 Ibid.
110 Ibid., p. 117.
111 Ibid., p. 118.
112 *"The imputation of wrongs, the distribution of responsibilities, perpetual accusation*. All this replaces aggression." Ibid.
113 Ibid., p. 116. And Nietzsche: "At the same time they are preachers of equality and tarantulas. They speak in favor of life, these poisonous spiders, even though they are sitting in their holes and have turned against life, because they want to do harm." *Thus Spoke Zarathustra*, trans. Adrian Del Caro (Cambridge: Cambridge University Press, 2006), pp. 77–8.
114 Nietzsche, *The Will to Power*, p. 364. For Deleuze's comments on this, see *Nietzsche and Philosophy*, p. 58.
115 *"On the denaturalization of morality*. To *separate* the action from the man." Nietzsche, *The Will to Power*, p. 165.
116 *Diagnostic and Statistical Manual of Mental Disorders*, 4th ed. (Washington, D.C.: American Psychiatric Association, 1994). Hereafter cited as DSM-IV.
117 Ibid., p. 775.

235

NOTES TO PAGES 62–75

118 Freud, *Civilization and Its Discontents*, p. 44.

119 DSM-IV, p. 298.

120 Hateloving, *l'hainamoration*, is a neologism invented by Lacan to designate the inextricable interaction between hatred and love. See Jacques Lacan, *On Feminine Sexuality: The Limits of Love and Knowledge*, trans. Bruce Fink (New York: W. W. Norton and Company, 1998), p. 90.

121 DSM-IV, p. 733.

122 See the DSM-IV's entry for "passive aggression" in its "Glossary of Specific Defense Mechanisms and Coping Styles" (p. 755): "The individual deals with emotional conflict or internal or external stressors by indirectly and unassertively expressing aggression toward others. There is a façade of overt compliance masking covert resistance, resentment, or hostility. Passive aggression often occurs in response to demands for independent action or performance or the lack of gratification of dependent wishes but may be adaptive for individuals in subordinate positions who have no other way to express assertiveness more overtly" (p. 756).

123 Blanchot, *The Infinite Conversation*, pp. 231–32.

124 Whether this resentment is of the order of psychosis or of severe neurosis.

125 Blanchot, *The Infinite Conversation*, p. 238.

126 D. W. Winnicott, "Hate in the Counter-Transference," *Journal of Psychotherapy Practice and Research* 3, no. 4 (Fall 1994), pp. 348–56.

127 Denys Ribas, "La Vie de Donald Woods Winnicott," in *Donald Woods Winnicott*, ed. Denys Ribas (Paris: PUF, 2003), pp. 6–34.

128 Christine Voyenne, "'La Haine dans le contre-transfert' (1947), 'Le Contre-transfert' (1960), commentaire des articles de D. W. Winnicott," conference presentation, 2010, p. 4.

129 Quoted in Clare Winnicott, "D. W. W.: A Reflection," in *The Collected Works of D. W. Winnicott: Volume 12, Appendices and Bibliographies*, ed. Robert Adès (Oxford: Oxford University Press, 2016), pp. 295–310, here p. 300.

130 Deleuze, *Nietzsche and Philosophy*, p. 117.

131 "It is thus that, in 1910, Freud writes: 'every analyst's achievement is limited by what his own complexes and resistances permit, and consequently we require that he should begin his practice with a self-analysis and should extend and deepen this constantly.' [Trans. note: Sigmund Freud, "The Future Prospects of Psycho-Analytic Therapy," in Freud, *Collected Papers*, Volume 2, trans. supervised by Joan Riviere (New York: Basic Books, 1959), p. 289. Didactic analysis will be proposed at the Fifth Congress of the IPA in 1918" (Voyenne, "La Haine . . .," p. 2).

132 D. W. Winnicott, "Anxiety Associated with Insecurity," in *Through Paediatrics to Psycho-Analysis* (New York: Basic Books, 1975), p. 99, cited in Voyenne, "La Haine . . .," p. 3.

NOTES TO PAGES 76–88

133 Voyenne, "La Haine . . .," p. 2.
134 Ibid., p. 3.
135 D. W. Winnicott, "Metapsychological and Clinical Aspects of Regression within the Psycho-Analytical Set-Up," in *Through Paediatrics to Psycho-Analysis*, pp. 285–86, cited in Voyenne, "La Haine . . .," p. 4.
136 Voyenne, "La Haine . . .," p. 12.
137 Montaigne, *The Complete Essays*, p. 19.
138 Ibid.
139 Quoted in ibid.
140 Ibid., p. 33.
141 Ibid., p. 73.
142 Behind this entire second part, which is devoted to the historical question of collective resentment, lies a background of the "mother," not in the sense of some feminization of the question, but simply to underline in a metaphoric and hermeneutic manner, a refusal of separation—for we are proceeding along a Möbius strip with three "sides" (bitterness, the mother, the sea [*l'amer, la mère, la mer*]). Leaving behind the fantasy of original unity and of the breast that is forever protective and loving, and moving beyond the eternal desire of wanting to be protected, are both necessary in order to move beyond resentment. We are all separate from one another: certainly we are linked by sublimation and by work, but we are nonetheless separate, alone, and unprotected. The human vocation is inseparable from separation from one's mother (or father)—in other words from all oceanic protection and restoration. We must mend ourselves all alone: yes, we are helped by others, by the world, by the forms of creation that we invent when confronted with the reality of the world; but in the end, we must act alone. We must move from the mother to the sea [*aller de la mère à la mer*].
143 Theodor W. Adorno, *Negative Dialectics*, trans. E. B. Ashton (New York: Continuum, 1973), p. 33.
144 Ibid.
145 Theodor W. Adorno, "Anti-Semitism and Fascist Propaganda," in *The Stars Down to Earth, and Other Essays on the Irrational in Culture* (London: Routledge, 1994), pp. 219–20.
146 Adorno, "Freudian Theory and the Pattern of Fascist Propaganda," in *The Culture Industry: Selected Essays on Mass Culture* (London: Routledge, 1991), p. 146.
147 Adorno, *Minimia Moralia*, p. 164.
148 Adorno, "Scientific Experiences of a European Scholar in America," in Donald Fleming and Bernard Bailin, eds., *The Intellectual Migration: Europe and America 1930–1960* (Cambridge, Mass.: Harvard University Press, 1969), p. 362.
149 R. Nevitt Sanford, "Ethnocentrism in Relation to Some Religious Attitudes and Practices," in Adorno et al., *The Authoritarian Personality* (London: Verso, 2019), p. 220.

NOTES TO PAGES 88–101

150 Adorno, *Minima Moralia*, p. 129.
151 Ibid.
152 Ibid.
153 Adorno, *Dream Notes*, trans. Rodney Livingstone (Cambridge: Polity, 2007), p. 6.
154 In *The Human Stain*, the stain in question hides another, deeper one. Might there not be an infinite number of stains for every one of us?
155 Adorno, *Minima Moralia*, p. 33.
156 Ibid., p. 8.
157 Ibid., p. 47.
158 Ibid.
159 Ibid., p. 46.
160 Ibid., p. 15.
161 Ibid., p. 18.
162 Ibid., p. 178.
163 In his books *Evolutionary History of the Modern Drama* (1909) and *History and Class Consciousness* (1923).
164 As Jean Ferrette writes: "It fell to Kostas Axelos and Jacqueline Bois in 1959 to introduce into French Marxism the terms *reification* and *reify*, which translate the German words *Verdinglichung* and *verdinglichen*. The German words *Versachlichung* and *versachlicht* were translated as *thingification* and *thingified*. . . . For several years prior to this, there had been no way of expressing this in French: *reification* and *reify* [*réification et réifier*] were only invented, respectively, in 1917 and 1930, by Julien Benda." "Les (més)aventures de la réification," *Anamnèse* 6 (2010).
165 Max Horkheimer and Theodor W. Adorno, *Dialectic of Enlightenment*, trans. John Cumming (New York: Continuum, 1989), pp. 133–34.
166 Ibid., pp. 136–37.
167 Ibid., p. 137.
168 Nathalie Heinich, "Sublimer le ressentiment. Elias et les cinq voies vers une autre sociologie," *Revue du MAUSS*, v. 44 n. 2 (2014), pp. 290–98, here p. 290.
169 Ibid.
170 Ibid., p. 291.
171 Ibid., p. 295.
172 Playing on Lacan's famous concept of the "Name of the Father"—*le Nom-du-père*—we might refer to this form of knowledge and the position of power that it seeks as that of the *Nom-des-pairs*, the naming of one's peers or colleagues.
173 Heinich, "Sublimer le ressentiment," p. 297.
174 Adorno, *Negative Dialectics*, p. 163.
175 Adorno, *Minima Moralia*, p. 85.
176 Adorno, *Negative Dialectics*, p. 407.
177 Ibid., p. 408.

NOTES TO PAGES 101–107

178 Ibid. See also Éliane Escoubas's excellent preface to Adorno's *Jargon de l'authenticité. De l'idéologie allemande* (Paris: Payot, 1989), pp. 7–37, especially her remarks on the specificity of Adorno's style.

179 If Adorno is an after-Auschwitz poet, Paul Celan is another. In an article devoted to Celan, the psychoanalyst Michel Bousseyroux has sought to grasp what is at play in the moral and civilizational obligation to write in the language of the perpetrators: "What poetry can one write *after* Auschwitz? What is it possible to write that would *still* be poetry after Auschwitz, above all if this poetry is written by a Jew writing in German, *in the very language of the perpetrators?* It is to this question that the experience of Paul Celan leads us. In a letter from 1946 (a year after the liberation of Auschwitz), he writes: "I will tell you how difficult it is for a Jew to write poems in German. When my poems are published they will no doubt also reach Germany and— let me say the horror—the hand that will open my book has perhaps shaken the hand of the one who murdered my mother . . . And it could get even more horrible . . . But this is my fate: to have to write German poems." Michel Bousseyroux, "Quelle poésie après Auschwitz? Paul Celan: l'expérience d'un vrai trou," in *Au Risque de la topologie et de la poésie. Élargir la psychanalyse*, edited by Michel Bousseyroux (Toulouse: Érès, 2011), pp. 302–23. Celan quotation cited in Pierre Joris, "Preface," in Paul Celan, *Microliths, They Are, Little Stones: Posthumous Prose*, trans. Pierre Joris (New York: Contra Mundum Press, 2020), p. iv.

180 Adorno, *Minima Moralia*, p. 87.

181 Ibid.

182 Ibid.

183 Stefan Müller-Doohm, *Adorno. Une biographie*, trans. Bernard Lortholary (Paris: Gallimard, 2004), p. 363. Citations are from Adorno, *Notes to Literature*, trans. Sherry Weber Nicholson (New York: Columbia University Press, 2019), pp. 76 and 61.

184 See Müller-Doohm, *Adorno*, p. 365.

185 [Trans. note: see Adorno, *Noten zur Literatur II* (Frankfurt am Main: Suhrkamp, 1961), p. 198.]

186 Samuel Beckett, *Endgame & Act Without Words I*, trans. Samuel Beckett (New York: Grove Press, 1958), pp. 1–2.

187 Ibid., p. 13.

188 Ibid., p. 5.

189 Ibid.

190 Adorno and Horkheimer, *Dialectic of Enlightenment*, p. 171.

191 Ibid., p. 209.

192 Ibid.

193 Ibid.

194 Wilhelm Reich, *The Mass Psychology of Fascism*, trans. Vincent R. Carfagno (New York: The Noonday Press, 1970), pp. 200–1.

NOTES TO PAGES 108–115

195 Ibid., p. 201.
196 "Selfishness is a passionate and exaggerated love of self that brings man to relate everything to himself alone and to prefer himself to everything. Individualism is a reflective and peaceable sentiment that disposes each citizen to isolate himself form the mass of those like him and to withdraw to one side with his family and his friends, so that after having thus created a little society for his own use, he willingly abandons society at large to itself." Tocqueville, *Democracy in America*, p. 482. Here, selfishness and individualism are differentiated, even if we see what can bring them together. For all that, democratic individualism is not what others have called individuation, which is an absolutely decisive process for the development of a subject and a state of law.
197 Reich, *The Mass Psychology of Fascism*, p. 201.
198 Ibid., p. 202.
199 Ibid., p. 102.
200 Ibid., p. 83.
201 Ibid., p. 84.
202 As Reich states: "We must get into the habit of paying strict attention to precisely what the fascist has to say and not to dismiss it as nonsense or hogwash. Now we have a better understanding of the emotional content of this theory, which sounds like a persecution mania when it is considered together with the theory of the poisoning of the nation." Ibid., p. 101.
203 Ibid., pp. 202–3.
204 Ibid., p. 203.
205 [Trans. note: see ibid., p. xxix.]
206 André Grimaldi, "L'éducation thérapeutique: ce que nous apprennent les patients," *Obésité* 4, no. 1 (March 2009), pp. 34–8.
207 Reich, *The Mass Psychology of Fascism*, pp. 203–4 [translation modified].
208 Ibid., p. 217.
209 Ibid., p. 218.
210 Ibid.
211 Ibid., p. 218.
212 Ibid., p. 63.
213 Ibid.
214 Ibid., p. 80.
215 Ibid., p. 63.
216 Ibid. p. 337.
217 Ibid.
218 The analysis of the phenomenon of resentment reveals the complexity with which the individual is confronted: the subject is in need of (re)narcissization so that he does not tarry within resentment. This is what André Green named "primary narcissism," which is absolutely

NOTES TO PAGES 116–123

necessary for the subject, and which is linked to a subdued form of self-confidence, or at least a feeling of stability in the face of one's own internal chaos. By contrast, an exacerbation of narcissism in the absence of self-awareness is detrimental, and can ally itself in an extremely productive way with a resentment of victimhood. From this standpoint, Medea is a terrible and indeed terroristic Narcissus, convinced that she has been offended, seeking justice: she is the very archetype of the resentmentist drive.

219 Reich, *The Mass Psychology of Fascism*, p. 347.
220 Ibid., p. 348.
221 "It almost looks as if analysis were the third of those 'impossible' professions in which one can be sure beforehand of achieving unsatisfying results. The other two, which have been known much longer, are education and government." Sigmund Freud, "Analysis Terminable and Interminable," trans. James Stratchey, in *On Freud's "Analysis Terminable and Interminable*," ed. Joseph Sandler (London: Karnac, 2013), p. 35.
222 Ibid., p. 3.
223 Ibid.
224 Ibid.
225 Ibid., p. 11.
226 Ibid., p. 12.
227 Ibid., p. 18.
228 Ibid.
229 [Trans. note: ibid., p. 37. Freud takes the second term from Alfred Adler.]
230 Reich, *The Mass Psychology of Fascism*, p. xiii.
231 Ibid., p. 220.
232 Ibid., p. 163.
233 Ibid., p. 355.
234 Ibid., p. 358.
235 Ibid.
236 Ibid., p. 355.
237 Ibid., pp. 349–50.
238 [Trans. note: *Le Fascisme en action* is the title of the French translation of Robert O. Paxton's *The Anatomy of Fascism*, discussed at length by Fleury in this chapter.]
239 Georges Sorel, quoted in Robert O. Paxton, *The Anatomy of Fascism* (New York: Alfred A. Knopf, 2004), p. 4.
240 Paxton, *The Anatomy of Fascism*, p. 4. Paxton recalls here the etymology of the word "fascism": "The Italian *fascio*, literally a bundle or sheaf, [recalling] the Latin *fasces*, an axe encased in a bundle of rods that was carried before the magistrates in Roman public processions to signify the authority and unity of the state. Before 1914, the symbolism of the Roman *fasces* was usually appropriated by the Left" (ibid.):

241

NOTES TO PAGES 123–135

from Rome to the Italian revolutionaries of the end of the nineteenth century, it was used to evoke the solidarity of militants, unionists, and nationalists.

241 For the following lines, see also Cynthia Fleury, "La Chronique philo. Les Français dans la guerre," *L'Humanité*, 10 May 2019, https://www.humanite.fr/la-chronique-philo-les-francais-dans-la-guerre-672009.

242 Cited in Pierre Laborie, *Penser l'événement*, 1940–1945 (Paris: Gallimard, 2019).

243 Paxton, *The Anatomy of Fascism*, p. 12.

244 Ibid., p. 9.

245 See ibid., pp. 9–11.

246 Ibid., p. 10.

247 Ibid., p. 58.

248 Ibid., p. 11.

249 Ibid., p. 17. Paxton also discusses Benjamin's "The Work of Art in the Age of Mechanical Reproduction": "Benjamin quotes Marinetti on the beauty of the just-completed Ethiopian War: '. . . [war] enriches a flowering meadow with the fiery orchids of machine guns. . . .'" Quoted in Paxton, ibid., p. 258, n. 72.

250 Ibid., p. 17. Mussolini's words are also cited in Richard Bosworth, *The Italian Dictatorship: Problems and Perspectives in the Interpretation of Mussolini and Fascism* (London: Arnold, 1998), p. 39.

251 Emilio Gentile, *Qu'est-ce que le fascisme? Histoire et émancipation* (Paris: Gallimard, 2004), p. 361.

252 Ibid., p. 445.

253 Tweet by Donald Trump, 3 January 2018.

254 George Orwell, *1984* (London: Secker and Warburg, 1949), p. 11 and elsewhere.

255 Paxton, *The Anatomy of Fascism*, p. 85.

256 Rainer Maria Rilke, *Duinio Elegies*, in *The Selected Poetry of Rainer Maria Rilke*, trans. Stephen Mitchell (New York: Vintage, 1984), p. 377.

257 Cynthia Fleury, *Métaphysique de l'imagination* (Paris: Éditions d'écarts, 2000).

258 Vladimir Jankélévitch, *L'Enchantement musical. Écrits 1929–1983* (Paris: Albin Michel, 2017).

259 My book *La Fin du courage* (Paris: Payot, 2011) opens with a reflection on "glue" that is not far removed from that of Paxton.

260 Paxton, *The Anatomy of Fascism*, p. 147.

261 Ibid., p. 209.

262 Ibid., p. 27.

263 Raul Hilberg, *The Destruction of the European Jews, Volume 3* (New York: Holmes & Meier, 1985), p. 1007.

264 Ibid., pp. 1007–8.

265 Frantz Fanon perfectly described this phenomenon in *The Wretched of*

NOTES TO PAGES 136–141

the Earth, specifically concerning acts of torture during the Algerian War. He notably discusses the case of a European inspector losing his temper with his wife and children after the "events." Interestingly, the inspector does not complain directly about the need to torture; he even recognizes that he must do it in a rigorous manner, and that there is no question of giving the responsibility to someone else who would end up getting the glory for making the prisoners speak. He recalls that torturing requires "'a feel for it,'" knowing when to torture and when to stop, and above all letting the victim believe that there is hope for survival: "'It's hope that makes them talk.'" Fanon then makes a loose link with the fact that the inspector goes crazy after regularly torturing the "'enemies,'" and that he beats his wife and his children. Instead of calling torture into question, he asks the doctor to "'straighten me out.'" Fanon comments: "This man knew perfectly well that all his problems stemmed directly from the type of work conducted in the interrogation rooms, though he tried to blame everything on 'the troubles.' As he had no intention of giving up his job as a torturer (this would make no sense since he would then have to resign) he asked me in plain language to help him torture Algerian patriots without having a guilty conscience, without any behavioral problems, and with a total peace of mind." Frantz Fanon, *The Wretched of the Earth*, trans. Richard Philcox (New York: Grove Press, 2004), pp. 198–99.

266 Speech by Himmler at the Gruppenführer meeting at Poznań, 4 October 1943. Cited in Hilberg, *The Destruction of the European Jews, Volume 3*, p. 1008.

267 Ibid., pp. 1008–9.

268 "Another terrifying yet surprising anecdote from Himmler's personal diary: it seems that, surprising though this may seem, he was sensitive to the sight of blood. He describes how he almost fainted when, during the execution of some Jews in Belarus, a piece of brain landed on his coat." "Le journal intime du nazi Heinrich Himmler retrouvé en Russie," *Midi Libre*, 4 August 2016, https://www.midilibre. fr/2016/08/04/le-journal-intime-du-nazi-heinrich-himmler-retrouve-en-russie,1375644.php.

269 "According to *Mashable*, more than 1,600 appointments were recorded in Himmler's personal diaries." Ibid.

270 Raul Hilberg, *Perpetrators Victims Bystanders: The Jewish Catastrophe 1933–1945* (New York: HarperPerennial, 1993), p. 20.

271 See Cynthia Fleury, *Mallarmé et la parole de l'imâm*, especially the chapter "Le Tombeau d'Anatole," which is the title of the poem Mallarmé dedicated to the death of his son. A child's death is impossible to mourn. Mallarmé's work carries the resonance of this silent cry, of these infinite tears. "De-birth" [*Le "désenfantement"*], a notion I developed while reflecting on the analytic cure (see my book *Le Soin est un humanisme* [Paris: Gallimard, 2019]), describes not only mourning

NOTES TO PAGES 142–153

for the child who has lived, but also that of the child who was never born, who was longed for but will never arrive.

272 Achille Mbembe, "L'universalité de Frantz Fanon," in Frantz Fanon, *Oeuvres* (Paris: La Découverte, 2011), p. 9.

273 [Trans. note: see Vladimir Jankélévitch, "Should We Pardon Them," trans. Ann Hobart, in *Critical Inquiry* 22 (Spring 1996), pp. 552–72, here pp. 554–65.

274 Mbembe, "L'universalité de Frantz Fanon," p. 10.

275 Ibid.

276 Ibid.

277 Ibid., p. 11.

278 Ibid., p. 12. [Trans. note: this word translates "déclosion." It should be understood not in the sense of divulging information, but of removing that which encloses or closes off.]

279 Ibid., p. 19.

280 Frantz Fanon, *Black Skin, White Masks*, trans. Richard Philcox (New York: Grove Press, 2007), p. xii.

281 Aimé Césaire, *Discourse on Colonialism*, trans. Joan Pinkham (New York: Monthly Review Press, 2000), p. 43; cited in Fanon, *Black Skin, White Masks*, p. xi.

282 Fanon, *Black Skin, White Masks*, p. xii.

283 Ibid., p. xii.

284 Ibid., pp. xiii-xiv.

285 Ibid., p. xii.

286 Ibid., p. 42.

287 Ibid., p. 48.

288 Minkowski, cited in ibid., p. 54.

289 Minkowski, cited in ibid., p. 55 [translation modified].

290 Guex, cited in ibid., p. 57.

291 Aimé Césaire, cited in ibid., p. 64.

292 Ibid., p. 16 [translation modified].

293 Ibid.

294 Ibid., p. 24.

295 Ibid., p. 89.

296 Ibid., p. 92.

297 Ibid., pp. 92–3.

298 Stéphane Mallarmé, *Selected Letters of Stéphane Mallarmé*, trans. Rosemary Lloyd (Chicago: University of Chicago Press, 1988), p. 74.

299 Ibid.

300 Fanon, *Black Skin, White Masks*, p. 119.

301 Ibid., pp. 163–4.

302 Ibid., p. 164 [translation modified].

303 Ibid., p. 167.

304 Ibid. [translation modified].

305 Ibid., pp. 185–6 [translation modified].

NOTES TO PAGES 154–166

306 Ibid., p. 201.
307 Ibid., p. 204.
308 Ibid.
309 Ibid.
310 Ibid., p. 205 [translation modified].
311 Frantz Fanon, *A Dying Colonialism*, trans. Haakon Chevalier (New York: Grove Press, 1965), p. 27.
312 Fanon, *Black Skin, White Masks*, p. 204.
313 I love Laing's writing, and also the way he practiced care. But he was strongly critical—at times rightly so—regarding this practice. Those who shoot high often crash, often make mistakes—and give rise, precisely because of their errors, to important advances made by others who are in their debt.
314 Fanon, *A Dying Colonialism*, p. 123.
315 "The compulsory visit by the doctor to the *douar* or village is preceded by the assembling of the population through the agency of the police authorities. The doctor who arrives in this atmosphere of general constraint is never a native doctor but always a doctor belonging to the dominant society and very often to the army." Fanon, *A Dying Colonialism*, p. 121 [translation modified]. Even if the doctor were native, this would change nothing: he could also be suspected of some sort of allegiance to the authoritarian order, which would yet again render his care ineffective.
316 Ibid., p. 128 [translation modified].
317 Ibid., p. 130.
318 Alice Cherki, "Préface," in Frantz Fanon, *Les Damnés de la terre* (Paris: La Découverte, 2002), p. 9.
319 Jean-Paul Sartre, "Preface," in Frantz Fanon, *The Wretched of the Earth*, trans. Richard Philcox (New York: Grove Press, 2004), p. l.
320 Ibid., p. lii.
321 Ibid., p. liii.
322 Ibid., p. lv.
323 Ibid.
324 Fanon, *The Wretched of the Earth*, p. 2.
325 Fanon, *A Dying Colonialism*, p. 99.
326 [Trans. note: The reference is to Henry Corbin, *Mundus Imaginalis; or, The Imaginary and the Imaginal* (Boston: Golgonooza Press, 1976).]
327 Fleury, *Métaphysique de l'imagination*. See especially the entry for "the imaginal sea" in the glossary.
328 Friedrich Hölderlin, "Remembrance," in *Poems and Fragments*, trans. Michael Hamburger (Ann Arbor: University of Michigan Press, 1966), p. 491.
329 Fanon, *The Wretched of the Earth*, p. 136 [translation modified].
330 Ibid., p. 137.
331 Ibid., p. 138 [translation modified].

NOTES TO PAGES 167–180

332 Ibid., p. 172 [translation modified].
333 Ibid., p. 170.
334 Ibid., p. 172.
335 Ibid.
336 Ibid., p. 179 [translation modified].
337 See Jean Khalfa, "Fanon, Revolutionary Psychiatrist," in Frantz Fanon, *Alienation and Freedom*, trans. Steven Corcoran (London: Bloomsbury Academic, 2018), p. 168.
338 Fanon, quoted in ibid., p. 170.
339 Frantz Fanon, *Altérations mentales, modifications caractérielles, troubles psychiques et déficit intellectual dans l'hérédodégénération spino-cérébelleuse* (thesis written to obtain the rank of doctor of medicine, 1951), quoted in Khalfa, "Fanon, Revolutionary Psychiatrist," p. 171.
340 Khalfa, "Fanon, Revolutionary Psychiatrist," p. 188.
341 Ibid., p. 199.
342 Ibid., p. 201.
343 Fanon, *Alterations mentales*, quoted in Khalfa, "Fanon, Revolutionary Psychiatrist," p. 204 n. 2.
344 Frantz Fanon, "Trait d'Union," in *Alienation and Freedom*, pp. 280–81.
345 "The past, present and future must comprise human beings' three predominant interests; it is impossible to see and achieve anything positive, valid and lasting without taking all three elements into account." Ibid., p. 283.
346 E. M. Cioran, *Tears and Saints*, trans. Ilinca Zarifopol Johnston (Chicago: University of Chicago Press, 1995), p. 39 [translation modified].
347 E. M. Cioran, *The Trouble with Being Born*, trans. Richard Howard (New York: Seaver Books, 1976), p. 147.
348 Ibid., p. 4.
349 Ibid., p. 193.
350 Ibid., p. 139.
351 Ibid., p. 119.
352 Ibid., p. 19.
353 Ibid., p. 18.
354 Ibid., p. 21.
355 Ibid., p. 20.
356 Ibid., p. 153.
357 Cioran, *Tears and Saints*, p. 49.
358 Amina Azza Bekkat, "Introduction: with Fanon," in Fanon, *Alienation and Freedom*, p. 312.
359 Fanon, quoted in ibid., pp. 313–14.
360 Frantz Fanon, "Our Journal," in Fanon, *Alienation and Freedom*, p. 315.

NOTES TO PAGES 180–195

361 Ibid.

362 Fanon, *Black Skin, White Masks*, p. 24.

363 Fanon, "Our Journal," in Fanon, *Alienation and Freedom*, p. 315.

364 [Trans. note: Groupe hospitalier universitaire de Paris.]

365 Erving Goffman, *Asylums: Essay on the Social Situation of Mental Patients and Other Inmates* (Chicago: Aldine Publishing Company, 1962), p. 14.

366 Fanon, "Our Journal," in Fanon, *Alienation and Freedom*, p. 318.

367 Pierre Macherey, "Il n'y a pas de bon sens de l'histoire," interview with Jean-Philippe Cazier. *Chimères* 83, no. 2 (2014), p. 33.

368 This classification is quite clearly "false" in that it is too binary, but it allows us to understand the deep antagonism between the different currents of society.

369 Fanon, "Our Journal," in Fanon, *Alienation and Freedom*, pp. 347–48 [translation modified].

370 Vladimir Jankélévitch, *Forgiveness*, trans. Andrew Kelley (Chicago: University of Chicago Press, 2005), p. 102.

371 Ibid., p. 103.

372 Ibid. Per Jankélévitch: "The philosophy of good riddance is a caricature of forgiveness. . . . If there is no other path to forgiving than that of good riddance, then let there rather be *ressentiment*! For in this case, it is *ressentiment* that would imply seriousness and profundity. At least in *ressentiment* the heart is committed, and this is why it is a prelude to cordial forgiveness" (102–3).

373 Axel Honneth, *The I in We: Studies in the Theory of Recognition*, trans. Joseph Ganahl (Cambridge: Polity, 2012), p. 194.

374 Ibid., p. 195.

375 Ibid.

376 [Trans. note: Cynthia Fleury, *Les Irremplaçables* (Paris: Gallimard, 2015).]

377 Richard Thaler received the Nobel Prize in 2017 for his work on behavioral economics.

378 Honneth, *The I in We*, p. 195 [translation modified].

379 Ibid.

380 Ibid.

381 Ibid., p. 196.

382 This and the following paragraphs, which concern hatred, defamation, and lying, have been taken from the following article: Cynthia Fleury, "La Haine se ment," in *Dis-moi qui tu hais*. À propos de quelques formes contemporaines de la haine, special issue of *Le Diable Probablement*, 11, ed. Anaëlle Lebovits-Quenehen.

383 Plato, *Republic*, trans. G. M. A. Grube, revised by C. D. C. Reeve. In Plato, *Complete Works*, ed. John M. Cooper, associate ed. D. S. Hutchinson (Indianapolis: Hackett, 1997), p. 382b–382c. See also Pierre Sarr, "Discours sur le mensonge de Platon à saint Augustin:

NOTES TO PAGES 195–203

continuité ou rupture," *Dialogues d'histoire ancienne* 36 n. 2 (2010), pp. 9–29.

384 Plato, *Republic*, p. 383b–383c.

385 Ibid., p. 382c.

386 On this issue, see also my article "Typologie des mensonges dans l'espace public: quelle régulation numérique?," *International Review of Sociology* 15 (2015).

387 Plato, *Republic*, 389b.

388 Ibid.

389 Ibid., p. 414b.

390 Ibid., p. 415a.

391 Jacques Rancière, *The Philosopher and His Poor*, trans. John Drury, Corinne Oster, and Andrew Parker (Durham, N.C.: Duke University Press, 2003), p. 29.

392 Julia Kristeva, *Nations Without Nationalism*, trans. Leon S. Roudiez (New York: Columbia University Press, 1993), p. 29.

393 [Trans. note: Fleury refers here to Freud's discussion of the primal horde in *Totem and Taboo*.]

394 Sigmund Freud, "Instincts and Their Vicissitudes," trans. James Strachey. In Freud, *The Standard Edition of the Complete Psychological Works of Sigmund Freud*, vol. 14 (London: The Hogarth Press and the Institute of Psycho-Analysis, 1957), p. 139.

395 Genesis 4:9 (New International Version).

396 Bernard Stiegler, *La Télécratie contre la démocratie* (Paris: Flammarion, 2006), pp. 71–2.

397 Molière, *The Misanthrope*. In Molière, *The Misanthrope, Tartuffe, and Other Plays*, trans. Maya Slater (Oxford: Oxford University Press, 2008), act I, scene 2, p. 218.

398 Freud, *Civilization and Its Discontents*, p. 92.

399 Quoted in Nicole Loraux, "Of Amnesty and Its Opposite," in *The Divided City: On Memory and Forgetting in Ancient Athens*, trans. Corinne Pache with Jeff Fort (New York: Zone Books, 2004), p. 154. Also quoted in Michel Naepels, "Il faut häir," *Genèses* 69 no. 4 (2007), p. 144.

400 Marc Angenot, "Nouvelles figures de la rhétorique: la logique du ressentiment," *Question de communication* 12 (2007), p. 68.

401 Marc Angenot, "Le Ressentiment: Raisonnement, pathos, idéologie," in Michael Rinn, ed., Émotions et discours: *L'Usage des passions dans la langue* (Rennes: Presses Universitaires de Rennes, 2008).

402 Ibid.

403 Angenot, "Nouvelles figures," p. 71.

404 "Illness is a positive, innovative experience in the living being and not just a fact of decrease or increase." Georges Canguilhem, *The Normal and the Pathological*, trans. Carolyn R. Fawcett and Robert S. Cohen (New York: Zone Books, 1991), p. 186 [translation modified].

248

NOTES TO PAGES 203–214

405 "But illness is not simply disequilibrium or discordance; it is, and perhaps most important, an effort on the part of nature to effect a new equilibrium in man. Illness is a generalized reaction designed to bring about healing; the organism develops an illness in order to get well. Therapy must first tolerate and, if necessary, reinforce these hedonic and spontaneously therapeutic reactions. Medical technique imitates natural medicinal action (*vis medicatrix naturae*)." Ibid., pp. 40–1 [translation modified].

406 Angenot, "Nouvelles figures," p. 74.

407 Hermann Broch, *Théorie de la folie des masses*, trans. Didier Renault and Pierre Rusch (Paris: Éditions de l'éclat, 2005), p. 13.

408 Ibid., p. 8.

409 Ibid., p. 14.

410 Ibid., p. 20.

411 Ibid., p. 45.

412 Ibid., p. 48.

413 Ibid., p. 47.

414 Simone Weil, *Correspondance familiale, I*, in *Oeuvres completes*, vol. 8 (Paris: Gallimard, 2012), p. 8.

415 As Robert Chenavier says, "Simone Weil was never cast out of her childhood." Chenavier, "Avant-propos," in ibid., p. 16.

416 Ibid.

417 Cited in ibid., p. 21.

418 See Simone Weil, Écrits de Marseille, in *Oeuvres completes*, vol. 7.

419 Chenavier, "Avant-propos," p. 21.

420 Weil, *Correspondance familiale*, p. 438.

421 Ibid., p. 467.

422 "Certainly, they had a painful conception of existence, like all those whose eyes are open. But their pain had an object; it had a meaning with respect to the bliss for which man is made, and from which the hard constraints of the world deprive him. They had no taste for misfortune, catastrophe, disequilibrium. On the other hand, in the work of so many moderns (notably Nietzsche, I think), there is a sadness linked to the privation of the very meaning of happiness: they need to annihilate themselves." Ibid., p. 475.

423 Broch, *Théorie de la folie des masses*, p. 48.

424 Ibid.

425 Ibid.

426 Ibid.

427 Ibid.

428 Ibid.

429 Ibid.

430 Ibid.

431 Ibid.

432 Ibid., p. 62.

NOTES TO PAGES 214–224

433 Ibid.
434 Ibid.
435 Ibid.
436 See Georges Nivat, "Préface," in Fyodor Dostoyevski, *Crime et Châtiment* (Paris: Gallimard, 1975).
437 Fyodor Dostoyevsky, "12 September (1865): Fyodor Dostoyevsky to M. S. Katkov," *The American Reader*, https://theamericanreader. com/12-september-1865-fyodor-dostoyevsky-to-m-n-katkov/.
438 Ibid.
439 Ibid.
440 Fyodor Dostoyevsky, *Crime and Punishment*, trans. David McDuff (London: Penguin, 1991), p. 307.
441 Louis Aragon, *Le Roman inachevé* (Paris: Gallimard, 1956), p. 176. On this theme, see Fleury, *Pathologies de la democratie*, especially the chapter entitled "De la Frustration à la violence généralisée."
442 Joris-Karl Huysmans, *The Damned (Là-bas)*, trans. Terry Hale (London: Penguin, 2001), p. 4.
443 Ibid.
444 Joris-Karl Huysmans, *Against Nature*, trans. Margaret Mauldon (Oxford: Oxford University Press, 1998), p. 186 [translation modified]. These words appear in a preface the author wrote twenty years after the novel was first published.
445 Ibid., pp. 55–6 [translation modified].
446 Huysmans, *The Damned*, p. 230.
447 D. W. Winnicott, "The Tree," cited in F. Robert Rodman, *Winnicott: Life and Work* (Cambridge, Mass.: Da Capo Press, 2003), p. 290.
448 Nietzsche, *Thus Spoke Zarathustra*, p. 174.
449 Ibid.
450 Ibid.
451 Ibid., p. 175.
452 *Tremendum* is literally the "sacred shiver" typical of the experience of the sublime and of (divine) awe.
453 *Amor fati* (literally, "love of fate") is Nietzsche's ethical and metaphysical theory indicating that Zarathustra's wisdom is based on the capacity to love becoming, to welcome it as the very power of the living and the real.
454 Ibid.
455 Ibid., p. 77.
456 Ezra Pound, *The Cantos of Ezra Pound* (New York: New Directions, 1996), p. 3.
457 Ibid., p. 541.
458 Jonathan Pollock, "Éclatement et dissolution du sujet dans *Les Cantos* d'Ezra Pound." *Revue Silène*, 2008, http://www.revue-silene.com/f/ index.php?sp=liv&livre_id=107, p. 4. Pollock cites Anne Cheng's *Histoire de la pensée chinoise*.

NOTES TO PAGES 224–226

459 Pound, *Cantos*, pp. 541–42.
460 Ibid., p. 407.
461 Ibid., p. 822.
462 Ibid., p. 478.
463 Alongside Antoine Fenoglio, I have been developing this art of furtiveness through the concept of *verstohlen*, which teaches the production of undetectable foundations, the durability of which can be used to create institutions allowing individuals to be reassured about that which cannot be stolen from them. See Cynthia Fleury-Perkins and Antoine Fenoglio, "Le Design peut-il aider à mieux soigner? Le Concept de *proof of care*," *Soins* 834 (April 2019), pp. 58–61.